Dissenting Women in Dickens' Novels

Dissenting Women in Dickens' Novels

The Subversion of Domestic Ideology

Brenda Ayres

Contributions in Women's Studies, Number 168

Greenwood Press
Westport, Connecticut • London

Library of Congress Cataloging-in-Publication Data

Ayres, Brenda, 1953–
    Dissenting women in Dickens' novels : the subversion of domestic
ideology / Brenda Ayres.
        p. cm. — (Contributions in women's studies, ISSN 0147-104X ;
no. 168)
    Includes bibliographical references and indexes.
    ISBN 0-313-30763-6 (alk. paper)
    1. Dickens, Charles, 1812–1870—Characters—Women. 2. Dickens,
Charles, 1812–1870—Political and social views. 3. Feminism and
literature—England—History—19th century. 4. Literature and
society—England—History—19th century. 5. Women and literature—
England—History—19th century. 6. Domestic fiction, English—
History and criticism. 7. Dissenters in literature. I. Title.
II. Series.
PR4592.W6A97   1998
823'.8—dc21   98–12151

British Library Cataloguing in Publication Data is available.

Library of Congress Catalog Card Number: 98–12151
ISBN: 0-313-30763-6
ISSN: 0147-104X

First published in 1998

Greenwood Press, 88 Post Road West, Westport, CT 06881
An imprint of Greenwood Publishing Group, Inc.

Printed in the United States of America

The paper used in this book complies with the
Permanent Paper Standard issued by the National
Information Standards Organization (Z39.48–1984).

10 9 8 7 6 5 4 3 2

Copyright Acknowledgments

The author and publisher gratefully acknowledge permission for use of the following material:

Fred Kaplan, ed., *Oliver Twist* (1993) and Jerome H. Buckley, ed., *David Copperfield* (1993)
are reprinted courtesy of W. W. Norton & Company.

To my mom,
　　　Norma Jean Shearer Ayres

The first feminist I ever knew,
who,
after a lifetime of contemplation
　　　　　and observation
could only conclude
that when God took out one of Adam's ribs,
He must have taken out more
than what He had meant to.

Contents

Abbreviated Titles and Sources

PP   *The Pickwick Papers*. 1836. Ed. and introd. Edgar Johnson. New York: Dell, 1964.

OT   *Oliver Twist*. 1837. Ed. Fred Kaplan. New York: Norton, 1993.

NN   *Nicholas Nickleby*. 1838. Afterword. Steven Marcus. New York: Signet, 1980.

OCS *The Old Curiosity Shop*. 1840. Ed. Angus Easson. New York: Penguin, 1972.

BR   *Barnaby Rudge*. 1841. Ed. and introd. Gordon Spence. New York: Penguin, 1973.

MC   *Martin Chuzzlewit*. 1843. Ed. and introd. Margaret Cardwell. Oxford: Oxford University Press, 1982.

D&S *Dombey and Son*. 1848. Boston: DeWolfe, Fiske & Co., n.d.

DC   *David Copperfield*. 1850. Ed. Jerome H. Buckley. New York: Norton, 1990.

BH   *Bleak House*. 1852. Afterword. Geoffrey Tillotson. New York: Signet, 1964.

HT   *Hard Times*. 1854. Eds. George Ford and Sylvère Monod. New York: Norton, 1990.

LD   *Little Dorrit*. 1855. Ed. John Holloway. New York: Penguin, 1967.

TT   *A Tale of Two Cities*. 1859. New York: Bantam, 1981.

GE   *Great Expectations*. 1860. Introd. Edward Wagenknecht. New York: Washington Square Press, 1956.

OMF   *Our Mutual Friend*. 1864. Afterword. J. Hillis Miller. New York: Signet, 1964.

ED   *The Mystery of Edwin Drood*. 1870. Concluded by Leon Garfield. New York: Pantheon, 1980.

Acknowledgments

In my early teens I began a sweet love affair with Dickens' novels. In the 1970s I became a woman when women enthusiastically were burning the bras of womanhood. The combination of passions—for Dickens, who had long been thought of as a patriarchal bully, and for female liberation—formed a fiery marriage of sorts that eventually produced this study.

The people and situations that informed my reading of Dickens' novels are too numerous to mention here, but I am most grateful to the University of Southern Mississippi, which gave me, when a doctoral student a number of years ago, the language and strategies to engage in dialogue about gender issues that had long plagued me. In particular, I wish to thank Professor Anne Wallace and the late Professor Harry McCraw for their guidance and company through Victorian and feminist studies.

I also owe an immeasurable debt to my dear friend and colleague Professor Jo Culbertson Davis of Williams College in College City, Arkansas, for her conscientious reading of this project and belief in it.

I am also grateful to Middle Georgia College (MGC) where I taught English while working on this manuscript. I came to rely heavily on its library staff for interlibrary loans that kept me current with scholarship. Dr. Valerie D'Ortona, my chair and friend at MGC, helped me understand myself as female, puzzling with me over those who were of the opposite sex. To Valerie and all of my colleagues and employers at MGC who gave me opportunity and incentive to continue my impassioned probe into gender study, I am most thankful.

And finally, most of all, let me express my love and appreciation for my dearest sister, who, since we were little girls, believed that I would grow up and someday have books with my name on them. Well, Sue, here is my first one!

1

Introduction: Domestic Ideology and the Dickens Text

We post-Victorians have much to thank our predecessors for: their rich corpus of stories, characters, and ideologies has greatly influenced our worldview. My appreciation and awareness of personal and social information, though not restricted to Dickens, certainly and frequently turns to him, as I think it must for many Western readers. Take Dickens' Scrooge and Western notions of Christmas, for example. Take Dickens' portrayal of Miss Havisham, the ideogram of the jilted spinster. Take Dickens' biting criticism of industrialism in *Hard Times*.

Given the pedagogical nature of Victorian novels, regardless of plot, setting, and character, their texts are politicized, filtered through their authors' value schemes, social moorings, and conscious purpose in writing. In a way very similar to Roland Barthes' description of how photography manipulates a viewer, the texts want to control what readers are to perceive:

The text directs the reader through the signifieds of the image, causing him to avoid some and receive others; by means of often subtle dispatching, it remote-controls him towards a meaning chosen in advance. . . . The text is indeed . . . society's right of inspection over the image. . . . The text has thus a repressive value and we can see that it is at this level that the morality and ideology of a society are above all invested. ("Message" 40)

Whether or not Dickens developed scenes and characters deliberately to propagate domestic ideology is not the issue here. His text does overtly manipulate and does "articulate the interests" of a particular group of people—specifically of males who maintain certain beliefs about a woman: what her natural limitations should be, what her domestic and moral aptitudes and conduct should be, and what part she should play in society. The Dickens text on the surface is normative; its attitudes of approval or disapproval toward divergent female behavior are salient—if not through biased details used to describe the woman, then by judgment or chastisement of her through plot.

These strategies are at work in, say, *Our Mutual Friend* when Eugene Wrayburn looks through a window to see Lizzie Hexam for the first time. She is the image of a long-suffering, devoted, adoring daughter with only one purpose, to attend to her father and her brother. The text portrays the heroine in ideological terms. Dickens probably did not describe the scene with the conscious idea of affirming an ideology, but his text does attempt to affirm domestic ideology. Eugene is careless, indolent, and unambitious because he is not situated within a family—no one is dependent upon him and no fine woman steers him to higher moral good. Naturally, he is drawn to the light in Lizzie's window like a man who has been living a cold and dark existence. Lizzie is seated, naturally, in front of a hearth, waiting longingly and lovingly for her father to arrive. She is an iconographic manifestation of domestic ideology, an image that frequents Dickens' works. The text depicts her favorably because she conforms so well to the angel-in-the-house typology.[1] The text instructs women to behave likewise and men to expect women to do so. If the narrative fails to make this disposition clear, then the plot does so by rewarding in a sense Lizzie's behavior with marriage to one of the novel's heroes, Eugene.

Even as Dickens' text overtly promotes an ideology of womanhood, however, at the same time it modifies and subverts that ideology. Lizzie epitomizes filial obedience, but she suffers terrible deprivation and hardship as a result. The reader first meets her on the Thames with her father, searching for dead bodies to be robbed. Lizzie assists her father but under duress. The text makes it clear that Lizzie finds this occupation both revolting and socially and morally unacceptable—just as an angel-in-the-house would. Yet, if she is to be "good," she must obey her father. Similar conflicts in the same novel exist through the daughter/father relationships that involve Jenny Wren and Bella Wilfer. By presenting patriarchal authority as malevolent or lame, the text posits dangerous pitfalls to that domestic ideology that places power in the hands of gender and not necessarily of good character. If Dickens teaches that a daughter should serve her father (and this most assuredly is a constant throughout his novels), why are the fathers not ideologically sound? That is, why are they incapable of ruling women, providing a living, and being, in general, "good" citizens?

At one point in the novel, Lizzie's brother tries to coerce her into a marriage to an obvious villain, Bradley Headstone. Whether her marriage to Eugene is a reward for good behavior is questionable for, throughout the novel, Eugene has been portrayed as her moral and spiritual inferior, who has dishonorable intentions toward her. Such examples are gaps suggesting the vulnerability of women in submitting to male authority. This is a notion at flagrant odds with patriarchal rule and substantiates the claim that the Dickens texts reflect a struggle with rather than an advocacy of patriarchal power.

Another form of gender power comes into question through the male/female relationships in *Our Mutual Friend* (and elsewhere). According to John Ruskin and his contemporaries, women were empowered to raise those around them to higher moral ground.[2] How is it then that Jenny and Lizzie cannot save their fathers or protect themselves from their fathers' profligate ways? Why does Bradley Headstone try to murder the man Lizzie loves instead of going about doing good deeds as a result of his love for her? Why cannot Bella convert her mother or her sister into an angel-in-the-house? The depreciation of the angel's ability to sow and reap goodness is a severe undercutting of ideological dynamics.

Our Mutual Friend also produces some women who are independent and can survive in the world without a man, a situation that definitely threatens the social ordering of man and woman in domesticity (an illustration discussed in Chapter 4). Jenny Wren, a dressmaker and a "cripple," supports not only herself but also her father (who drinks his own wages away). Lizzie works in a factory to finance her brother's education. And Bella succeeds, when her father has not, in gaining social advancement through a marriage suit. She, apparently, has been more insightful and sexually powerful in selecting a marriage partner who will ultimately help realize her social goals.

Through such gender depictions in *Our Mutual Friend* and throughout other texts from the Dickens canon, three areas of conflict complicate domestic ideology: (1) patriarchs do not automatically deserve the respect they command from their privileged social positions; (2) women, regardless of being exemplars, are unable to effect moral or social change; and (3) many women succeed (they are happy and do not die of brain fever or end up in the workhouse, Newgate, or, worst of all, America) outside domesticity.

The nuclear middle-class family in Western civilization is a relatively new phenomenon, first entrenched as a required bourgeois social configuration in the Victorian society. Along with at least two maidservants, one horse, a groom, and of course an odd number of children who could survive infancy, the middle-class household had to consist of a man and his wife, both performing their prescribed divisions of labor. The woman gave herself over to the rearing of children and overseeing of servants, housecleaning, food preparing, mending and sewing, shopping, flower arranging, and performing other domestic tasks. The man earned wages, paid the bills, oversaw the livery, attended to political and legal matters, and went to war if necessary.

Such subscription was endorsed time and time again in advice books. The most widely read of these was Sarah Ellis' *The Women of England* (1843), which emphatically differentiated gender roles. The man was called to a vocation that cultivated and required a worldly and selfish spirit. As for the woman, her "appropriate part [was] to adorn that station wherever it may be, by a contented mind, an enlightened spirit, and an exemplary life" (114). This ideological function of gender was for the furthering of the British empire.

Clearly it was the woman's responsibility to counteract the onslaught of evil in the world by dedicating herself solely to the social and moral well-being of the male folk. The family, as the famous evangelical expert of late eighteenth-century manners Hannah More, described it, was the "Christian haven in a disrupted world."

This social organization extended beyond a division of labor; people were expected to behave according to socially defined gender codes. The woman was supposed to be soft, meek, quiet, modest, submissive, gentle, patient, and spiritual. The image of the ideal woman from this period has been described in Barbara Welter's well-known article "The Cult of True Womanhood," which defines feminine virtues as "piety, purity, submissiveness, and domesticity" (152).[3] She was the angel-in-the-house. The man was to be aggressive, assertive, rough although gentlemanly, tough-skinned, self-controlled, and independent—able to compete well in the marketplace and to do his job as a citizen in a manly way and to rule his household.

People believed conforming to these roles was best for them and for their nation.[4] Didactic literature often reinforced this notion, instructing readers in how to adhere to "proper" behavior. "Fiction was expected to preach," Andrew Blake observed in his study of the ideological content of nineteenth-century novels. Instead of just being reflective, "fictional literature can be seen as active within society, as being aimed at particular readerships within it, of presenting, to that specifically chosen audience, certain types of information and attitude, and helping to form or change attitudes and behavior" (8). Instruction, besides entertainment, was what the Victorians expected from their reading.

The nineteenth-century novel, with its intrinsic moralizing, helped regulate behavior for the middle class (especially in regard to treatment of women). Terry Eagleton confirmed this effect: "Literature is a vital instrument for the insertion of individuals into the perceptual and symbolic forms of the dominant ideological formation" (*Criticism* 52). As if responding to the moralizing of the Victorian novel, Eagleton summarized: "Ideology adapts individuals to their social functions by providing them with an imaginary model of the whole, suitably schematized and fictionalized for their purposes" (*Ideology* 151). Literature and other forms of art naturally further an author's ideology, for they engender fictive worlds into which they draw a reader and thus immerse him or her in that ideology.

Blake regarded the Victorian novel not only as a social and cultural artifact that historians could read in order to identify the dominant ideologies of past societies (13), but also as a set of thoughts and feelings and expectations that Victorians could discuss in the public way, to modify, solidify, and then impel into action either by social enforcement or political action (for instance, through legislation in the House of Commons[5]). That Victorian fiction often served as a vehicle for ideological modification and debate is a point that Richard Altick has made:

Never before had the novel been so tightly and extensively involved in the events of the day. It was not simply a matter of a new didacticism appearing to replace the one that had languished. . . . When ideological concerns of various sorts increasingly animated the public mind, the art of fiction was prepared to express and debate them in imaginative frameworks. Fiction, in short, met the social needs of the hour. (52)

Through literature, the Victorians were specifically indoctrinated by an ideology that translated a concept of ideal woman into expected modes of behavior.

The question throughout this study is to identify where and when the Dickens' novel fails to promote this ideology. Insofar as he has often been referred to as a domestic tyrant and patriarchal bully, it is hard to imagine how such subversive texts squeaked from Dickens' pen. One might be tempted to accuse him of having greatly benefited from domestic ideology: there was Catherine, who bore him ten children and suffered at least two miscarriages in sixteen years. She was the woman he described in letters as dumpy, dull, and domestically inept.[6] There were her sisters, the youngest, whom he adored, and the other, who helped raise his children. When tired of his "Christian haven in a disrupted world," he secured a Deed of Separation from his wife and turned to a young actress.

Dickens wielded more power to determine his life than did the women he knew. That makes him a patriarch enjoying privilege in a patriarchal society. But just how much power and privilege can patriarchs enjoy in a society built upon illusions? Beginning with a mother who seemed intent on leaving him in a blacking factory, working as a law clerk when he had other ambitions, and then discovering that marriage was not all that he had been led to believe it should be, why would he not produce a text characterized by convulsions, contortions, contradictions, and gaps whenever he depicted the ideology of domesticity at work?

Not being a Victorian, other than a passionate Victorian reader, I cannot imagine how a fictive world that reflects a real world, regardless of its didactic leadings, can consistently support such restrictive and essentializing models of people and modes of behavior. Whether consciously or not, the Dickens text could not and did not achieve these ends. That there would be contradictions in Dickens' text in relation to domestic ideology should not come as a surprise; the critics have not been able to agree in their assessments of Dickens' portrayal of women.

The very nature of "ideology," according to Andrew Blake, is that there is never a dominant ideology, but multiple ideologies that "conflict and compete, and do not necessarily produce uniformity." In other words, a Victorian novel would not represent a singular expression of domestic ideology within its covers. After all, not every middle-class Victorian embraced the regimen of domesticity as if it were one's national and religious duty to do so. Ideologies, however, "exert fundamental control over the boundaries of cultural practice" (38). For all their didactic posturing and colonizing efforts, Victorian novels evidence a struggle for power and contain pockets of resistance against conformity. Ideologies are sources of power that fight through such apparatuses as literature and other forms of art for hegemony—as John Thompson argued in his study of ideological theory: "[Current literature] is linked to the process of sustaining asymmetrical relations of power—that is, to the process of maintaining domination" (4). The ideology of domesticity is an "illusionary perception" translated into reality by a dominant gender group. It defines how men and women should perceive women, not how they should know women.

Paul Ricoeur theorized that "ideology, then, designates initially some distorting, dissimulating processes by which an individual or a group expresses its situation but without knowing or recognizing it" (2): distorting, in that they do not reflect reality but the "relation" to "conditions of existence." That is, what can be and often is distorted is one's interpretation of how he/she "fits" into the world (233–34).[7] Dickens' ideological expression of gender behavior undergoes much distortion on the printed page. Overtly his text reinforces and contributes to the cult of domesticity, but—although often covertly—also alters that representation at the same time. The very nature of writing individualizes what might be considered a dominant ideology, because the writer is a reflector at best who will distort according to his own personal agenda.[8] David Aers supported and explained this theory:

Writing is a social activity necessarily immersed in a diversity of contemporary practices, ideological forms and problems: its minute particulars articulate forms of life and outlook, imaging and displaying the writers' attitudes towards received ideology and existing circumstances, but also performing concrete work on that ideology and those circumstances by virtue of the very process of writing. (2)

Besides factoring in the individual who constructs the ideology in writing and will thus perform work on that ideology, this study considers the characteristic of text itself, which Barthes called a "ready-made veil." Translating "text" as "tissue," Barthes surmised that behind text "lies, more or less hidden, meaning (truth) . . . that is worked out in a perpetual inter-weaving; lost in this tissue—this texture—the subject unmakes himself, like a spider dissolving in the constructive secretions of its web" (*Pleasure* 64). This description applies well when investigating Dickens' ideological op-erations in his novels. The text finely delineates and urges domesticity as the ideal social code for middle-class society, but in that text runs a current of questions, gaps, and conflicts that fail to brace that ideology. Indeed Kimberley Reynolds and Nicola Humble consider the text to challenge or-thodoxy through its "hints, elisions and contradictions" (16).

A discussion, therefore, of Dickens' portrayal of women in light of do-mestic ideology would be incomplete without identifying sites in Dickens' text that modify, shadow, or distort that ideology. Toward that end, this analysis examines representatives of a cast of dissenting women whose ac-tivities and functions depart from gender orthodoxy in ways similar to those that the religious dissenters of Dickens' day struggled to break free from governmental regulation and Anglican doctrine. The "Free Church-men" (as they became known in the 1890s) were the nonconformists in many new denominations (Methodists, Baptists, Presbyterians, and Con-gregationalists) who believed in the freedom of the individual to interpret the Scriptures and to obey God according to the dictates of one's own heart. The dissenting women who populate Dickens' fictive haunts are noncon-formists, too, albeit, for the most part, under a veil of conformity. Socially perceived as religious icons of virtue and purity, they were, in fact, icon breakers and individuals ascribing to their own behavioral codes.

Dickens' women are anything but stereotypical. They cause disruptions in the text that make their reality ever so accurate, their silences ever so telling, and their complex dynamics authentic phenomena from the Vic-torian archives of sexual politics.

NOTES

1. The reference is to the term made famous by Coventry Patmore's poem. Al-though the poem was not published until 1854, by which time Dickens had already serialized ten novels, the concept does not trace its origins to Patmore. That a woman should be regarded as an angel of the house or hearth is such a recurrent theme throughout the nineteenth century that it is not in fact anachronistic in the discussion of Dickens' works prior to 1854. The term is hyphenated throughout this study to designate its function as a single "ideological apparatus" (Althusser's term; see note 7).

2. See *Sesame and Lilies* in which Ruskin defined women's mission ("the type of eternal truth"): "The soul's armour is never well set to the heart unless a woman's hand has braced it; and it is only when she braces it loosely that the honour of manhood fails" (57).

3. Drawing from the history of the language that has defined a cult of woman-hood from mid-Victorian times, several terms are used interchangeably in references

to domestic ideology: womanhood, domestic ordering, enclosure, gender definition, and domesticity. Such terms indicate those viewpoints that restricted women to a domestic identity based upon their gender, a perspective that is at the core of domestic ideology.

4. Many studies have considered how Victorian morality emerged as a reaction against the courtly and somewhat lascivious practices of the eighteenth century. Such assessments can help the modern reader to understand that many twentieth-century attitudes toward sexuality and gender roles have not always dominated Western culture and to trace their origins to only the previous century. Joan Kelly's work provides a historical context for Victorian prudery and domesticity as it surveys the British trajectory of women's roles, freedoms, and restrictions. Kelly theorizes that domesticity grew out of an economical and sexual–political atmosphere and pinpoints when women lost public power (1–52). Gordon Rattray Taylor analyzes specific areas of repression and addresses how and why they came into existence. He believes that historical periods form into two cycles: the first he labels as "matrist"—when the mother image dominates, resulting in a socially permissive period. "Patrist" is what he terms the alternate cycle in which the father figure dominates, resulting in a repressive period. Taylor argues that the seventeenth and eighteenth centuries were a time of sexual freedom and liberties reflected in dress, customs, laws, sexual preferences, and so forth. The Victorians lived during the second cycle.

Two other studies are useful in analyzing Victorian sexual anxieties arising out of the nuclear family, newly emerging during the end of the 1700s. See Tania Modleski's *Loving with a Vengeance: Mass Produced Fantasies for Women*, 16–77; and Raymond Mise's *The Gothic Heroine and the Nature of the Gothic Nature*, especially 4–7, 50, and 239–51.

5. Blake writes: "Novels did not exist in some precious literary vacuum . . . Eliot's *Adam Bede* had also been quoted in the House of Commons—not an unusual occurrence. The novel, then, was public property in a way in which family life and letters were not: it gave people a chance to discuss domestic ideology in public without touching on their own domestic secrets" (72).

6. See Slater's chapter, "Catherine: The End of the Marriage" (135–62).

7. Ricoeur is working with Althusser's ideas, and Althusser is working with Marx's ideas. Althusser defined "ideology" as "the system of the ideas and representations which dominate the mind of [an individual] or a social group" ("Apparatuses" 239). Ideology, according to Althusser, "always exists in an apparatus, and its practice, or practices"; although illusionary, its "existence is material" ("Lenin" 166). One might share in an ideological perception—a "doing what one 'ought' " ("Apparatuses" 243)—for example, that a husband and wife form the foundation of a family structure. Marriage, then, as sanctified by religion, society, and government, becomes the apparatus that carries the ideological concept. Althusser proposed that a novel might also serve as an apparatus to convey the ideal ("Lenin" 223).

Whereas Marx saw ideology as "an imaginary construction" that exists in a theoretical, dreamlike state (159), Althusser viewed ideology as "imaginary relationships of individuals to their real conditions of existence" (162). People play out their existence through an "illusionary perception of reality": what they perceive to be the truth but what is only reality to the extent that people believe their system to be truth ("Apparatuses" 241). Ideology, then, is an arbitrarily defined system of beliefs and perceptions as to how people should relate to each other. The ideological apparatus (to use Althusser's terminology) is superimposed upon reality in order to govern individuals, "realized in institutions, in their rituals, and their practices" (249).

The key concepts of Althusser's theory useful to this study are "arbitrary" and "imaginary." In viewing gender relationships through domestic ideology, one finds their construction and definition to be arbitrary and contrived to regulate social behavior—but neither innate, nor immutable, nor necessarily altruistic. These are conclusions that will be inevitable throughout this discussion of Dickens' conflicted notions of domestic ideology.

Göran Therborn expanded the dynamics of Althusser's apparatus in a way also useful to this study: "[Ideology] refers to that aspect of the human condition under which human beings live their lives as conscious actors in a world that makes sense to them to varying degrees. Ideology is the medium through which this conscious-ness and meaningfulness operate" (2). In order for people to make sense out of their lives, they consciously play out roles that they either construct for themselves or subscribe to and that seem likely to guarantee a certain quality of life. Such is the nature of gender roles: they are not providential. According to Althusser's terms, the ideology constructs "imaginary relationships" between men and women not necessarily based on any reality that might have naturally meted such characteristics and functions to genders ("Lenin" 162).

8. For instance, Dickens' agenda was influenced greatly by the encounters he had with women. Much scholarship has sought to identify the patterns of hostilities in Dickens' work as well as his propensity to deify women, by tying these patterns to incidents in his life. Both attitudes were bound to distort his expression of domestic ideology. Michael Slater, for one, in *Dickens and Women*, produced a viable study by aligning biographical data to Dickens' formation of female characters. Doris Alexander's persuasive later study considered the people who influenced Dickens' creation of characters. And Arthur Adrian made much of Dickens' relationship with his mother, which led, according to Adrian, to the struggle for satisfactory maternal images throughout his novels. Harry Stone's effort to discern what he called "love patterns" in Dickens' novels is rather reductive, though helpful in ascribing meaning to Dickens' presentation of women. Stone surmised that Dickens' construction of the angel type registered a repeated search for a heroine who would not disappoint him ("Love" 6–8), unlike those in his life who broke his heart (his mother, Mary Hogarth, and Maria Beadnell). However, the study here does not explore why the text got on the page, but how, once there, it contradicts itself. Some biographical reference may be helpful in explaining some of those contradictions, but such a perspective does not direct this study.

PART I

Choices, Bosoms, and Dampers

In creating Dora and Agnes in *David Copperfield*, Dickens set up a dichotomy between two types of women. The text seems to promote Agnes as the more acceptable mate for a young middle-class gentleman because she complies with the angel-in-the-house ideal. Apparently the text would have the reader believe that David's first marriage is a mistake: he married a child–woman who cannot run a household, cannot counteract encroaching worldly trials (earning a living) that conspire against his well-being, and cannot mother his children. Dora is the first dissenting woman whose portrayal in text becomes the focus of this study. She is not deliberately rebellious in her dissent: she is simply unable to effect the domestic deportment expected of her; therefore, she does not conform to the "proper" notions of womanhood. Dickens eliminates her before she produces offspring who, without a proper role model, will similarly be unable to conform to gender expectations. This has been the traditional interpretation of the novel's dilemma of love. It seems to fit nicely into a stock viewpoint of Victorian domestic ideology.

Chapter 2 identifies where the narrative of *David Copperfield* contradicts the advocacy of Agnes as ideal woman. The text seems to favor Dora as a wife and subtly countermines what the most popular advice manuals of the day said about the kind of woman who would make a man a perfect wife. It also covertly criticizes and undermines an ideology that destroys a woman who cannot realize the domestic ideal. Even more subversive than this activity is the text's telling portrayal of a man who seems miserable when he should be happy and who seems happy when he should be miserable, all because he is naturally at odds with social constructs of what is to produce nuptial bliss.

David and his women are not the only Victorians victimized by domesticity. Chapter 3 identifies gender tensions in *Barnaby Rudge*, tracing the dissent of Martha, an older woman who not only fails to care for her husband, govern her servant, or tend to the house, but also conspires against her husband's well-being. On the surface, the text's main objective seems to be to correct women like Martha. However, alongside the rising violence of the Gordon Riots (which erupted, interestingly, out of hateful reaction to those dissenters, the Catholics), a wife's rebellion heightens until, at the climax of both, Gabriel Varden subdues her. Martha's struggle, however, has left gaps and revealed conflicts that complicate and suggest alternate versions of ideologies that undercut domesticity.

Although the text tries to manipulate the reader to be critical of Martha, and even more so of her servant, that acrid dissenter Miggs, it is uneven in this effort. Chapter 4 examines the general discomfort and disdain with which Victorian society regarded spinsters as represented in and complicated by the text. Miggs negotiates her way through courtship rites, observes failed ideology apparent in her master's marriage, and finally becomes an independent woman who attacks tenets of domesticity. *Barnaby Rudge*, like *David Copperfield*, covertly but severely casts doubt on what was to be considered an ideal gender code by which men and women were to abide.

2

The Women of *David Copperfield*: The Choice of an Undisciplined Heart

Traditionally, *David Copperfield* has been read with a focus on the David/ Dora marriage as the book's central conflict. Crucial to that conflict has been the novel's dichotomy between two types of women, represented by Agnes and Dora.[1] The text seems to teach that a woman like Agnes Wickfield is the ideal mate for a young middle-class gentleman—she typifies the angel-in-the-house by demonstrating piety, domestic efficiency, submissiveness, self-denial, and subservience. To show what happens to a man who does not marry such a paragon of virtue, Dickens has David marry Dora Spenlow. Although in love with her, David suffers as no gentleman should because of his wife's inability to comply with domestic ideology. Not intentionally rebellious, nevertheless she is this study's first dissenting woman, a woman who does not conform to the domestic ideal. The novel, however, conflicts in its assessment of *both* Agnes and Dora.

David writes his narrative ten years after marrying Agnes. This couple becomes situated within the framework of domesticity, where David can realize his worldly career because he now has a wife who tends well to him and his hearth. Seemingly, arriving at this gender-based organizational scheme has been the novel's point of destination all along.

In actuality, David recalls his first wife with great passion and intense loss, describing her with language charged with desirability. When he recounts the history of his relationship with Agnes, David seems to respond to his second wife as if he were a patient who has to take medicine. With striking omission, he describes Agnes in only shadowy detail. All in all, he implies, "I should be enraptured by this woman because she is the perfect example of womanhood, but I miss my Dora." One must wonder whether the text is promoting the second Copperfield marriage as a model or, rather, is evaluating the price and clouding the merits of gender division of roles within marriage.

Once David and Dora set up housekeeping, the first Mrs. Copperfield fails to enact her wifely part, and, as a result, the Copperfield domestic sphere conspicuously contrasts with what was expected of a middle-class home, as outlined in Sarah Ellis' *The Wives of England* (1843). Dickens might have read or at least been familiar with its tenets, for this advice book was widely read and known when he began work on *David Copperfield* (1849). The ideology it constructs also forms the locus of the novel's pedagogy: "At home it is but fitting that the master of the house should be considered as entitled to the choice of every personal indulgence" (28–32). This description contrasts sharply with the Copperfield household when David, struggling to write and to support his household by working as a parliamentary reporter, returns to his home—the place that is supposed to be his sanctuary away from the cares of the world. The housekeeper, Mary Anne Paragon, by virtue of her name and her profession, should be able to keep David's house, but not if the mistress of the house cannot manage her. Paragon is the ironic metonymy for Dora, who fails in matters of the house. As such, Dora (Dickens seems to say) falls far short as a paragon of womanhood.

David is tender in his remonstrance with Dora. The narrator overtly means for the reader to sympathize with David in the scene when he is asking his wife only to speak to their housekeeper about dinner. He has been waiting to eat for over an hour and will have to leave shortly for a job that will keep him out past midnight. The day before, the dinner was so late, he was able to eat only half of it. The day before that, he was forced to eat uncooked veal in a hurry, and it made him sick. It would appear that the reader is not to consider whether Dora is also suffering from hunger, however. After all, as Gail Houston observed in this novel and in *Dombey and Son*, the male is always supposed to be hungry and the female, nurturing (92). The Copperfield state of culinary affairs signals the unacceptable management of the household: a well-set table symbolizes contentment, material sufficiency, and a well-ordered family in which everyone is properly acting out his or her role.[2]

When David lists his grievances about the homemaking, Dora responds by crying because she thinks he is calling her a "disagreeable wife." He protests that that is not what he said, but Dora persists, "You said, I wasn't comfortable!" David returns, "I said the housekeeping was not comfortable!" (537; ch. 44). Although this sounds like a simple tiff between a husband and wife, Dora's conclusion signals an important issue: "It's exactly the same thing!" Through the course of this dialogue, Dora charges David for confusing who she is with what she can and cannot do as a domestic manager. Although David insists that that is exactly what he is determined not to do, Dora astutely recognizes that that merger of identities (woman and household manager) is the crux of the conflict.

Dora has never been trained to take care of a house, but David expects her to do so as if all women were natural housewives. If Dora cannot make his home comfortable, then she is the problem, not the housekeeping. What else can Dora *be* if she cannot *do?* Here lies the dilemma of domestic ideology that is posed by the text. Even though David may say otherwise, his constant behavior and criticism reinforce that Dora must not have identity outside her role as housewife. The text will support this theme by killing Dora. Yet the text has given her identity by presenting her case, a charge directed to the heart of domestic organization that reduces woman to a doer-unto-the-man instead of allowing her *to be* unto herself.

Because David loves her, despite her failure as housekeeper, then, Dora's plight is also David's sorrow. They both suffer not just because they cannot grow into an ideal couple, with each performing his and her proper domestic roles—a conflict that is well defined on the surface of the text—but because they cannot perform roles within a social system that will not accept any deviation or adjustment to domesticity as it must be in marriage. This is a crisis more subtly conveyed that opposes domesticity but is just as legitimately present in the text as is the more apparent moralizing for domesticity.

Elizabeth Langland, in her article "Nobody's Angels," investigates the "Victorian myth" (as it permeates *David Copperfield*) that defined a woman as one who by her nature diffuses a charm and order that turn a home into a refuge from the capitalist competition of the commonplace (291–98). Dora stands in the way of David's climbing the social and economic ladder (Raina 100–101). If she does not take care of the home front, he cannot function effectively in the marketplace. These are the gender dynamics of the Victorian nuclear family. Dora's inability to fulfill her domestic function results not only in organizational chaos, but also in loss of status for David, who aspires to be a middle-class gentleman (Langland, "Angels" 298). In the novel's reproduction of domestic ideology, there is no other option but to eliminate Dora, even as Dora herself expects her death and asks Agnes to take her place. Langland understands Dora to be David's "first mistaken impulse of an undisciplined heart" (*DC* 558 and 560; ch. 45; and 587; ch. 48).

On the surface of Dickens' text, Langland would appear to be correct. In a scene that follows soon after the domestic argument, David is again distraught over dinner arrangements. As he complains about getting sick because he had to gulp down uncooked veal, the text urges sympathy toward David and criticism of Dora because the text has also provided an earlier scene when the bachelor David deals with uncooked mutton at the hands of the tyrannical Mrs. Crupp. The scenes become connected when

David refers to the present housekeeper, Mary Anne, as "Mrs Crupp's daughter in disguise," and that connection raises the question of why he would expect Dora to be able to supervise the servants better than he. Notwithstanding the admission that he, too, is a novice at marriage and has much to learn, he seems to have come into this marriage with a set of gender expectations: the woman is innately equipped and required to rule the home, and the man to rule the world outside the front door. However, Dora's inability to fulfill her socially prescribed gender role is not the result of her childishness; instead, she remains childish so that she will not have to fulfill that role. Dora—as a result of her class upbringing—has not been trained to become an angel-in-the-house. Among the Victorian middle class, in which the dominant ideology is domesticity for women, no other options are available for the wedded Dora except becoming a housekeeper and mother.

Dora has been raised in a well-to-do family, tended by servants and pampered by her father and aunts alike. She has never had a mother to teach her how to manage a household. This is a crucial point, for women were expected to train other women to be wives and mothers. Without such training, Dora demonstrates that division of labor defined by gender is indeed arbitrary. She does not innately know how to perform a domestic role. Hence the cult of domesticity must be perpetuated through a deliberate, conscientious indoctrination: women are not born housekeepers. This idea in itself is subversive text.

Besides, had Dora married as her father had intended, a wealthy husband would have hired a professional housekeeper and butler to oversee the servants and make sure the house operated properly. Dora's class made her an ornament, a "plaything," a cultivation that did not serve her well when she married beneath the genteel class. The cult of domesticity is a middle-class construction.

It is that quality of ornamentation that makes David fall in love with her in the first place. She does not possess an Agnes-like face with the "tranquil brightness" of an object illuminated by the light through a stained glass window. Nor has she a basket full of keys that indicate she can control her house, nor the wisdom to advise David about finding a job to raise money to support his aunt and Mr. Dick or about avoiding friends who exert a bad influence. These descriptions, of course, fit Agnes—a sister—a woman he *does not love* (romantically). David, married to Dora, will never have a house in splendid working order, but neither will he be bullied and oppressed by a competent but acrid female domestic, as are Mr. Pott *(PP)*, Joe Gargery *(GE)*, Mr. Bumble *(OT)*, and Mr. Snagsby *(BH)*. Nevertheless, David is miserable because his marriage is not what he believes a marriage should be:

I did feel, sometimes, for a little while, that I could have wished my wife had been my counsellor; had had more character and purpose, to sustain me and improve me by; had been endowed with power to fill up the void which somewhere seemed to be about me; but I felt as if this were an unearthly consummation of my happiness, that never had been meant to be, and never could have been. (545; ch. 44)

David, in many respects, acts like a phallocentric male who expects his companion to act as angel-in-the-house. He bemoans the lack of a wife whose sole existence is making him a better person and ensuring his happiness. This attitude is not an individual one; his discontent arises from social conditioning. An 1832 article, which appeared in an American magazine, articulates what a man should expect from a wife:

See, she sits, she walks, she speaks, she looks—unutterable things! Inspiration springs up in her very paths—it follows her footsteps. A halo of glory encircles her, and illumines her whole orbit. With her, man not only feels safe but is actually renovated. For he approaches her with an awe, a reverence, and an affection which before he knew not he possessed. (qtd. in Douglas 46)[3]

With this bill typically representing ideological expectations, no wonder David is going to end up with Agnes and not recognize his affection for her, the angelic wife.

Aunt Betsey tries to modify this perspective. When her aid is enlisted, she reminds David of the second marriage that killed his mother, suggesting that he could very easily turn into a Mr. Murdstone. Dora is already a replica of Clara Copperfield: "ringleted and lovely but [she] can't do anything practical" (Manning 73). Perhaps the narrative calls for more elasticity in defining womanhood. When Clara Copperfield was alive, Clara Peggotty provided the mothering, and Clara Copperfield, the dancing (Dora also dances). The women were doing just fine without a man. In this particular household, two women bore the same first name: one was domestic and the other was not and would never be, regardless of a husband's discipline. Nevertheless, they were both women even if Victorian ideology would erase the one that did not conform to the prescribed image. They were both women who loved David and were loved by him but provided that love in different feminine ways. Once a patriarch enters the equation, such women as Dora and Clara Copperfield cannot survive; both dancers do die. The text, in depicting such a tragedy, notably does not champion heterosexual marriage framed by a rigid gender ideology.

If there is any woman in the novel who represents an alternate woman who crosses gender lines and yet survives, it is Aunt Betsey. She is the female head of a household who mothers not only an orphan outcast, but also a childish man. Sometimes she is described as eccentric and masculine (as perceived by Dora's aunts) (509; ch. 41). Because she is still married, does not live with her husband, but gets along quite well without him, the text, in overtly advocating heterosexual relationships in which gender lines are clearly drawn, cannot depict her as having desirable "normal" feminine physical qualities. However, complicating her portrait are illustrations of her performing domestic tasks and adding that "woman's touch" to make David's life more comfortable (454; ch. 37). As Sylvia Manning succinctly indicates, Aunt Betsey is masculine in her independence, but she has a feminine heart (73).

Some critics have perceived her as being androgynous and reproducing that androgyny in David (Edwin Eigner, for one; 141). Then Pam Morris' suggestion makes sense that David's feminine side as Daisy is also represented in the feminine Dora as Blossom. But when David denies his femininity by overpowering it with masculine sexual need for Agnes, then his feminine side, Dora, dies (67–76).

Many critics assess David as pre-Oedipal in his relationship with Dora. One might begin with Arthur Adrian's important work on Dickens' search for a good mother through his novels, which was caused by the unsatisfactory image of his own mother. One might also consider David Holbrook's identifying in Dickens' work the male fear of the mother's removing her breast. According to his theory, Dickens' men never move into an Oedipal stage with their mothers. Men are terrified of sexual desire, so women are usually killed before they become sexual creatures, or men are constantly betrayed by women who cease to be ideally pure. Dickens, to Holbrook, could never resolve the ideal and the libidinal.

Then one might turn to Gail Houston, who argues that David loses the breast to his brother and recognizes his mother's sexuality in the Murdstone marriage. At these crucial psychological junctures, the transition is not smooth, because the mother and the brother die. David is unable to receive nurturing from Mrs. Micawber, who already has twins at her breasts. He becomes sexually awakened through his knowledge of Emily and then Rosa, and finally through Uriah's lust for Agnes, after he fails to receive nurturing from Dora, who is herself searching for a breast (102–22). By the way, Harry Stone also sees the Uriah/Agnes development as important to David's own development; only Stone understands Heep to represent David's darker side, the hidden passions that he has had to suppress in his relationship with Dora. Heep's aggressive pursuit of Agnes allows David to recognize and follow his own sexual impulses *(Night* 118–24).

Finally, one would complete an understanding of the psychological growth of the male as depicted by Dickens through Pam Morris' study. Morris theorizes that the two Claras represent David's psychological split between a desirable Oedipal mother and a pre-Oedipal nurturer (67). The death of David's brother signifies the death of his own infancy (75–76). At Yarmouth, he is ready to be sexualized by Little Em'ly's own struggle to transfer her affections from her uncle to her cousin. Morris refers to this situation as David's "fantasy displacement of a sexually desirable mother" (67). If Morris had continued this line of thinking, she might have recalled that shortly afterward, Little Em'ly is seduced by Steerforth, and later David courts Dora. Morris does identify Dora's death as David's "death of youthful visionary self" (72), but then might have speculated that David was finally ready for a sexually mature relationship with Agnes. When once David related to both Little Em'ly and Agnes as brother to sisters, his sexuality seems to mature in the following scene, first in relation to Little Em'ly, then, by association, to Agnes: "I thought I saw sitting, by an open port, with one of the Micawber children near her, a figure like Emily's; it first attracted my attention, by another figure parting from it with a kiss; and it glided calmly away through the disorder, reminding me of—Agnes!" (683; ch. 57). At this point Little Em'ly is the fallen woman, having had a sexual affair with Steerforth. She is no longer the asexual little girl of his youth. Agnes' kiss is like a symbolic transfer of Em'ly's sexuality to Agnes, or at least David's revelation that Agnes, like Little Em'ly, is not just a sister anymore.

However, other critics evaluate David's psychological drama, Dora's death, and Aunt Betsey's influence differently. Doris Alexander, for one, pairs the aunt with Miss Havisham as "prototype feminists" who are angry at the way men treat women (132). This observation can be supported by the text when Aunt Betsey gives David her own name instead of respecting his patriarchal name. As if denying his gender, she constantly compares him to his sister Betsey, who exists only in the aunt's mind. The sister is the aunt reproduced in David and is a denial of maleness. After all, Aunt Betsey's experiences with patriarchy have not been positive. In every situation in which she submits herself to male authority, she suffers: her vagrant husband returns after having abandoned her, and she dutifully surrenders all of her cash. She relies upon Mr. Spenlow to invest the rest of her money only to lose it because of Heep's malpractice. Consequently, she preaches to David to be firm and self-reliant. These are Aunt Betsey's own unfeminine qualities that she would instill in her adopted son whom she regards as a daughter. Aunt Betsey signifies herself; she is an independent woman, but her (or the text's) perception of gender is embroiled. Through all of her nonconformity, the text does not retaliate as it does with other women who are independent and refuse to be submissive female types (such as Miggs in *Barnaby Rudge*, Sally Brass in *Old Curiosity Shop*, and Mrs. Joe in *Great Expectations*[4]). Because of David's constructive relationship with Aunt Betsey, he should be able to appreciate diversity in women, to recognize that not every woman has to be an angel-in-the-house to make a man happy or a marriage successful. Unfortunately this is a lesson he does not learn in time, but one that the text seems to teach through his experience.

Knowing David's expectations of a wife, Aunt Betsey advises him to try to reform Dora, and failing that, to set aside his expectations: "Estimate her (as you chose her) by the qualities she has, and not by the qualities she may not have. The latter you must develop in her, if you can. And if you cannot . . . you must accustom yourself to do without 'em" (538–39; ch. 44). In order to return to the old happiness they once both knew with each other, David resolves to adapt to his young wife rather than to continue fathering her into maturity as Murdstone had his mother. Given this decision, the seminal critic Barbara Hardy views David as a persona that "reveals—or rather *betrays*—Victorian limitations which the author does not see but which the modern reader most certainly does" (124). Either David realizes that he may continue to endorse an ideology that causes him only pain or he may defy that ideology and perhaps again experience the happiness of his early relationship with Dora before she was to become a housewife. David entertains Victorian expectations of what a wife should be but then decides to accept Dora as she is; however, Hardy adds, Dora "is not what he wants or needs" (124). Actually the text consistently does affirm that Dora *is* what David wants. Unfortunately, if he also wants the trappings of middle-class status, then he needs a woman like Agnes who can run his household and enhance his status. The text reveals the severity of ideology by discarding the woman who does not fit into the schema.

Although many critics have argued against him,[5] G. K. Chesterton faults Dickens for depicting David's marriage to Dora as a mere flirtation. Chesterton holds that the text entices the reader to fall in love with Dora and believe that the marriage should last a lifetime. When David later marries Agnes, the reader sees it as "nothing, a middle-aged compromise, a taking of the second best, a sort of spiritualized and sublimated marriage of convenience" (133). Despite language intended to manipulate the thoughts and feelings of its reader, the text often fails to sway in only one direction. This is the conflicted Dickens.[6] This is the Victorian who tries to advocate a certain marriage ideal and perfect wife type, all the while creating desire for something outside domestic ideology. The text would have us prefer Agnes to Dora because the former represents the perfect angel-in-the-house. It would also have us become irritated at Dora's inadequacies. Yet it portrays Dora as a delightful, charming woman who brightens the world around her. She is the romantic free spirit that resists structure and regulation, making an unfortunate, ill-timed appearance in a society that exacted structure and regulation with an almost religious fervor.

Chesterton reasons that the reader should not condemn Dora for her poor housekeeping skills; instead, despise the demands of housekeeping:

It is better to marry a human and healthy personality which happens to attract you than to marry a mere housewife; for a mere housewife is a mere housekeeper. . . . David Copperfield and Dora quarreled over the cold mutton; and if they had gone on quarreling to the end of their lives, they would have gone on loving each other to the end of their lives; it would have been a human marriage. But David Copperfield and Agnes would agree about the cold mutton. And that cold mutton would be very cold. (134–36)

Chesterton identifies within the text an advocacy of a marriage that does not conform to Victorian ideal. Further, Chesterton finds the David/Dora struggle to represent more accurately a believable marriage beset with both joy and conflicts than does the David/Agnes relationship. If the text is indeed trying to persuade the reader that David's second marriage is a domestic model that the reader should imitate, then it needs to give as much— if not more—evidence that the second marriage is as at least as viable as the first, and that it is more conducive to the well-being and happiness of the parties involved. The text does not do this, leaving a crucial gap in its case for domestic ideology.

The text contains another severe gap: domestic ideology is well served when a young girl marries an older man, a situation that serves patriarchal politics in that the husband can finish the molding process begun by the father. Thus, the child can be formed into the woman who can best serve his needs.[7] Dora is literally called a child-bride. Besides the sensual description that defines her in text, Albert Guerard considers the portrayal as an "idealized virgin," coupled with the fantasy (David's) of being married to such, deliberately provocative (71). In all the erotic desirability that Dickens would invest in her youthfulness, the text fails to connect where fantasy meets reality, when Dickens attempts to incorporate both in the same narrative. The text supports domestic ideology in which marrying a young woman is to be encouraged, but the text conflicts with itself. One of the problems that Thomas Vargish identifies is Dickens' failed attempts to reconcile his ethereal notions of women with sexual desire (111–2). Another problem is that Dora, because she is childish, cannot run her household, but this was no problem for Agnes when she was only ten years old and in charge of her father's house. Would the text have us believe or not believe that a child can manage the complex, demanding operations of a Victorian home?[8] Domesticity, in its male fantastical fictionalization of woman, would have her manage the difficult and exacting tasks of running a typical middle-class Victorian household and at the same time be a helpless, dependent juvenile. David wants both, but he cannot have both.

Besides finding inconsistencies in Dickens' construction of an ideal marriage (represented by Agnes/David), many critics have faulted Dickens for creating shadowy characters, and of all of them, Agnes is cited most.[9] In truth the only physical description of her is similar to the following: "Although her face was quite bright and happy, there was a tranquility about it, and about her—a quiet, good, calm spirit—that I never have forgotten; that I shall never forget" (194; ch. 15). Either she is ascribed saintly and ethereal characteristics or she is described in terms of how she serves the men in her life. This is how the text portrays the expression on Agnes' face and defines her beauty in one scene: "There was such deep fondness for him, and gratitude to him for all his love and care, in her beautiful look" (238; ch. 19). She exists only as a reflection of the male. Instead of concrete details about her, the text describes the outside (190) and the inside (194) of the house, as well as Mr. Wickfield's clean attire (192). Every characteristic reaffirms her ideological representation as a domestic caretaker: "serene," "modest," "gentle," "sweet," and similar adjectives do not physically describe Agnes. In this failing, the text denies her physicality and essence.

In contrast, the criteria for defining Dora seem to be physical and sensual. It is true that the reader is never told what color Dora's curls are, but at least she does have curls, as well as dimples, a pink complexion, small hands and feet. The narrator describes the color of her dress, hat, and ribbons. When Dora talks to David, she plays with his buttons. She wears a gold watch. She touches a dog. It is not much to go on, but she appears to have flesh and blood, unlike Agnes, who is described only as having a "heavenly face" and seems not to exist in this physical world for the lack of detail surrounding her.

And Dora is a sensual character with a tiny mouth that forms into a rosebud. Her ability to arouse David is apparent in the following passage:

[Jip] was mortally jealous of me, and persisted in barking at me. She took him up in her arms—oh my goodness!—and caressed him, when I tried; and then she beat him. It increased my sufferings greatly to see the pats she gave him for punishment on the bridge of his blunt nose, while he winked his eyes, and licked her hand, and still growled within himself like a little double-bass. At length he was quiet—well he might be with her dimpled chin upon his head!—and we walked away to look at a greenhouse. (336; ch. 26)

In mentioning jealousy, the text establishes Jip and David as equal competitors for Dora's attentions. As she picks up the dog and caresses him and beats him, David clearly projects himself into Jip's place. They have not yet reached the greenhouse (a site of much sexual activity) when David is so distracted by Dora's continued physical and adoring attentions to Jip that he narrates, "If it had lasted any longer, I think I must have gone down on my knees on the gravel, with the probability before me of grazing them, and of being presently ejected from the premises besides" (337). To this day—that is, David's present as he is writing his reminiscence—the racy scent of a geranium leaf recalls the earlier sensations brought on by "a quantity of curls, and a little black dog being held up, in two slender arms, against a bank of blossoms and bright leaves." Such language connotes sexual display.

Virginia Carmichael also views the text as meaning for Dora to be perceived as a titillating object of desire, in apparent contrast to Agnes: "David's passion for Dora was sexual and he explicitly insists that his feelings for Agnes are not" (665). In comparison to a physical Dora, Agnes is an emblem. Angus Wilson dismisses her as "the first of the group of heroines who mark the least pleasing, most frumpy, and smug vision of ideal womanhood that he [Dickens] ever produced" ("Heroes" 20). She is a Mary type of woman,[10] one who is so good that Dickens cannot think of her in fleshy terms. Not only does the character lack concrete physical description, there is nothing sexual about her, whereas Dora emerges out of an abundance of sensual detail. Richard Barickman et al. note a similar desexualization of the nineteenth-century novel's domestic woman: "As part of the shift from an erotic to a domestic center, the courted woman tends to be valued for her ability to sustain family life, to maintain or restore moral, emotional, and spiritual integrity for the household, rather than for any distinct erotic qualities" (9). Michael Slater offers an explanation of the value shift: "The virtual absence of any serious presentation of woman in 'the lofty character' of sanctifying wife relates to Dickens's extreme difficulty in reconciling the sexual with the domestic ideal."[11] That absence (aside from any biographical consideration) illuminates why the text, in its pedagogic promotion of domesticity, equates purity with absence of sexuality. As Merryn Williams points out, Dickens makes a connection between housekeeping and moral influence (77–8), necessitating that the woman manifest saintly qualities that were understood as being nonsexual. The following passage exemplifies Agnes as both housekeeper and moral nurturer:

In good time [Agnes] made tea; and afterwards, when I brought down my books, looked into them, and showed me what she knew of them (which was no slight matter, though she said it was), and what was the best way to learn and understand them. I see her, with her modest, orderly, placid manner, and I hear her beautiful calm voice, as I write these words. The influence for all good, which she came to exercise over me at a later time, begins already to descend upon my breast. (201; ch. 16)

Agnes inconspicuously introduces order and, therefore, calm wherever she goes, as in the scene when she sets up Aunt Betsey in a room after the aunt has lost all of her money. Aunt Betsey is able to survive the catastrophe because Agnes hangs the bird cages just as they used to hang in the cottage, and she finds David an additional job: she maintains order. Even if she is not described by physical detail, her actions are quite physical and practical. Instead of being, she does, and her doing ensures the moral well-being of those around her.

By the same token, Dora's poor housekeeping does not affect only her and David. The reader is to understand that it morally corrupts all of the servants who work for them, that their thievery is the direct result of Dora's failure to exert a moral influence. Sarah Ellis charged women: "You have deep responsibilities; you have urgent claims, a nation's moral worth is in your keeping" (*Women* 6). By regulating the moral and spiritual climate of the home, multiplied by thousands of homes, women were seen as the preserver of British values, especially during a time when men engaged in competitive practices in the work force. Dora's failure in this area is by far the most severe violation of domestic ideology.

Some critics fill in the gap between Agnes and Dora by construing Dickens' preference for a combination of both women as wife (or wives). For example, Edwin Charles writes: "David was wanting—though he does not know it—a combination of the beautiful child–wife Dora, and the calm, sagacious, practical, seraphic Agnes" (524). Or another way to put it is that Dickens (as one might suspect most Victorian men who were conditioned to expect an angel-in-the-house partner did) desired both the sexual and the angelic in the same woman (Stone, *Night* 396). The text cannot reconcile both types in one woman. The Agnes/Dora nexus mirrors the ideology's expectations that an ideal woman would be both a virginal Mary and a voluptuous Bathsheba. The Dickens text demonstrates that Dora will never become an Agnes even if the latter were to tutor her; neither will Agnes ever give the kind of pleasure to David that he received from Dora. That is why, after marrying Agnes, David writes about Dora with the passion of one still in love with her, and it is also why he constantly refers to Agnes throughout his love affair and marriage with Dora. On David's first wedding day Dora is "so fond of Agnes that she will not be separated from her, but still keeps her hand" (533; ch. 43). David envisions the three of them as necessary to create a happy home: "I remember cherishing . . . a fancy as if Agnes were one of the elements of my natural home. As if, in the retirement of the house made almost sacred to me by [Agnes'] presence, Dora and I must be happier than anywhere" (414; ch. 34).[12]

Most critics who support the Dora-the-mistake interpretation do not accept the ménage à trois theory. They might cite Dora's deathbed speech to David, which sounds the note of finality to the young couple's relationship: "Oh, Doady, after more years, you never could have loved your child-wife better than you do; and, after more years, she would so have tried and disappointed you, that you might not have been able to love her half so well! I know I was too young and foolish. It is much better as it is!" (647; ch. 53). They figure (as does Audrey Lucas) that Dickens has to kill off Dora before David becomes disillusioned with her, before he comes to resent her for not being Agnes, and before Dora loses her charming effect on him by growing fat and old. Dickens killed, nearly killed, or stunted many of his young heroines (like Little Nell [*OCS*], Rose Maylie [*OT*], and Jenny Wren [*OMF*]), transforming them into Keatsian "unravished bride[s]."[13] Thus he not only glorifies Agnes, but kills Dora, who failed as an earthly angel, so that she can become a heavenly angel. Dickens had no other choice, for Dora had no other options in Victorian society (as Dickens must have supposed) if she was incapable of being a proper Victorian wife but still was a desirable Dickensian character.[14]

Another refutation of the idea that Dora was a mistake lies in the narrative itself. A now-married-to-Agnes David is writing the Dora chapters. If he is someone who is really in love with his wife and can retrospectively consider his first marriage a mistake, he displays contradictory emotions. For example, during his remembrance of Dora, David says, "I had not been walking long, when I turned a corner, and met her. I *tingle* again from head to foot as my recollection turns that corner, and my pen shakes in my hand"(335; ch. 26; emphasis added). The "tingle" happens ten years after marriage to Agnes. Recalling the ring of forget-me-nots that he had bought for Dora, he writes that it was "so associated in my remembrance with Dora's hand, that yesterday, when I saw such another, by chance, on the finger of my own daughter, there was a momentary stirring in my heart, like pain!" (413; ch. 33). More than a nostalgic recollection of young love, the reminiscence vibrates with yet vigorous sexual desire for Dora, made more vivid by the association of the ring and flowers with defloration and the vagina. Although Dora may have passed her marital ring to Agnes, the flowers, by their very name, indicate that she will not be forgotten.

The text itself clarifies Dickens' intentions with Copperfield's first marriage. So conspicuous are the intertwining of events in the Strong marriage with David's, the similarities between the two marriages, and the impact on David of the Strongs' reconciliation that a discussion of David and Dora is incomplete without serious consideration of this other struggling marriage.

Annie Strong, now twenty, has been married several years to a man who has known her since she was six months old and had been a good friend of her father's. From this point on, the Strongs' marriage mirrors the Copperfields'. Dr. Strong married a woman too inexperienced for marriage, but he has the intention, like David, of forming her character (turning her into a proper wife). She, like Dora, "was very young, and had no adviser" (559; ch. 45). Also like Dora, she thinks that someone else could have made her husband a "worthier home" and that she was "unsuited" to his "learning and wisdom" (559).

Annie is charged with sexuality, like Dora. Edwin Eigner recalls that Mr. Spenlow warns Agnes to stay away from Annie as if she poses some threat to his daughter's purity (64). The night that Annie loses her cherry-colored ribbon, and David notices that it is in her cousin's hands, Annie returns without the ribbon and is pathetically pale and soon faints. She significantly says of the ribbon that "she had had it safe, a little while ago, she thought, but it was not worth looking for" (212; ch. 16). David describes her, after the meeting with Jack, at the Doctor's feet: "But with such a face as I never saw. It was so beautiful in its form, it was so ashy pale, it was so fixed in its abstraction, it was so full of a wild, sleep-walking, dreamy horror of I don't know what. The eyes were wide open, and her brown hair fell in two rich clusters on her shoulders, and on her white dress, disordered by the want of the lost ribbon" (212; ch. 16). In the sketch by Phiz, Annie is portrayed as a fallen woman who sits at her husband's knees as if to beg forgiveness. Her bodice exposes much breast as if the dress has been torn. She seems to be kneeling on one leg. The outline of the other limb defines a sensually plump leg that is slightly, provocatively turned out. Her hair is disheveled and careless over bare shoulders and bosom. She does not look like an "innocent" woman.

The text has attributed much sensual detail in its description of Annie as it has of Dora. Both are enticing women who complicate the notion of essential Victorian woman in much the way that Elizabeth Langland suggests (in an earlier article): "Characters often spring to life in contexts that individualize rather than reinforce their representative natures" *(Society* 72). Nevertheless, the text responds to both women as threats to domestic order. The implication is that Annie is at fault because her sensuality is so provocative that a man is driven to rape her (symbolized by the loss of ribbon). What needs to be reconciled here is why Dora dies but Annie does not and why and how Annie is embraced by her husband as if the rape had been *his* fault.

Annie (like Dora) is indeed in love with her husband and finds all of her happiness solely in him. He says that by marrying her, he had wanted to provide "a refuge, for her, from the dangers and vicissitudes of life" (521; ch. 42), just as David should for Dora.

Although Dickens is adamantly opposed to women marrying for pecuniary reasons (as in the Granger/Dombey marriage [*D&S*]), and seems not to encourage December/May marriages (as in the Summerson/Jarndyce proposal [BH]), he promotes the Strong marriage by implying that they will live happily ever after—a particularly rare projection for Dickens, who often treats marriage and happiness as two states that cannot possibly exist together.

When David tries to depart from nuptial conventions, he makes an odd declaration: "For I knew, now, that my own heart was undisciplined when it first loved Dora; and that if it had been disciplined, it never could have felt, when we were married, what it had felt in its secret experience" (588; ch. 48). "There can be no disparity in marriage like unsuitability of mind and purpose," Annie Strong tells him, grateful that her husband, who is very much her senior, has saved her from the "first mistaken impulse of [her] undisciplined heart." Both of these conditions (the disparity and the impulse) refer to her irresponsible, disreputable cousin whom she loved as a girl. Does David realize that he has made a mistake in marrying Dora? Is his "secret experience" those unvoiced doubts that he married someone inappropriate and too young for him? Are they not very similar to the doubts that plagued Dr. Strong, and was not the doctor willing himself to die (as was Dora) in order to free his spouse to marry someone more suitable? Instead of trying to reform Annie as David does Dora, Dr. Strong defies domestic ideology by allowing Annie the freedom to be who she is and to be happy in that state, and even to enjoy marriage, albeit with someone else, who can love her as she is and not what she should be. These are the attitudes and actions of a benevolent patriarch. Through him, the text challenges the structure of domesticity on behalf of women as well as men by accepting a woman who is not an ideal.

The Strong marriage is an encouragement to David that his marriage can succeed as well. Gwendolyn Needham observes that the resolution of the Strongs' domestic unhappiness occurs only after David wonders whether he will ever know happiness because of marriage to Dora (100). The Strongs' reconciliation is necessary in the novel, according to Needham, to teach David that he has made an unsuitable union with Dora (98) and that this realization is to give him hope, peace, and resolution about his present marriage to Agnes. However, the resolution of the Strong marriage is an affirmation that David—in marrying Dora—has married correctly, just as Strong has in marrying Annie. When Annie says, "There can be no disparity in marriage like unsuitability of mind and purpose" (558; ch. 45), it is up to David to change his mind and purpose about his marriage—that is, to relinquish his expectations of what Dora should be and to accept who she is. When Annie thanks her husband for saving her "from the first mistaken impulse of [her] mistaken heart" (558), she is, of course, referring to Jack Maldon. The question is, as David repeats these lines to himself, which mistaken impulse does he refer to? Does he see, while narrating his past, that he made a mistake in his treatment of Dora and that she, after all, had been the best choice for him (as Annie was for Dr. Strong) or that he made a mistake in marrying Dora, and now that he's married to Agnes, all is right? The ambivalence in the text is the text's ambivalence toward the very marriage ideal that it tries to exemplify.

Marrying impulsively was also warned against in *Oliver Twist*. Mrs. Maylie tries to dissuade Harry from marrying the angelic Rose because she is blemished. As discussed more fully in Chapter 8, the mother counsels that impulses that lead people to want to marry do not last. Yet, in this case, Harry's impulse is right. Rose does prove to be the perfect match. Since this novel predates *David Copperfield*, one might consider its implications in evaluating what the Dickens text has to say about marrying for love.

If Dora had survived, she might have become like Annie. This is neither an unsupported nor an unimportant speculation, for the text indicates striking similarities in behavior between the two women. In one scene Annie sits watching her husband read his dictionary. He urges her to go to bed for she must be tired, and watching him read must be boring. She begs him to let her stay. In a scene that is nearly identical, Dora watches as David writes. He entreats her to go to bed, and she entreats him not to send her away. Both women specifically encourage their men in each literary pursuit;

thus, they are performing, as aesthetic nurturers, that role as Victorian women that, to Dickens, is their highest duty. And both men protect vulnerable young women from the snares of the world, such as marrying a vagabond like Jack or ending up spinsters like Miss Lavinia and Miss Mills or being abandoned like Aunt Betsey.

The evidence of the successful Strong marriage implies that David and Dora could have been happy had David been able to forgo his expectations. By being willing to free Annie instead of disciplining her to his will, as Murdstone has Clara, and David to a less severe degree, Doctor Strong surrendered his patriarchal power. David was not able to do this, so he ended up with Agnes. Chesterton would have readers believe that Dickens made a mistake in creating Dora and then marrying her to David. Dora developed into a problem for David, so Dickens simply dispensed with her by killing her (134). Dora's death is an important and integral part of the entire novel that critiques a hostile set of conventions that made no room for a woman to survive if she did not conform.

David expresses hope that "lighter hands than mine would help to mould her character, and that a baby-smile upon her breast might change my child–wife to a woman" (588; ch. 48)—in other words, motherhood would cause Dora to conform to a standardized version of woman—but "[i]t was not meant to be. The spirit fluttered for a moment on the threshold of its little prison, and, unconscious of captivity, took wing" (588; ch. 48). By "spirit," does the text refer to the unborn child or Dora? It seems that the text, through death, is releasing both the child and Dora from a prison. It seems that Dora dies because her pregnancy represents the system of expectations imposed inappropriately and fatally on a woman not cut out to be a wife or mother in David's terms.

If the "spirit" refers to the unborn child escaping from its "little prison," does the text subtly imply that the child would never have done well in this world under the dubious auspices of Mrs. Copperfield (as was the case of poor Kate and Nicholas, who had to put up with an insipid mother in *Nicholas Nickleby*)? If there had been a Little Dora, would she not have suffered the same disadvantages as Mama Dora, who had no mother to train her how to be a "woman"? The novel has made much of Agnes' close resemblance to the picture of her mother; domesticity is reproduced in women by women. The text foregrounds a support of the patriarchal system that defines women within a domestic enclosure by eliminating the child (as well as the mother for the same reason), because she could neither survive nor be happy in Victorian society, unable as she would be to assume the angel-in-the-house role. If the text decides that Providence did indeed take Dora and her child, then Providence is a powerful advocate of domestic ideology with an omnipotent arm that enforces its tenets and executes its judgments. Whether or not an act of mercy, the removal of two nonconformists from society displays the merciless rigor of a system that

insists upon standardizing men and women. The prison reference signals a
gap that can be read as an unfavorable perspective toward domestic ideology, namely, that the entire patriarchal regime is an intolerable prison,
especially to women like Dora and to the only kind of offspring that Dora
types could produce.

The specific scene that precedes her death (and has much to do with it)
occurs in yet another chapter, entitled "Domestic" (ch. 48). Aunt Betsey is
visiting Dora when they both notice that Jip is not his usual energetic self.
Betsey tells Dora that Jip is getting too old to "race with" Little Blossom.
This knowledge is a shock to Dora: there are some rather complicated
undercurrents at work here in what Jip symbolizes. When Betsey suggests
that she will give Dora a replacement dog, the aunt may be implying the
reproduction and replacement of Dora through giving birth. Dora quickly
rejects the suggestion. More likely, Jip represents Dora as she is at present,
and his death signifies the death of Dora before she can be born again as
a woman who better conforms to Victorian standards. This would explain
Dora's response of alarm in this scene—after all, "Jip" is short for
"Gypsy," a fitting description of the freedom-loving, carefree spirit that has
characterized Dora. Furthermore, Dora is associated with Jip by Miss Lavinia's and Aunt Betsey's references to her as a pet.

Jip, also, as a stand-in for David (conveyed in passages that depict the
dog as the object extension of Dora's passion), represents that same spirit
in David that he suppresses in order to assume middle-class status. The
death of Jip will mark the end of Dora's identity, and she realizes it: "I
couldn't be such friends with any other dog but Jip; because he wouldn't
have known me before I was married, and wouldn't have barked at Doady
when he first came to our house." He represents the end of her options—
not her childhood, as some might think. Dora, in moaning, "I couldn't care
for any other dog but Jip," is not resisting the necessity to grow up, but
the necessity to become a woman who has no other definition than as a
wife and mother, roles that she has not been designed to fill.

Immediately after this scene, Dora's condition deteriorates so rapidly that
she is soon bedridden, doomed never to get up again. When she dies, Jip
"comes very slowly back to [David], licks [his] hand, and lifts his dim eyes
to [David's] face. . . . He lies down at [David's] feet, stretches himself out
as if to sleep, and with a plaintive cry, is dead" (647; ch. 53).

Laurie Langbauer theorizes why Dickens kills off the woman, in her
treatment of *The Old Curiosity Shop*, which, because *David Copperfield*
presents a similar case, is apropos to this study:

Nell's sacrifice to the closure of the novel suggest [*sic*] the way it needs to project
out, to pursue and kill off, what are really its own dissatisfactions with closure and
all that closure implies. The male order projects its own dissatisfactions with order
onto a woman so that it can indulge these feelings at a distance, converting its own

discomfort and even disturbing rebelliousness into a form that is displaced and manageable. By ultimately killing the woman off, that order seems to get rid of its dissatisfactions. (137).

Just as Dickens might have projected his own frustrations with the ideological system onto a woman in *The Old Curiosity Shop* (in the way Langbauer describes) so that those frustrations could be contained and handled, likewise he might have constructed a romance between David and Dora that creates desire from something outside ideology. Langbauer considers "how romance becomes for the novel the imaginary locus of dissatisfaction, rebelliousness; it becomes the traditional epitome of that which challenges or escapes restraint, namely, desire itself" (129). The identification of romance with desire—that unsatisfiable "want of something" which Dickens felt propelled *him* through life—suggests too the way romance inhabits whatever attempts to reject and disclaim it (130). By "romance," Langbauer refers to a type of writing that meanders and defers narrative closure, which one can identify as characteristic of Dickens' romance in the David/ Dora relationship. The text indicates that David is torn between his passion for Dora and his expectations of an ideal wife. By desiring Dora, David (and Dickens) must then deal with his frustrations about those expectations rather than about Dora's failure to fulfill them. When Dickens destroys Dora, he also causes great sorrow to David and thus registers his own feelings of unsettled concerns with domesticity.

Leavis and Leavis read the text as conveying the moral that a man should not marry a woman only for her charm and beauty, and they argue that critics have fallen off-track by "not seeing David's first marriage from the woman's (Dora's) point of view, but, instead, solving David's problem by the easy expedient of removing her by death and, even worse, exonerating David from guilt for it by representing her as willing to die in order not to be a burden" (106). The narrative, by the absence of Dora's story, *does* tell woman's story. It is a tale without a voice. Dora is a woman who cannot write her own text, and *that* is her text. David, the writer, is narrating not only his autobiography but hers as well, and all she can do is to sit and hold his pens and get ink all over her.[15] He has the power (the phallic pen) to define her according to his inclinations, and the resulting narrative completely writes her out of the text (she becomes nondistinct; she is covered with ink).

Besides, Dora does not know how to signify her own life. If she had been given a pen, she would not have known how to write her story any differently than has David; she does die so that Agnes can become David's wife.

Michael Slater applauds Dickens' creation and presentation of Dora: "Whether she be considered primarily as an individual character or as the embodiment of a critique of women's position in Victorian society, Dora is one of the most impressive achievements of this middle period of Dickens's work" (250). Not only does the narrative portray her as a desirable woman, it grants her more complexity, Slater says, than it does David in understanding human relationships (248–49). She is more perceptive than David in recognizing the futility of their situation and obligingly dies so that he can be happier without her.

The David/Dora/Agnes text is fuller when amplified by the parallel construction of the Strong marriage, but it is also diminished by the absence of women's text. Where are the stories of the women in *David Copperfield*? There are so many gaps in the narrative about them that these gaps signal the lack of power that the women had to make their own place in the novel, in a relationship, or in society.

The text indexes another unwritten story: if David could have learned flexibility from the Strong marriage and had the strength to resist a prefabricated design of a marriage unsuitable to the two partners involved, Dora would have represented a revolutionary new image of desirable woman and preferred wife. Such an outcome would have posed a threat to domestic economy; nevertheless, all of the pointers toward that possibility are embedded in the text.

NOTES

1. See discussions by Virginia Carmichael, G. K. Chesterton (129–31), A. O. J. Cockshut (115), Edwin Charles (232–54), and Audrey Lucas (711).

2. As discussed in Chapter 3, the Vardens enjoy a feast that is carefully described at the end of *Barnaby Rudge* that indicates order: the wife is finally submitting to her husband and nurturing him physically and spiritually as a good wife should.

3. *Ladies' Magazine* 3 (1832): 83–84.

4. For further discussion on Miggs, see Chapter 4; for Miss Sally and on Mrs. Joe, see Chapter 6.

5. For instance, Audrey Lucas disagrees with Chesterton. He insists: "Dickens has made it abundantly clear that Dora was David's first and wrong love," and Agnes "is intended from the beginning to be the right wife for David. She is preselected" (711).

6. It is not surprising that the text is conflicted, for John Forster records Dickens' attention to these two women, Agnes and Dora, as he struggled to decide whether Dora should die (letter to Forster May 7, 1850; qtd. in part on 101).

7. For excellent discussions about the Victorian daughter as an ideal wife, see Jenni Calder (98–117) and Deborah Gorham (38–46).

8. Elizabeth Langland alludes to the rigor of operating a Victorian household in "Nobody's Angels" (290–304). Other good sources are Leonore Davidoff and Catherine Hall's *Family Fortunes* and Mark Girouard's *Life in the English Country House*. Several novels written by women also make vivid the grueling tasks that faced the Victorian housewife, such as Elizabeth Stuart Phelps' *The Story of Avis* and Susan Warner's *The Wide, Wide World*.

9. Examples of such criticism include the following: Michael Slater regards

Dickens' portrayal of her as "clichéd" (248), "a religious ikon, an inert figure" (251), and "lifeless" (253). John Forster writes: "Dora . . . is more attractive than the too unfailing wisdom and self-sacrificing goodness of the angel–wife, Agnes" (vol. 2: 119). Crediting Dickens for intentionally ignoring Agnes' physicality in order to portray her soul, Juliet McMaster, nevertheless, finds that "Agnes's attributes seem slack and unconvincing" (7). And Gwendolyn Needham views her as "the victim of David's romantic sensibility; he has etherealized her into a superior being, a removed spirit whose rays warm his heart and guide his path" (96).

10. A Mary type of woman might refer to Mary Hogarth (the author's sister-in-law, who died at seventeen in his adoring arms) or the Virgin Mary—it does not matter which, for Dickens seemed to think of them in much the same way.

11. Michael Slater concludes that Dickens' angel-in-the-house icon could only be a single woman without a child who adopts something of a husband and acquires a child somehow, thereby producing a replica of a family that she is to protect and nurture but only without any sexual and other physical indications (312). Thus with Agnes, as with Little Dorrit and Little Nell, we have young women (Agnes is only ten when we are told she is the "little housekeeper") who are mothers to their fathers. Mr. Wickfield's puerile obedience to her is evident in this passage: "After dinner, Agnes sat beside him, as of old, and poured out his wine. He took what she gave him, and no more—like a child" (438; ch. 35).

12. The following passage from *David Copperfield* draws a sketch not unlike that etched of Catherine, Georgina, and Dickens by Daniel Maclise (1843), reproduced on the cover of Slater's *Dickens and Women*: "I never was so happy. I never was so pleased as when I saw those two sit down together, side by side. As when I saw my little darling looking up so naturally to those cordial eyes. As when I saw the tender, beautiful regard which Agnes cast upon her" (515; ch. 42).

13. See Slater's chapter 5.

14. Other critics recall the Maria Beadnell romance and concur with Dora, who tells David that it is better that she dies now before "Doady" tires of her (647; ch. 53). Similarly Dickens wrote to John Forster: "It is better for the precious coquette to die at an early age rather than to turn into 'a toothless, fat, old, and ugly' [Maria's description of herself to Dickens in 1855], repulsive old coquette" (vol. 1: 51).

15. For discussion of the significance of women and writing, see Chapter 10, which analyzes this theme in *Bleak House*.

3

Barnaby Rudge's Mrs. Varden: The Buxom

"Whether valued as a nursery of civic virtues or as a refuge from the tensions of society, the family was worshipped throughout the Victorian period," begins Anthony Wohl in his analysis of the nineteenth-century family. The famous Victorian essayist John Ruskin did indeed propagate this veneration in his well-known "Of Queen's Garden" speech, describing the home as a spiritual oasis, a refuge that forfended the cares of the world and provided comfort, strength, and healing: a "place of Peace, the shelter, not only from all injury, but from all terror, doubt, and division" (59). It would seem in *Barnaby Rudge* that Dickens likewise extols the family by providing a text that wars against its dissolution in the midst of a value system that is in constant flux. Set against the violent backdrop of the Gordon Riots, the text foregrounds a desperate struggle to form and maintain invincible family units. Nevertheless, the text is as violent a force against the family as the rebellion it depicts.

Raised to a religious icon, the home necessitated an angelic guardian supplied by the wife and mother, who, in turn, became another religious icon. Baldwin Brown inscribed this aspect of domestic ideology in his 1866 sermon "The Home Life: In the Light of Its Divine Idea":

I know women whose hearts are an unfailing fountain of courage and inspiration to the hard-pressed man, who but for them must be worried in life's battle . . . and who send forth husband or brother each morning with new strength for his conflict, armed, as the lady armed her knight of old, with a shield which he may not stain in any unseemly conflicts, and truth, righteousness and God. (qtd. in Houghton 351–52)

The religious implications and armor analogy reflect what Ruskin articulated a couple of years earlier: "It is the type of an eternal truth—that the soul's armour is never well set to the heart unless a woman's hand has braced it; and it is only when she braces it loosely that the honour of manhood fails" *(Sesame* 57). When one holds this portrait of the ideal woman in a domestic context against the portrait of Martha in the Varden family, the novel, in its endorsement of domestic ideology, becomes extremely problematic and satirical in ways that deflate and distort the assumed value of the hearth.

Overtly, Dickens was not unlike other Victorian writers who cherished the family[1] and believed that the mother should provide its heart. The Dickensian good mother was represented as plump and buxom. The bosom, emblematic of nurturing, is, to Dickens, the single most important indicator of a good woman. (Conversely, "bad" women are flat-chested.) He assigns that part of a woman's anatomy as her signifier. Before her transformation, Mrs. Varden is often referred to as "the buxom" (the description is used as a noun). In the early part of the novel, Dickens satirically singles out this gender synecdoche to accentuate her failing to perform her expected role as nurturer.

Above all, the good woman (with a full bosom) could set a good table—a concrete demonstration of providing and ordering for her family: "For women to provide and/or dispense food is a sign that the natural order of things is maintained" (Ingham 30). As if to emphasize the abundance and well-being that a good home would provide, Dickens took pains to describe the layout of a table prepared by her hand—for example, this domestic scene made possible by the "buxom," Mrs. Varden:

There [Gabriel] sat, watching his wife as she decorated the room with flowers for the greater honour of Dolly and Joseph Willet, who had gone out walking, and for whom the tea-kettle had been singing gaily on the hob fully twenty minutes, chirping as never kettle chirped before; for whom the best service of real undoubted china, patterned with divers round-faced mandarins holding up broad umbrellas, was now displayed in all its glory; to tempt whose appetites a clear, transparent, juicy ham, garnished with cool green lettuce-leaves and fragrant cucumber, reposed upon a shady table, covered with a snow-white cloth; for whose delight, preserves and jams, crisp cakes and other pastry, short to eat, with cunning twists, and cottage loaves, and rolls of bread both white and brown, were all set forth in rich profusion. (714; ch. 80)

This scene occurs at the end of *Barnaby Rudge.* The members of the Varden household are finally performing their gender-defined tasks (such as Gabriel's watching his wife busy at her domestic duties). Consequently, the objects in this well-ordered household respond with animated happiness and harmony. They are the most and best they can be. The tea kettle not only sings gaily but has done so for a *full* twenty minutes and chirps as no kettle has ever chirped before. The china not only is the genuine article but is undoubtedly real—no facsimile here. The mandarins are not poor rice-fed Chinese but are round-faced and hold up *broad* umbrellas. The ham is transparent: an unadulterated cut of meat baked to its finest beneath a honey glaze. The lettuce is cool green; the cucumber, fragrant; the table, shady; the cloth, snow white; the cakes, crisp—every item is perfect. The text suggests that when a woman conforms to ideological prescription, not only is her family well off, but the world suffers no poverty, pollution, disease, impurity, or other meanness or deformity. If all women would so comply, what an ideal world this would be.

The Dickensian canon reproduces many of the buxom types, such as Mrs. Bagnet, "as fresh as a rose and as sound as an apple," who is also busy at food preparation *(BH 396)*. Another, Mrs. Pegler *(HT)*, has sacrificed everything so that her son can be a success. When this son refuses to be associated with her, she virtuously suffers in silence, spying on him to reassure herself that he continues to do well. Others are exceptionally "buxom" because they take orphans to their breast: Mrs. Bouncewell *(BH)*, Mrs. Maylie and Mrs. Bedwin *(OT)*, Peggotty *(DC)*, Polly and Jemima Toodles *(D&S)*, Mrs. Jarley and Mrs. Nubbles *(OCS)*, and Mrs. Grudden *(NN)*.

Perhaps even superior to this company is the buxom landlady who acts as surrogate wife and mother to men, like Mrs. Whimple *(GE)* and Mrs. Lupin in *Martin Chuzzlewit*: "The mistress of the Blue Dragon was in outward appearance just what a landlady should be: broad, *buxom*, comfortable, and good-looking, with a face of clear red and white, which by its jovial aspect at once bore testimony to her hearty participation in the good things of the larder and the cellar" (25; ch. 3; emphasis added). In contrast, when Sally Brass feeds her servant only "two square inches of cold mutton" *(OCS* 351; ch. 36), she is Dickens' antipathetic expression of a nonbuxom woman. Since Dickens had originally planned to make Sally the mother of the Marchioness, her inability to provide sustenance for her own daughter underscores her image as nonbuxom when the buxom symbolizes nurturing.

The "buxom" also contrasts to Mrs. MacStinger *(D&S)*, who terrifies Captain Cuttle; Mrs. Billickin *(ED)*, characterized by "[p]ersonal faintness, and an overpowering personal candour" (183; ch. 21); Mrs. Crupp *(DC)*, who, in contrast to being described as buxom, is indicated, significantly, as stout (302; ch. 23); Mrs. Raddle *(PP)*—although tenants' not paying their rent might make any landlady act less than a lady (472; ch. 32); the Misses Pecksniffs *(MC)*, who take a perverted delight in starving their unfortunate boarder, Tom Pinch; and Mrs. Martha Bardell *(PP)*, who, having mistaken that Mr. Pickwick has proposed to her, causes his imprisonment for breaking his alleged marriage promise.[2]

Another category of care providers includes schoolmistresses who are notably absent of bosoms. They are women teaching little boys, and very few teaching little girls, such as Miss Edwards *(OCS)* and Miss Twinkleton *(ED)*—both of whom are single. It would appear that the text would not have a married woman, if she is a good woman, teach outside the home, and definitely not teach males—as if a woman should not be allowed to exercise any authority over males, even young ones. Those who violate this principle are depicted as sadistic types, such as Mrs. Squeers *(NN)*, Miss Monflathers, who ridicules Little Nell *(OCS)*; and Mrs. Pipchin *(D&S)*.

Finally, Dickens' novels are populated by wives and mothers who, instead of providing moral support, have made it their mission to make men miserable. Under this caption are Mrs. Pott *(PP)*; Mrs. Sowerberry and Mrs. Bumble *(OT)*; Mrs. Spottletoe, who has a "bony figure and masculine voice" *(MC 50*; ch. 4); Mrs. Snagsby *(BH)*; and Mrs. Wilfer *(OMF)*. I have not included in this list those women who make the lives of their husbands and offspring miserable through ineptness or unbalance (such characters are handled with Dickensian humor). The women who defy patriarchal restraints, however, are masculinized, like Miggs *(BR)*, Sally Brass *(OCS)*, and Mrs. Joe *(GE)*.[3]

From the foregoing survey, one would assume that Dickens had devised a typology of women based on their varying degrees of compliance and noncompliance with his notions of domesticity. Although a useful exercise in many ways, this classification is an inaccurate method of ascertaining a full identification of each character. Dickens' characters are not just types. They are elements set within contexts crucial to and inseparable from plot, theme, and narrative dynamics. It simply will not do to pull a character out of Dickens' text without considering the narrative that sustains the character and interacts with it, and without considering it as part of a whole. Isolating a Dickens character from the novel is like studying a piece of a puzzle by itself without a view of the larger picture.

In keeping with this theory, I intend to look more closely at a "buxom" within the context of the novel: Martha in the environment of *Barnaby Rudge* provides conflicting and complicated portrayal of a woman that challenges Dickens' own overt perceptions of domestic ideology. Instead of just contrasting acceptable and unacceptable behavior to reinforce approved motherhood, the Dickens text creates a "buxom" who has the potential to be a care giver but subverts the role.

The locksmith's wife is the profile of an angel-in-the-house seemingly gone awry. First described as "plump and buxom" as well as "short" *(BR* 102; ch. 7), she appears to be presented favorably, for such a description usually implies a worthy woman. At best the reader is to hope that Mrs. Varden will reform and that, judging from the love and respect with which Gabriel regards her, there was a time when she better exemplified her "womanly" part.

The reader is expected to hope that because of her husband's long-suffering, patient, and kind nature, she will be won over. The text, as purveyor of domestic ideology, here has taken an unusual turn. Gabriel has been given the wife's role: that is, through *his* angelic goodness he will lead his wife to repentance. Since Gabriel has been partially desexed (because his wife will not brace his armor as Ruskin prescribes), his male lack of power is supplanted by the power that Victorians ascribed to their females: to provide the spiritual force in the home. Since Martha has perverted this faculty and has failed to temper it with humility and self-abnegation, the text delegates the office to Gabriel—temporarily, however, and toward the goal of converting Martha. It would not be acceptable to allow this reversal of roles to become a standard.

At the beginning of the novel, Martha demonstrates the piety that is expected of the housewife, but she has taken it to a zealous, brainless, destructive extreme. The text overtly mocks this type of woman: "Like some other ladies who in remote ages flourished upon this globe, Mrs. Varden was most devout when ill-tempered. Whenever she and her husband were at unusual variance, then the Protestant Manual was in high feather" (85; ch. 4). Instead of converting her into a humble wife dedicated to serving her husband, religion has become a weapon that she brandishes at her humble husband. About his wife's fervor Gabriel philosophizes: "All good things perverted to evil purposes, are worse than those which are naturally bad. A thoroughly wicked woman, is wicked indeed. When religion goes wrong, she is very wrong, for the same reason" (474; ch. 51). His indictment of zealots is twofold: first, that religion is a woman (if it eludes patriarchal control), and second, that a wicked woman is the worst wickedness, which is the same as religion (something otherwise good, like obedient women) gone bad (or gone to the devil). The transgressions against Judaism–Christianity (or patriarchal religion) are not only socially wrong, but morally and damnably sinful.

Furthermore, the narrative indicates that this use of religion as a weapon against mankind (precisely) is characteristic of women throughout history and in all cultures. As such, Martha Varden falls into that camp of religious zealots that receives much acrimony from the Dickensian narrative. Most of her cohorts can be found in *Bleak House*: Mrs. Chadband, Mrs. Jellyby, Mrs. Snagsby, Miss Barbary, and Mrs. Pardiggle.[4] Although other ladies fit into this company, the *Bleak House* zealots do not repent; they are capable of spreading only misery.

The satire in *Barnaby Rudge* attempts to veil an otherwise flagrant conflict in domestic ideology. Here is Mrs. Varden performing the primal task of angel-in-the-house by devoting herself to religious fervor. Were not women charged with the duty of fostering a spiritual environment in the home? The text may overtly mock the angels who become too spiritual—which is a rather contradiction of terms—but the text also covertly represents a woman's unhappiness within domesticity, for Martha *is* an unhappy woman. However, the text does not ask us to sympathize with her. Instead, it would have us sympathize with the gentle husband who suffers from her mood swings. Yet, here is a woman bound by domestic restraints and expectations and made miserable as a result.

Elizabeth Langland, in "Nobody's Angel," argues that middle-class women were "less constrained, imprisoned, and passive than the victim[s] discerned in conventional gender-inflected interpretations" (303). Her study pronounces female complicity in that part of domestic ideology that allowed them to share "class politics of power" with men, reaffirming their family's class status and managing the lower classes (294). Langland acknowledges that women lacked privilege in "gendered politics of power" and states that the Victorian power systems did oppress these women, but she reinterprets the Victorian woman as having found domestic agencies of power through which she could channel her managerial skills (295). Although positively complicating the picture of the ideal woman and crediting her with laudable abilities, Langland still essentializes women in much the same way as does Sarah Ellis—a generalizing that Langland herself criticizes. Where Ellis prescribes a single set of acceptable behavior and attitudes for the "true English woman," Langland proposes that the middle-class housewife wielded tremendous power within the domestic sphere through moral influence, religious sway, education of children, supervision of household staff, and outward display of social status and decorum. Both writers reduce the middle-class woman to a singular type of woman firmly entrenched within domesticity, even if the former portrays her as an angel-in-the-house, and the other, as "nobody's angel." What of women like Martha Varden who fell short of the domestic ideal?

Surely Dickens was not consciously proposing that society provide professional opportunities for women outside the home. By not considering that women may not only lack abilities and interests inside the home, but may also possess varying abilities and interests that exceed the scope of home, the text creates a gap in much the same way that other ideological apparatuses created in Victorian times continue to be a problem today with regard to gender generalizations. Martha's spirit will finally be broken and her energies redirected to the only valid ministry open to her, that of housewife.

Such an outcome for Martha might seem inevitable especially with a text that overtly disperses domestic ideology, but it was not inevitable in other nineteenth-century texts, especially those written by women, for example, Mary Taylor's *Miss Miles*. Although it was not published until 1890, Taylor worked on this novel throughout her life and had completed three hundred pages of it by 1852, just a decade after the first printing of *Barnaby Rudge*. Four women in the novel struggle to find employment outside the home that will either benefit them financially or gratify them intellectually.

Maria opens her own school; Sarah becomes a professional singer; Dora, a professional lecturer. In order to relieve the debt of her family, Amelia wants to take in work or hire herself out. Her family, too proud to allow one of its daughters to labor for a living, forbids her to do so. This attitude throws her into such a state of frustration and despair that she dies. All four women strive for self-sufficiency and the two who do marry do not relinquish that quest. Janet Murray, who has written an introduction to *Miss Miles*, observes the same: "The two marriages at the end of the novel are based on equality and mutual respect. The women's occupations bring them a good living and a satisfying connection to the public world" (xxiii).

This is just one novelist from the period who vocalized the gap evident in *Barnaby Rudge*. That gap is the position in society that someone like Martha should have been able to fill, outside domesticity, that would have allowed her to be a constructive member of society and experience more satisfaction with herself. She obviously could not manage her servant and would not serve her husband; she is Dora Copperfield who survived pregnancy. When Martha visits the Maypole bar, she is amazed at the apparent domestic skills at work. The text tells: "Her housekeeping capacity was not large enough to comprehend them. She was obliged to go to sleep. Waking was pain, in the midst of such immensity" (210; ch. 19). Mrs. Varden is a woman who fails as a domestic manager, and such failure, in light of the lack of any other vocation, gives her great pain. The text may want us to believe that her fanatic observation of religious practices is the source of her unhappiness, but Martha is a woman who has turned to religion as the only acceptable outlet for her nondomestic interests.

Nancy Cott, in *The Bonds of Womanhood*, reasons that many nineteenth-century women became deeply involved with religion and religious activities because only through the church were they able to exercise their intellectual powers.[5] Within the Christian community, they were able to define themselves without their husbands even if religion did preach subordination to men. Inside this social group they could bond, gain moral support, and share feminine understanding (127–90). Besides, only through religion were women granted any license to excel—it was the only conduit allotted to them through which they could extend themselves outside the home, such as through philanthropic work. The Dickens text resists women who circumvent patriarchal order through religion but, in so doing, also registers feminine dissatisfaction with restriction to a domestic role.

Cott makes another point relevant to Martha's story, that women were more preoccupied with death and therefore with religion—and understandably so, in view of the high mortality rate of childbirth (138). Although the text might have portrayed women given to a spiritual bent as neglectful of their earthly duties (as was Mrs. Jellyby), a disposition to be spiritually minded could be expected when, without birth control methods, women faced a serious and real risk of dying in childbirth. One might recall the deaths of Dora and Clara *(DC)*, Agnes *(OT)*, the first Mrs. Dombey *(D&S)*, and a score of young people in every Dickens novel who are orphans from birth. Martha often talks about dying. Since a major expectation for a woman was to reproduce, Martha's expression of fear is a reaction to a hazard of domesticity.

In addition, although Martha has already borne one child, she may have been experiencing a death ever since—either because she has had to conform to domesticity as a result of motherhood or because she has failed to conform and then witnessed her husband's bestowing all of his affection on their daughter. Perhaps there is not a specific cause of her malaise, but Martha is a woman who is preoccupied by death because of her lack of happiness and hope in her life.

Besides her religious excess, Martha exhibits a capricious ill temper. But, as she counsels her daughter about the duties of womanhood, the text voices her pain:

Mrs Varden entreated her to remember that one of these days she should, in all probability, have to do violence to her feelings so far as to be married; and that marriage, as she might see every day of her life (and truly she did) was a state requiring great fortitude and forbearance. She represented to her in lively colours, that if she (Mrs V.) had not, in steering her course through this vale of tears, been supported by a strong principle of duty which alone upheld and prevented her from drooping, she must have been in her grave many years ago. (229; ch. 21)

All of this is the discourse on womanhood, an office that apparently does not agree with Mrs. Varden. Marriage has required that she "do violence to her feelings" and endure a life that is unbearable. Although the text has been penned by Dickens, the unfairness of the ideological constriction forces woman's voice to erupt through a male text. Whether Dickens consciously or unconsciously expresses here, as he does elsewhere, the difficulties of domestic ideology is not the point. The perspective of a female in dissent becomes apparent through Mrs. Varden's behavior.

Mrs. Varden's opposition to the Willet romance (for instance, when she throws Joe's crocuses and snowdrops out the window) might be explained by her view of marriage. Crocuses and snowdrops are flowers of spring, which often bloom before the last snows disappear. Mrs. Varden's discarding of the nosegay might represent her opposition to her daughter's having to bloom into womanhood when womanhood and wifehood seem to go hand in hand. Mrs. Varden regrets and resents her own constricted life-style and despairs that it is the only option for her daughter. She is, however, realistic about Dolly's prospects and determines at least to settle her well. The better off the husband, the easier life will be for Dolly (with servants' handling most of the domestic tasks). The problem with Joe is that his father will not let him take responsibility at the inn, so his ability to provide for a wife is shaky at best. Also, he seems to have Gabriel's approval, and Martha may be afraid that her husband's choice of suitors for his daughter would produce a marriage similar to her own.

Such frustrations may also explain her alliance with Miggs (who is even more frustrated about male expectations of females). The servant is the only person who understands the locksmith's wife. Gabriel often turns to Miggs for her to explain what is wrong with his wife, for "nobody does know" but Miggs (204; ch. 19). The maidservant exhorts Dolly to pattern herself after her mother who has had "constantly to sustain afflictions in domestic life . . . but . . . always came up to time with a cheerful countenance" (230; ch. 22). Besides stating the source of Martha's unhappiness, Miggs also satirizes that aspect of ideology that requires the woman to suffer in silence and to maintain, at all cost, a pleasant disposition, which the text demonstrates that Martha is likewise unable to do (contrary to Miggs' unctuous assessment).

When Martha snaps at Gabriel, "I'm not a child to be corrected one minute and petted the next" (106; ch. 7), she attacks another aspect of domestic ideology: the treatment of women as children. This statement is a delightful slip of text in light of just such a portrayal of women in many of Dickens' novels.[6] This propensity of Dickens seems to be both an androcentric indulgence and a form of pedophilia. It is also a method (by reducing them to children) to make women more manageable and to exert male domination over them. Here in Martha's protest, where adoration of a child (Dolly) by her father pervades the text, is dissent against a male-gratifying treatment of women.

Miggs' satire is as directed against domesticity as is Martha's criticism. The servant does not focus on the mistress but, instead, on domestic expectations. When Miggs claims that her mistress embodies the "sweetness of an angel," the Miggs text ridicules the concept of angelhood within domesticity because Mrs. Varden denigrates the ideology of the domestic angel. Besides being the model of self-centeredness (which can be perceived in a more positive light, namely, Martha's battling for the right to selfhood) instead of self-sacrifice, Mrs. Varden does not suffer in silence as an angel type must. Martha complains to Joe, "You . . . never will know . . . what a woman suffers when she is waiting at home under such circumstances" (158; ch. 13). If indeed Martha has suffered, then she must abide by the rules and keep quiet rather than talk about it to just anyone who comes in off the streets.

Regardless of the reasons why Mrs. Varden is antidomestic and religiously zealous, she does not minister to her husband in the way Sarah Ellis advocated: "As it is the natural characteristic of woman's love in its most refined, as well as its most practical development, to be perpetually doing something for the good or the happiness of the object of her affection, it is but reasonable that man's personal comfort should be studiously attended" (Wives 28). Martha's religious activities minister unto herself, a sure violation of domestic code. A woman is to satisfy the desires of others, not her own (McKnight 118). However, the text also posits a woman's rejection of this concept of self-denial. Mrs. Varden cherishes a little bank, a collection box, that she keeps for the Protestant Association. This philanthropic activity is the only legitimate avenue through which she can experience the power and privilege of procuring her own income, even if the contributions are for an organization. She must also feel pleased that she is accomplishing something that promotes what she believes to be a good use of funds. Surely this could have been perceived as a higher cause than her husband's occupation, which provided only for his family. Martha's vocation connects her to the public, a route usually trafficked only by men. Her lack of knowledge about the nondomestic world makes her naïve about motives and intentions. Little does she know, at this point in the novel, that the funds for her noble association are distributed by men like Tappertit. Nevertheless, there is some poetic justice of a sort here that Martha would support an organization that is working toward insurrection (albeit over issues with which Martha could not sympathize). The text, each time it depicts Martha, carries elements of her discontent and rising rebellion against her own state of affairs.

The climax of the domestic sequences in the novel occurs when Gabriel destroys the bank. Resembling a red-brick dwelling house, the bank represents an alternate home to the one that Martha was supposed to domesticate. In an action that parallels the violence of the riots and the rapes, Gabriel—the home builder—smashes the bank, negating Martha's self-earned possession and the value that she placed on it. The breaking of the bank is the breaking of Martha as an independent woman who has been running counter to domestic doctrine.

The reader is to believe from what transpires after this crucial scene, that Gabriel assumes his rightful place of authority over his wife, that she repents of her rebellious ways, and that she is transformed into an angel-in-the-house.[7] Martha's sudden deference toward her husband evidences a gap in the text that can only suggest that when Gabriel broke Martha's bank, he broke her spirit.

An even greater gap looms in the sudden transformation of Dolly (a subject explored more thoroughly in the next chapter). The coquette will prove to be a better "buxom" than had been her mother. The novel subdues Dolly, too, by having her suffer two "rapes" and five years of absence from the man she loves. She also witnesses the subjugation of her rebellious mother and the eviction of a rebellious spinster. Dolly must learn—and through her lessons, so must the Dickens reader—that woman is to be whipped into a role of subservience to men. If she is not, there can be no happiness in the home.

Thus the novel's ending suggests that both couples—the Willets and the

Vardens—are cheerful and content, even after five years have passed since Mrs. Varden and Dolly have been conquered. The text also has exposed the pain that enforced compliance to domestic ideology has caused. Both women have had to undergo incredible suffering in order to be transformed into male-serving ideals, and their men have had to experience incredible suffering prior to these transformations. Almost the entire novel focuses on the gender struggle rather than on happiness within marriage. Marital bliss is almost a contradiction in Dickensian terms, a subject addressed more fully in the next chapter and not rehearsed here. From the perspective of this chapter, the reader will note that only two chapters in the novel (80 and the last) project the home as a happy resolution of all of the troubles that have plagued the cast of *Barnaby Rudge*. With Dolly's dowry, Joe can reopen the Maypole. It eventually develops into a farm as well as a tavern. The Willets have more children than can be counted who all seem happy and healthy. We are also to believe that Joe, Dolly, the locksmith, and Martha never age because "cheerfulness and content are great beautifiers" (735). Returning to the scene described at the beginning of this chapter with the singing tea kettle and the snow-white table cloth in the Varden household, the reader is to understand that the dissenting natures of Dolly and Martha have been bridled; the world of *Barnaby Rudge* enjoys order and happiness.

The moral of the story seems to be that such joy had been possible all along had only Martha taken her place in the family scheme. The text makes an abrupt attempt to persuade that when the woman complies to domesticity, marital and familial bliss reign. Martha's metamorphosis into a submissive, happy wife is unbelievable, as is Dolly's into a selfless, happy mother of a dozen or so offspring. Dickens seems to be extremely ambiguous about the absolute value of the home (Frances Armstrong 1–2, 151–52). Instead of constructing a positive family unit throughout the novel that culminates in the last chapters, the text has been busily revealing (if inadvertently) the misery that gender expectations have caused. Left in the balance are the doubts as to the stability and sanctuary that the home actually could provide for all of its members, especially for the woman who was supposed to be its guardian.

NOTES

1. Besides being Victorian and perpetuating domestic ideology to much the same extent as did his contemporaries, Dickens also probably idolized the family structure because his own as a child had been shattered at times by financial difficulties. His personal history probably accounts, too, for why, although the family was an ideal, so many of the families in his novels were broken and anything but wholesome.

2. Michael Slater argues that Dickens does not ridicule Mrs. Bardell for wanting

to marry Mr. Pickwick but for making hasty assumptions and for falling into the hands of devious lawyers (233). This does not diminish the threat that she poses to Pickwick and the suffering that she forces him to undergo.

3. For further discussion on Miggs, see Chapter 4; for Miss Sally and Mrs. Joe, see Chapter 6.

4. Because of these women, Mr. Jarndyce has been known to classify charitable people into two categories: "one, the people who did a little and made a great deal of noise; the other, the people who did a great deal and made no noise at all" (115). In *Bleak House* the women are not only mocking the ideal of self-denial by taking it to the extreme and forcing it on other people so that charity becomes a self-serving practice, they are also entirely too unquiet, a definite violation of the cult of domesticity, which requires the woman to demonstrate modest propriety.

Dickens' intense dislike for evangelism and sanctimonious philanthropy is discussed in Zabel ("Dickens" 1–4), and religious women are examined in greater detail in Chapter 7.

5. For further study of women's empowerment through religion, see Ann Douglas' *The Feminization of American Culture*, especially 6–18. Also see Henry Nash Smith's "The Scribbling Women and the Cosmic Success Story" and Barbara Welter's *Dimity Convictions* (84–89).

6. For excellent illustrations of Dickens' treatment of women as children, see *Martin Chuzzlewit*, in particular: Merry Pecksniff (10; ch. 2 and 71; ch. 5), Mary Graham (26; ch. 3 and 414–17; ch. 30), and Ruth Pinch (119; ch. 9 and 504; ch. 37 and 513–18; ch. 39). For an in-depth study of these three "little women," see Chapter 5.

7. George Gissing questions the permanence of this transformation in that he cynically believes that a woman of her age and her advanced deterioration of womanly virtues can be changed. In fact, he does not comprehend how women like her have managed to survive the evolutionary process. Of her sour and sulky behavior he writes, "It is an odd thing that evolution has allowed the persistence of this art, for we may be quite sure that many a primitive woman paid for it with a broken skull" *(Critical* 137). Gissing is another Victorian who seems to advocate the domination of a woman's rebellious spirit even if it means destroying her.

4

The Spinster of *Barnaby Rudge*: "Born to Be a Damper"

Miggs violates two decorum principles in Dickens' manual for proper female behavior: she conspires against her own sex, and she repeatedly attempts to be the initiator in a sexual relationship. When Gabriel Varden declares (close to the end of the novel), "She was born to be a damper" (717; ch. 80), he not only expresses an evaluation of Miggs' character but also articulates a prevalent frustration apparently felt toward spinsters by his middle-class culture. If the ideal state for England was for men and women to be married, and for men to work in the public job force and for women to tend to concerns of the hearth, then what would society do with the approximately one-and-a-half million (nearly one-half of the total female population) who were unmarried?[1] Such creatures were simply dampers on an otherwise happy construction of society into family units in which they just did not belong.

Needless to say, the uncomfortable presence of spinsters also posed a threat to domestic ideology. If domesticity was to form the unshakable foundation that made England indomitable, spinsters who could not complement domesticity without upsetting the family structure were as dangerous as termites to a wooden house.

The text portrays Miggs as both a pest and a serious threat; in so doing, it also uncovers (perhaps unwittingly) the repressive and depreciative side of domesticity as people tried to work out its principles in daily life.

A scene that epitomizes a problematic view of domestic ideology occurs during the Gordon Riots in the novel. Jealous of Dolly Varden, who attracts the man she has been urgently pursuing, Miggs betrays Dolly and

Emma during their collective captivity, an action that serves much more in this single scene than just to further plot. When Mr. Dennis intends to separate Dolly from the others in order to rape her, Miggs delights in the prospect of Dolly's suffering a "severe practical lesson" (636; ch. 70). For this attitude Dickens' text will both mercilessly chastise Miggs and circumvently exonerate her.

The text throughout the novel ambivalently treats Miggs as the betrayer of her sister. By being unmarried and not conforming to the womanly ideal, she does not come under domestic government. By remaining outside domesticity, the spinster—if she enjoys any well-being and independence—upsets a social organization based upon gender because she demonstrates that a woman need not be married in order to fend for herself and to know happiness. The text in this novel, through its development of Miggs, also undercuts the whole of domesticity by implying that men and women are in a self-built prison that restricts their behavior according to gender, and that only unmarried women like Miggs who cross over gender lines secure freedom.

One must not absolve Miggs as if she were just reacting as a brutalized victim at the hands of that "monster master" Gabriel Varden. (Indeed, the kind and good-natured locksmith is also a suffering victim in this book.) Nor might she be recommended as an effective feminist model who escapes patriarchal confines and establishes a satisfying, independent life outside domesticity. This chapter will closely consider the language that describes her, the attitudes toward her expressed by the people within her domestic milieu, her negotiation of an understanding of domestic ideology, and those elements that emerge because of her that communicate societal conflicts with domestic politics.

The text overtly maligns women like Miggs by physically contrasting them to the angel-in-the-house. Thus Miggs stands in sharp relief against her archrival Dolly (an angel "in the making"). For example, the narrative reports that Miggs is "addicted to pattens in private life," so that her feet appear big and clumsy, in contrast to the diminutive, fleshy, and sensual characteristics of Dolly. Dickens' characterization of Miggs as "addicted to them in private life" may imply that she compulsively wears them even when she is not in a muddy public street. However, she may perceive her social environment (within the Varden household) as being like mud, a familial situation described in the previous chapter as a battleground over domesticity. Through the symbol of pattens, Miggs rises above the battle (as she often does with her supercilious attitude and private chuckles), protects herself from it (by acting as an ally to Mrs. Varden), or, in general, just makes a lot of noise to let people know that she too is battling the domestic fray even if or especially because she is not married.

As explained in the previous chapter, a sign of a good Dickensian woman is that she is buxom; the term refers not just to one part of her body but to a rotundness of overall physique. Soon after Dolly is introduced as "dimpled and fresh" (78; ch. 4) and immediately after Mrs. Varden is described as "plump and buxom" and "short," Miggs enters: "a tall young lady" (103; ch. 7). Lord George asks, when reading Miggs' name: "Is that a man?" and the answer follows that she is "the tall spare female" (345; ch. 36), which is to say that Miggs is named and sports a figure that resembles a man's. Accordingly, the illustrator Hablôt K. Browne (Phiz) depicts her as flat-chested. This womanly lack is to make her suit pathetic when she literally throws herself at the apprentice locksmith, who desires Dolly. As for Miggs, he observes "her deficiency of outline" (231; ch. 22).

Why Miggs desires Tappertit is unclear. The text does not portray him as an attractive character worth most women's aspirations. However, Tappertit is representative of the Dickens canon in his desire for the voluptuous female, in his objectification of the female, and in his double standard of expecting to attract physical beauty without regard to what he himself has to offer. Like many women, Miggs internalizes this value system. Were she desired, then she might think herself physically desirable; she has accepted the standards that have so long ruled Western courtship. Like most women then and today, Miggs feels compelled to prove her womanhood through the capture of a man.

Another way to evaluate her motives is to remember that Tappertit is intent upon dominating Dolly. Perhaps the act of domination sexually arouses Miggs. Such a theory would be in keeping with the portrayal of a spinster as a sex-craved object. The bachelor perceives himself as being tall and quite the ladies' man, able to "utterly quell and subdue the haughtiest beauty." The narrative extends Sim's power to "vanquishing and heaving down dumb animals, even in a rabid state" (79), as if dominating the female were the same action. A woman as independent as Miggs might find it sexually exciting to be dominated by a man who is capable of pulling off that feat. Or perhaps instead of wanting to be dominated, Miggs is motivated by a desire to dominate the dominator, torment, and then destroy him. She means to overthrow patriarchal oppression and assert her own independence.

What is clear is that Tappertit is a hyperbolic embodiment of patriarchy. If Dickens creates Dolly as the epitome of female desirability, Tappertit acts as the patriarch that objectifies the girl and lusts after her. He is quite dwarfish in size, admires his own legs, and thinks quite well of himself (especially his male prowess). By the end of the novel he is unmistakably dwarfish because he has lost his highly valued legs. This development mirrors some of the reduction of power that patriarchy experiences throughout the entire novel.

Miggs and Tappertit have much in common. Like Miggs, Tappertit has an unrealistic perception of physical attributes and social aspirations. Because of his gender, he is privileged, but this power makes him over-confident and blind to his own deficiencies—a significant portrayal if Tappertit is the incarnation of patriarchy. Of course, Miggs does not enjoy the same privilege of power because of her gender, but then the text often muddles her gender, as noted. Within the Varden household, she wields much power. Both servants aspire to what their master and mistress possess but later reject it. Also like Miggs, Tappertit wants someone (Dolly) he cannot have and class status he also cannot have, by simply stealing it from the Vardens. Miggs and Tappertit are dissatisfied with their lives, and their rebellion is often directed against the domestic order that Varden represents.

Early in the novel, however, both seem to struggle to find a place in domesticity. Tappertit intends to marry Dolly or gain her by some other means. Miggs intends to marry Tappertit or gain him by some other means. Their aspirations are thwarted because Joe Willet is also in love with the dimpled lass, a complication that drives Tappertit, and then Miggs, to uncontrollable jealousy. Through these romantic conflicts, the text continues to undermine domestic ideology by exposing its conflicts and problems.

For example, in the scene in which Dolly is preparing to attend a party, Joe voyeuristically enjoys her sitting next to the window inside a chair that is to convey her to the party. Her sexuality is framed for his pleasure: "and her hand—surely she had the prettiest hand in the world—provokingly and pertly tilted up, as if it wondered why Joe didn't squeeze or kiss it!" Like a camera closing in on Dolly's bosom, the narrative entices with sensual details: "To think how well one or two of the modest snowdrops would have become that delicate bodice, and how they were lying neglected outside the parlour window" (159–60; ch. 13). The snowdrops have fallen from the nosegay that Mrs. Varden has tossed out the window. The flowers belonging to Joe project his desire for Dolly: he wants them to touch that "delicate bodice" on his behalf. By association with the snowdrops, the bosom becomes white, pure, delicate, and round (snowdrop blossoms resemble rounded bells). This might have been one of the scenes that Richard Barickman and his team had in mind when they studied "the coquettes, the angels, the dimpled innocents," in Dickens' and other male Victorians' works. They concluded that these character creations "sentimentalized masculine erotic desires" (17) and made them even more erotic and acceptable in family literature.

Patricia Ingham has observed a voyeuristic structure in several of Dickens' novels, as exemplified by Hawk with Kate *(NN)* and Jasper with Rosebud *(ED)* (36). She perceives Dickens' displaying to all men how one man can dominate a woman through sexual threat (36). This is the purpose and effect of voyeurism, even in Dolly's case, when Joe's actions seem innocuous, and Dolly's seem willing. However, Dolly is not an autonomous entity: she is not only the object of desire for Joe, she is the object of Dickens' voyeuristic creation.

Yet, the text does make Dolly desirable while it critiques what makes her desirable. Miggs watches Joe watch Dolly. In growing disgust, she declares that Dolly "ain't half as real as you think," suggesting that there is not much substance remaining of Dolly once stripped of outward beauty. This accusation is later confirmed by the text when Dolly proves to be a vain coquette. The text, by exposing the inner deficiency of Dolly, also critiques men for placing their value on outer show. The text articulates this criticism again through Miggs' perspective: "To see how Miggs looked on with a face expressive of knowing how all loveliness was got up, and of being in the secret of every string and pin and hook and eye, and of saying it ain't half as real as you think, and I could look quite as well myself if I took the pains!" (160; ch. 13). This is a statement of power and submission—an assertion that Miggs not only defines herself but Dolly as well, and that, as a woman, she has chosen to reproduce what she perceives to be patriarchal standards of desirability in Dolly. All the while Miggs will work through her objections until she finally rejects those standards.

Ironically, Miggs does not try to change Dolly (although the text does). Instead, in this early chapter, she tries to imitate her because she sees that Dolly gets what she wants and that the young lady's behavior seems to be desirable enough to attract men (including suitors and fathers). When Miggs issues little screams like Dolly (which seem to work for Dolly but not for Miggs) or when she faints like Dolly, one might find the narrative arguing against Miggs, who declares, "I could look quite as well myself if I took the pains" (160), for according to Victorian tenets, if a woman does not cultivate her inner person, her appearance cannot reflect a genuine womanly stature.[2] Miggs' frequent attempts to imitate the alluring Dolly Varden fail because she is nothing more than a vinegary, spiteful, man-hungry spinster. What the twentieth-century reader might understand, instead, is that the text is making it obvious that all women are not alike and cannot be alike, contrary to any ideological perception that would reduce all women to an angel type.

Regardless, when Miggs acts like Dolly, Simon falsely professes his ardor for her. Although he is doing so to be free of her, the display of courtship ritual could be read as a mockery of the Dolly/Joe courtship, satirizing it as pretense and arbitrarily prescribed behavior. This indeed seems to be a satire on the courtship procedures considered acceptable in the pursuit of domestic bliss. When Simon "eyes" her and, ironically, refers to her as "Angelic Miggs" (as if she is an angel-in-the-house), Miggs issues a typical Dolly-like scream. Overcome with relief that her "Simmun" is safe, she yields "to her woman's nature, immediately [becoming] insensible" (124; ch. 9): she faints into his arms as Dolly or Martha would have. The text identifies this behavior as being typically female. Sim responds as if he had unluckily caught the very serpent of Eden: "What a slippery figure she is! There's no holding her comfortably" (124; ch. 9). As soon as he leaves her, she immediately recovers, as would be expected of Dolly if Dickens would let the reader see that aspect of her behavior. Joe can be enthralled by Dolly's clinging to him after her confrontation with Hugh, but when Miggs clings to Simon, her embrace is described as "spider-like" (471; ch. 51).

At another time Miggs drops herself as a "lovely burden" into his arms, causing him to stagger and reel several paces back (575; ch. 64). This is supposed to be a funny scene and is, but, at the same time, it carries both realistic and symbolic meanings. Even though Miggs is tall, she surely must weigh less than Dolly, who could not have been a light burden. But Joe does not reel when Dolly "fairly ran into [his] arms" after her fright with Hugh with the only damage done, supposedly, to her hat. The incident with Miggs exposes one of the delusions about domesticity. A woman like Dolly, who will eventually develop into the ideal woman, represents a burden, not just to herself (by having to live up to an ideal), but also to the man who has to play his role in domesticity. To the Victorian, this meant carrying her financially and socially. In the eyes of the law, he was responsible for her (as Mr. Bumble learns to his great dismay in *OT*).

The burden might also be felt if the man's ideal might radically depart from the domestic model. Such a burden should not be wished on any man during this period, as illustrated in the case of David Copperfield, who suffered because of his love for Dora *(DC)*. However, some Victorian women writers might have not regarded this nonconformist desire as a burden. Many British women created enticing nonangelic protagonists in their novels, such as Emily Brontë with her Catherine Earnshaw, and Charlotte Brontë with her Jane Eyre (who, although meek and self-controlled at times, is, at best, a problematic angel, if she is one at all). These two heroines seem to attract two very different kind of men, who are both depicted as appealing: the impassioned Heathcliff and Rochester and the subdued Edgar and St. John.

Miggs, however, has to struggle to get a man and seems to be heavily satirized because she is an "old virgin" or a "fright"—to use a Victorian label for male-seeking spinsters.[3] Being single was not considered an ideal state in Victorian society. Even George Gissing felt sorry for Miggs: "We feel it is all a little hard upon women soured upon celibacy" (*Critical* 139). W. R. Greg, in his famous "Why Are Women Redundant?" (1876), discussed the plight of the single woman as he saw it: "There are hundreds of thousands of women—not to speak more largely still—scattered through all ranks, but proportionally most numerous in the middle and upper classes . . . who, in place of completing, sweetening, and embellishing the existence of others, are compelled to lead an independent and incomplete existence of their own" (276). Herein lies the tragedy of being single. A woman's virginity is of no use if she cannot relinquish it; a woman's existence means nothing if she cannot serve a man. Moreover, the Dickens text does not treat spinsters simply as superfluous; it responds to them as threats. Indeed the woman who holds on to her independence threatens the very core of domesticity. She is in an actual state of rebellion because she serves no one but herself. Further, because this self-gratification is not supposed to be actually self-gratifying, no man is safe when such ladies are loose, because these females surely must be on the prowl to form an attachment. Appropriately Miggs tries to ensnare Tappertit, who, by all accounts in the text, is no great prize. The text seems to convey the desperate plight of single women by drawing Tappertit as a despicable character and also as the only possible suitor available to Miggs.

Consequently, the text might grant sympathetic treatment to Miggs in her schemes to get a man. That the text does not suggests a few critical problems about domesticity. When Miggs conspires to lock Simon out of the house so that he will have to ask her for help, she performs a calculating and coquettish show abstractly no different from Dolly's when the latter refuses to see Joe before he leaves for the army and he comes to profess his love and say good-bye. Even though the text will chastise Dolly for this behavior, it is simply a part of Dolly's growing process to become an angel-in-the-house. Her coquetry charms her father and her suitors, and it seems to be agreeable behavior while she is her father's daughter and Joe's enticing belle. Although her coyness is a part of the courtship ritual to secure a mate, that coyness also cripples Joe and nearly kills him.

Further, Miggs' unctuous declarations of sympathy, her loyalty, and her encomium of her mistress are acts that mock Martha's affected display of the angel ideal (by Martha's fanatical demonstrations of piety, self-denial, and long-suffering). Both mother and daughter undergo change in this novel, turning supposedly into true angel types, but, in their doing so the narrative serves male fantasy. The text sets up Miggs as the antiwoman and as the freakish model that women should avoid becoming and men should avoid marrying. On the surface, the text satirizes her, reducing her to a spinster stereotype. Such character depiction is a shorthand for a much larger text that is not apparent in the narrative, in a manner that Richard Barickman et al. perceptively note: "Paradoxically, it is often the very blatancy of sexual stereotypes in these novels that alerts us to the complex, psychologically and socially accurate material that the novel is trying both to suppress and to explore" (19). The text does provide hints to Miggs' complexity. Close to the book's end, Miggs replaces her small, red leather purse in her pocket. The pocket is a recurring motif in *Barnaby Rudge* often associated with men, who, when overwhelmed by circumstances, thrust their hands into their pockets. For example, after having been told that he was unfeeling, the locksmith followed the wife and Miggs "with his hands in his pockets" (228; ch. 22). The explication of this action is extended when Tappertit puts the copy of his master's key into his pocket

(108; ch. 7 and 8). Interpreting the key as a phallic symbol (explained in fuller detail later) then the pocket becomes a protective device for sexual power—it is the restraint of passion.

Hence, when Dolly places Emma's letter (which is a declaration of love for Edward) into her pocket for safekeeping, her pocket holds something as sexually potent and vulnerable as a man's pocket. Dolly vows not to surrender the letter even at the point of death, resolving: "to defend her pocket (for the letter was there) to the last extremity" (215; ch. 20). Here the person who appears to be a threat is Mr. Haredale, Emma's uncle and guardian, but it is the Caliban of the story who robs her. Hugh is described as animalistic, a personification of unrestrained male sexuality; he is a man without pockets. There is no doubt from the rising violence and the threats that he makes that Hugh will rape Dolly if Joe does not intervene. As it is, Hugh steals both the letter (a love token) and her bracelet (given to her as a keepsake by Emma); he is stealing something deeply personal and valuable to a woman. The female pocket can be interpreted as a metaphorical safekeeping of woman's sexuality. In this scene, after having been threatened once by a male who is an authority figure and one who could easily dominate her, Dolly has removed the letter from her pocket and is carrying it in her hand when Hugh violently seizes both the bracelet and the letter. Thus he sexually (metaphorically) violates both Emma and Dolly.

This attempted rape scene is also full of erotic messages, to which Joe responds. When Dolly hangs onto him, she crushes "the cherry-coloured ribbons sadly, and put[s] the smart little hat out of all shape." The language is charged with sexual connotations that suggest that Dolly loses her virginity here, not to Hugh, but through the incident with Hugh that arouses Joe.

Dolly seems to provoke uncontrollable passion in the single men about her. Hugh's violence is just one of several incidents in *Barnaby Rudge* when Dolly is nearly raped.[4] Of course her coyness does not give men license to rape her, but she lives in an androcentric society where her beauty is understood to exist only for the pleasure of men and where men can take her at will. The more sexually vulnerable she appears, the more desirable the text makes her: "In the mean time, Dolly—beautiful, bewitching, captivating little Dolly—her hair dishevelled, her dress torn, her dark eyelashes wet with tears, her bosom heaving—her face, now pale with fear, now crimsoned with indignation—her whole self a hundred times more beautiful in this heightened aspect than ever she had been before" (537; ch. 59). Here Dolly's brutalization and terror are treated as eroticism and the text spins a male fantasy of female beauty.

The definition of what constitutes beauty reinforces domestic ideology. Dolly's roundness, rosiness, and dimples suggest that she will be a good nurturer to both children and husband; Emma's delicate shapeliness and fairness indicate her gentleness and transparency in the way that Karen

Halttunen finds typical of women depicted in this period. Halttunen theorizes that the consumptive complexion reflects a heroic quality affixed to
women and a trait of "sentimental typology," conveying that such women
possess delicate sensibilities and ingenuousness. The transparent complexion (often defined as frail and consumptive) is seen as a woman who has
nothing to hide; she is the genuine article—meaning that she is no trickster
trying to ensnare a man into a marriage that would make him unhappy
once he learned that his wife is no true angel-in-the-house (40–89).

The easy violation and theft by three rioters reflect the privilege of the
man over the woman. Dolly and Emma have cultivated positive domestic
traits. They could not, at the same time, develop techniques that would
protect them from being overpowered by a male. To do so would be behavior contrary to submissiveness and self-denial. The text, by placing
Dolly and Emma in such a potentially dangerous situation, illustrates by
hyperbole the vulnerable position that all women are in as a result of their
gender.

Dolly's terror at being nearly raped by Hugh should be absolutely justified—this is no pretense. But it seems that the seriousness of a possible
rape is downplayed by everyone but Miggs, who cheerfully contemplates
how such an event could destroy Dolly's reputation. Joe is "too happy to
inquire very curiously into the matter" because he has had the luck to
rescue Dolly and experience her crushed against him from fright. When he
determines to search for the missing letter and bracelet, his father admonishes him "to mind his own business and not make a fool of himself." After
all, women are only a "nonsensical mistake on the part of Nature" (222;
ch. 21). Mrs. Varden reproves her daughter for pining "over the loss of a
toy and a sheet of paper" (225; ch. 21).

George Watt discusses the attitude toward rape expressed in Victorian
works, emphasizing that women had no protection from rape, physically
or socially. The nineteenth century was unkind to women who were raped,
regarding them as culpable, as ladies who must have deserved to lose their
chastity. Once violated, they became fallen women, and the men went on
their way without repercussion or stigma (8).

The crux of the matter lies in what today might be considered a niggardly
esteem of women, as if there was no distinction between a rape and vol-
untary intercourse within the "legal" bounds of matrimony. Woman was
a mere object created for man's use. She was, as Mrs. Varden artlessly
defines her, only a toy (object) and a sheet of paper (a token signifier of
love), both devalued commodities because they are female.

The cause and effect of courtship display and rape is made explicit several times throughout the novel and conveys some of the complexities of
gender politics. The text, rather covertly, connects sexual domination over
a woman to ensnarement, manifested through marriage as a form of patriarchal enclosure. Overtly Dickens' text depicts the woman as an ensnarer

(as he does with the early Martha), but the text subverts this notion, expressing conflicts in its ideological expression of Victorian marriage. One such conflict is apparent in Simon's announcement to Dolly: "For how many years has it been my intention to exalt and ennoble you! I redeem it. Behold in me, your husband. Yes, beautiful Dolly—charmer—enslaver— S. Tappertit is all your own!" (543; ch. 59). Meanwhile, Dolly is held literally captive, helpless to resist him and powerless to save herself.

The reader is also told that after five years have passed with Dolly pining over Joe, she is still enslaving men: "When and where was there ever such a plump, roguish, comely, bright-eyed, enticing, bewitching, captivating, maddening little puss in all this world, as Dolly? What was the Dolly of five years ago, to the Dolly of that day! How many coachmakers, saddlers, cabinet-makers, and professors of other useful arts, had deserted their fathers, mothers, sisters, brothers, and most of all, their cousins, for the love of her!" (384; ch. 41). Even though this does not seem to be a liberating experience for Dolly either, the text reiterates a point highlighted earlier. Men are just as ensnared by this gender system as are women, for at this juncture, Dolly has outgrown the "little puss" of her childhood. She finally makes the following declaration to Joe:

You have taught me . . . to know myself, and your worth; to be something better than I was; to be more deserving of your true and manly nature. In years to come, dear Joe, you shall find that you have done so; for I will be, not only now, when we are young and full of hope, but when we have grown old and weary, your patient, gentle, never-tiring wife. I will never know a wish or care beyond our home and you, and I will always study how to please you and with my best affection and my most devoted love. (703; ch. 78)

All the while that she is supposedly "captivating," she is falling into a form of captivity as well. When Dolly tells Joe that he has taught her to "know" herself and his worth, she means that through the baptism of suffering[5] she has matured into a suitable marriage partner. Knowing who she is, is knowing her place at the hearth. Knowing his worth (instead of his necessarily knowing who *he* is) is recognizing his natural authority over her, thus knowing *his* place at the hearth. But how is the reader to believe that Joe can finally rule Dolly or—more to the point—rule his own passion for her, which has heretofore ruled him? Dolly's coyness resulted in Joe's going to war and then losing his arm, and in Tappertit's joining a rebellion and then losing his legs. Even after Dolly has matured, she is still playing flirtatious games. She coyly makes believe that she does not "care to sit on his side of the table" (715; ch. 80). Is he supposed to react differently to this tease than he did earlier?

Or is Dolly only appearing to act coy because she knows that such an act will charm, and that charm disguises her rebellion against submitting to male authority? This could be a covert reason hinted in text as to why the "mature" Dolly refuses to sit by her future husband.

Woman's sexuality seems to be regarded in this novel in no different way from any other animal's sexuality with the female species in a constant state of estrus. As long as the female is the youthful Dolly, basic courtship rituals not only are acceptable but are supposed to arouse the reader. If the female is the old virgin, Miggs, the display of passion and sexuality is totally unacceptable and disgusting.

Yet another attitude is at work in this narrative. In the scenes discussed thus far, Dolly's sexuality, aside from what appears to be innocuous coquetty, has been encoded. The reader needs to translate the signs and symbols in order to understand what the text is "not saying" about women's sexuality. The passionate Miggs is a different story. The narrative openly mocks and chastises her for being a blatant sexual being. Dennis Allen's theory historically situates these perceptions: "The erotic reserve of the Victorian novel is a complex reflection of the difficulty of reconciling nineteenth-century constructions of sex and sexuality with the larger ideological framework of the culture, a response to the contemporary perception that sex and sexuality threaten to disrupt the social order and the self" (xiii). Appropriately set with a backdrop of riots, the spinster's sexuality must be read as a threat, and the text must find a way to control it. Certainly Dickens' novels have done this with other passionate women, like Lady Dedlock *(BH)*, Edith Dombey *(D&S)*, and Nancy *(OT)*. All three die violent deaths as if the text were doling out sentences.

Miggs escapes this ending. The last scene between the Vardens and her illustrates these points. Varden pays Miggs as a final gesture of goodwill: "Miss Miggs clutched the bank-note from his pocket-book and held out to her; deposited it in a small, red leather purse; put the purse in her pocket (displaying, as she did so, a considerable portion of some under-garment, made of flannel, and more black cotton stocking than is commonly seen in public)" (720; ch. 80). She demonstrably stores the note in her secret place, flashing, as she does and has all along to Tappertit, her sexuality as a bargaining token in exchange for an attachment to a male. Note the reference to Varden's pocketbook and Miggs' pocket. There is a definite exchange going on here that has to do with sexual power. Varden displays his power through not just his gender, but through the money and class that have privileged him as a result of his gender. In response, Miggs displays her own sexuality, which she must believe to be the only source of socially legitimate female power and the only way that she knows to gain financial and social security. There, where she places her red leather purse, lies her most valuable commodity. The black stocking signs the path to her dark interior. The flannel and cotton characterize both her class and her protection of her private areas (by wearing practical material rather than a bright silk). Nevertheless, the show of so much stocking is a provocative act for a Victorian, but Miggs does it as if to taunt Varden: "I have it, and although you've paid, it's not for you or for any man." Indeed after the riot (which can be viewed as Miggs' personal riot, too), Miggs has become an outlaw, both legally and socially. Outside the jurisdiction of or even desire for domesticity, she now needs to find a way to live her life outside domesticity. Indeed the old service is over.

Remarking the change in Mrs. Varden in this late scene, Miggs acknowledges that her mistress has "grown so independent" (720), which is to say that Martha has finally been molded into the proper wife cast, and she no longer needs her alter ego, Miggs. The marriage advice Varden gives Dolly is "Never have a Miggs about you!" (206; ch. 19). Dolly and Mrs. Varden are to use their sexuality in order to fit both genders into their proper place within the domestic sphere. The use of sexuality (since it is a form of power because it manipulates men into their proper places, too) for any other purpose is intolerable.

Likewise Mrs. Varden has undergone a transformation, which is due to the removal of Miggs as well as the realization of her own sanctimonious attitude toward religion. By conforming to gender standards, "Mrs V. herself had grown quite young, and stood there in a gown of red and white: symmetrical in figure, buxom in bodice, ruddy in cheek and lip, faultless in ankle, laughing in face and mood, in all respects delicious to behold" (714; ch. 80). Mrs. Varden is now an angel-in-the-house; she is beheld. Previously Miggs had been her persona of passion; Miggs often expressed Martha's passion when Martha could not express it herself. Now that there is no more Miggs, Martha tries to rewrite her past as if she had been acting like an angel all along (715–16), denying that she had had any right to desire any passions or causes outside patriarchal parameters.

Miggs jeers at her, accusing her of having "been forced into submissions when you couldn't help yourself" (720). Martha's situation is abstractly no different from Dolly's when the daughter was imprisoned and dominated. The text once more reveals women's lack of power to choose. For example, as Miggs points out, Martha did not want Joe as a son-in-law, but that is what she got and she is supposed to like it.

Martha compares to Dolly in another problematic way. She, too, traditionally has practiced gender pretensions and that is how she "ensnared" Gabriel. Again Miggs offers her insight by recounting how Mr. Varden "went out fishing for a wife one day, and caught a 'Tarter.'" The text seems to moralize about how courting people do not see the real item because of gender disguises until after marriage, when their masks come off. The people in *Barnaby Rudge* are constantly wearing masks that exemplify their wearing of gender (as a set of ideological traits that are put on rather than borne naturally). This theme is also symbolized early in the novel when Gabriel attends a masquerade in order to find the Haredales. He pretends that the party had been all nonsense, but he obviously enjoyed guessing other people's identities and having his own discovered. As mentioned previously, Gabriel's sexual identity is in something of a quandary as a result of his wife's lack of submission.

Emma, our transparent heroine, has been forced to go to the same party and against her will. She wears a mask but takes it off because the room is too warm (83; ch. 4). Although she clearly rejects the mask, her taking it off does not mean that she has a face behind the mask. Throughout the novel she seems to be so transparent that she is a nonentity with no will of her own: Edward, Mr. Haredale, and Mr. Chester are constantly telling her what to do and feel.

Whether disguising an identity that does not conform to domesticity in order to secure a domestic situation or assuming a domestic identity because no individual identity has been allowed to grow underneath, the mask wearer fails to be the actual face that lies concealed underneath.

By the end of the novel, Mrs. Varden has put the gender mask on, and everyone is supposed to be happy as a result. The path of the novel does not seem to have been leading in that direction, however, but toward the resolution of a rebellion that has fermented throughout the text. The nature of this rebellion is symbolized in this scene during the riots:

At this same house, one of the fellows who went through the rooms, breaking the furniture and helping to destroy the building, found a children's doll—a poor toy—which he exhibited at the window to the mob below, as the image of some unholy saint which the late occupants had worshipped. While doing this, another man with an equally tender conscience (they had both been foremost in throwing down the canary birds for roasting alive), took his seat on the parapet of the house, and harangued the crowd from a pamphlet circulated by the Association, relative to the true principles of Christianity! Meanwhile the Lord Mayor, with his hands in his pockets, looked on as an ideal man might look at any other show, and seemed mightily satisfied to have got a good place. (600; ch. 66)

Significantly, "all the localized private revolts have their logical extension in the massive public uprisings of the Gordon Riots," and each individual's rebellion rises out of a household problem (Rice 84). The riot culminates in the destruction of a home—the symbol of domesticity. The doll, of course, reminds us of Dolly, regarded as "a poor toy." It is exhibited at the window as Dolly was earlier. The doll is denounced as an unholy saint (the angel-in-the-house likewise had been revered). A rioter disdainfully roasts canary birds, a reference that can be associated with the earlier references to Emma and Dolly as caged birds (536; ch. 58). Domesticity was sanctioned almost as a branch of Christianity; the rioters totally rebel against it while a mayor, with his hands in his pockets (significantly), does not intervene but seems "satisfied to have got a good place." So the mayor is like Gabriel, a patriarch who idly watches as all of this rebellion occurs (in Gabriel's case, the rebellion belongs to Mrs. Varden, Miggs, and Dolly—to an extent). Varden takes no measure to stop the insurrection because he feels confident in the power and righteousness of his system, which will endure. The rebellion will peter out and the culprits (women) will be dealt with.

As for Miggs, the text would have us believe that she becomes only more masculinized and, therefore, more miserable:

Miss Miggs, baffled in all her schemes, matrimonial and otherwise, and cast upon a thankless, undeserving world, turned very sharp and sour; and did at length become so acid, and did so pinch and slap and tweak the hair and noses of the youth of Golden Lion Court, that she was by one consent expelled that [sic] sanctuary, and desired to bless some other spot of earth, in preference. (734; ch. the last)

Miggs has never been and is not now an attractive character. She has not been portrayed as a desirable woman because she is not domestic. Although living with her sister and thus in a family environment, she is viciously mean to her nephews. Right after her last tirade with the Vardens, she falls on her nephew with tooth and nail, goes out onto the street where she sobs, and then "ensnares some other youth to help her home" (722). Obviously she is no care giver, but perhaps the text has her striking out against domesticity by attacking those who are even more vulnerable than women: children. Miggs' victims, however, are male children who she knows will grow up to have power over her.

After this family arrangement, she secures a position as turnkey for the County Bridewell, an institute that incarcerated prostitutes. The name and background of the prison add to the appropriateness of Miggs' employment there. Originally built as a royal residence, the palace was located at the site of St. Bridget's Well, a "medicinal spring" believed to have curative powers. Thus it was called St. Bride's Well, later abridged to Bridewell (Dixon 265). In 1552, Edward VI turned the building over to the City of London "for the setting of idle and lewd people to work" (qtd. in Cowie 351). By the end of the eighteenth century (when Barnaby Rudge is set), most of the inmates were prostitutes (Cowie 356–58), who suffered frequent severe whippings that were so well attended by the public, a gallery was erected to accommodate viewers "for the better witnessing the correction" (356).

"Bridewell" is an interesting name for a prison that can be taken in two ways as it works in the novel. Either the prison is society's way to protect domestic women (brides) from contamination by their sisters who are prostitutes or it serves as a reservoir (well) to store women until their services become of value again. Regardless of interpretation, the name does allude to domesticity and is significantly attached to a prison.

Miggs—having competed against 124 candidates for this job—is chosen apparently because she is the meanest of the lot. Perhaps this employment suits her:

It was observed of this lady that while she was inflexible and grim to all her female flock, she was particularly so to those who could establish any claim to beauty: and it was often remarked as a proof of her indomitable virtue and severe chastity, that to such as had been frail she showed no mercy; always falling upon them on the slightest occasion, or on no occasion at all, with the fullest measure of her wrath. Among other useful inventions which she practices upon this class of offenders and bequeathed to posterity, was the art of inflicting an exquisitely vicious poke or dig with the wards of a key in the small of the back, near the spine. She likewise originated a mode of treading by accident (in pattens) on such as had small feet; also very remarkable for its ingenuity, and previously quite unknown. (734–35; ch. the last)

The tone satirizes Miggs and insinuates that this profession is Miggs' punishment. She will hold this post for the next thirty years until her death *and never marry!* Good women like Dolly and Emma not only live happily ever after as married women, they reproduce a troop of little Joes, Dollys, Edwards, and Emmas—that is, they perpetuate the conformity to gender codes.

Yet the text does not speak of Miggs' suffering. Instead, she seems to be in a position to dole out judgment. The prisoners are women depicted by the text as beautiful, frail, and beguiling—dominated, male-serving females—whereas, Miggs is none of those and the text treats her as a social misfit and sadist. She attacks women who were able to market both their beauty and their passion in exchange for a living. Her spiteful actions toward the inmates partly arise from envy and bitterness. Additionally, I believe, through her, the text covertly strikes out against a system that has so much power over women that even if they exchange their sexual services for financial security to willing male clients, males imprison them. Miggs' acts of torment are no more severe than were the actual whippings that did occur at Bridewell under the sanctimonious approval of society.[6] This was ironical treatment of women in a place originally named as a place of healing.

The text is not overtly, or even covertly, saying that marriage is a form of prostitution (although I believe it does in *Dombey and Son* in its treatment of Edith Granger). Yet, when the Dickens text is closely examined, marriage does seem to be a security purchased only through the exchange of sex after a female candidate is successful in billing her sale of goods. The security is a delusion unless one can enjoy a measure of security in being in prison, for women, according to a perspective covertly present in the text, after the sale of themselves end up in a prison, and it is only women like Miggs, unwilling or otherwise, who remain outside the sale, and thus free.

Through Miggs, the text protests against the masculine subscription as to what constitutes beauty. In this novel beautiful women are in a literal prison, and Miggs, because of not being in the dimpled way, stands on the outside and executes judgment by the use of a key on those women who merchandise their beauty. The key symbolizes her freedom and the possession of phallic power to keep herself out of a prison—or patriarchal enclosure.

This key metaphor, along with frequent references to other keys—as well as, by extension, to prisons[7]—is crucial to gender politics in this story. This is no better demonstrated than by the golden key above Varden's shop, the book's first such reference. This key is a wooden emblem, not the metal of a real key. It is painted "vivid yellow to resemble gold" instead of being made of actual gold. It dangles, swinging "to and fro with a mournful creaking noise, as if complaining that it had nothing to unlock" (77; ch. 4). Although surely familiar with his own sign, Gabriel spends much time in "long and patient contemplation of the golden key" and makes "many such backward glances" (78) before stepping into the road. This "camera close-up" causes the reader to pay close attention to the key as if it holds some important meaning.

Simon makes a key so that he can come and go as he pleases in his master's house as if he were the master, a power that he wants not only in order to define himself, but also in order to dominate the master's daughter. The key, traditionally read as phallic power, becomes even more significant in the scene when Tappertit is returning to his master's house having illegally duplicated a key to gain entrance. Miggs (a probable virgin) plugs the lock, thus preventing Simon's key from penetrating the enclosure. Then Simon has to rely on her to open the door for him from the inside. Miggs cannot be raped.

The narrative also assigns the key as a phallic symbol that imprisons females. Mary Rudge, a victim and a prisoner of her husband, has locked herself in and has to unfasten both chains and bolts and turn a key to give entrance to the locksmith (101; ch. 6). When Miggs hears noise below in the house that may be caused by a prowler, she exclaims, "Oh! What a Providence it is, as I am bolted in!" (119; ch. 9), and later she explains to the mob that she is "locked up in the front attic" (571; ch. 63). Actually she has bolted herself in (119).

Covertly, this text presents Miggs as a woman imprisoned because she lives within a patriarchal network and wants to marry the locksmith's apprentice (in order to access his power with keys), but she realizes that she has not really been bolted in; she's free. That freedom is, nevertheless, severely restricted. She may from this point on live outside domesticity, but as such, she lives outside society. Her only choices all along have been either to imprison or be imprisoned. These are the only two options that anyone has had in this novel.

The keys in *Barnaby Rudge* unlock prisons (Mrs. Rudge's house, Miggs' social and sexual position, Newgate, and Bridewell). If the key is an emblem of male power, then the prisons exist to contain women (as well as men). Such allusions appear frequently throughout the novel—for instance, the reference to Dolly as "a poor bird in its cage" (638; ch. 71). She clearly is in danger of a powerful phallic violation and domination (when she is taken prisoner by the male rioters). In Phiz's illustration, Dolly delivers Edward's letter to Emma. In the parlor are two boxes with stuffed birds sitting on the fireplace mantel (representing Dolly and Emma as enclosures). There are also a bird in a cage, two fish in a bowl, and Dolly gazing at herself in a mirror as if her image were captive within that frame or captivated her. Around Emma are sketches, flowers, a mandolin—indicative of talents acceptable for a young lady. She reads the letter from Edward declaring his love for her and proposing marriage. These are all prison emblems. In fact, the narrative alludes to prison: "The chamber was somber like the rest for the matter of that, but the presence of youth and beauty would make a prison cheerful (saving alas! that confinement within them)" (211; ch. 21).

Gender limitations and restrictions enslave both female and male alike. When Gabriel first studies the golden key, he has doubts whether he rules over his castle. The key is neither metal nor gold; it is not the real thing; Gabriel lacks the power to lock his wife into a patriarchal prison. Rather, he himself is locked inside *her* prison for him; the key moans as if it has nothing to unlock. Only his relationship with his daughter gives him splendid pleasure. The rioters tear down his key and steal his daughter. When the daughter is restored and appropriately married to Joe and Martha becomes an agreeable wife, then the golden key is "hoisted up again in all the glory of a new coat of *paint*, and *shewed* more bravely even than in days of yore" (705; ch. 79; emphasis added). The italicized words qualify phallic power as arbitrary and tentative. Regardless, because of the restoration of Varden's authority, all is in proper hierarchical order in the household. Overtly the text places the home as the center of patriarchal Victorian society. Covertly the text, through the key images, potentially equates the home with a prison.

Miggs has her own key. Unfortunately, by possessing her own phallic power, she will suffer the worst fate that can befall a female in Victorian society: she will never marry. Granted, this was a serious handicap in the nineteenth century; single women had a difficult time surviving financially and socially. Therefore, marriage was to be the ultimate aim of every female. But marriage as a satisfactory way of life urged by the text also conflicts with the text. Throughout *Barnaby Rudge* the reader has witnessed the sad marriage of the Vardens and has learned of the miserable marriages of the Rudges, the Chesters, and the Bulls. The Tappertits seem to be at war, too, though Dickens describes their conditions as "great domestic happiness,"

only chequered by those little storms which serve to clear the atmosphere of wedlock, and brighten its horizon. In some of these gusts of bad weather, Mr Tappertit would, in the assertion of his prerogative, so far forget himself, as to correct his lady with a brush, or boot, or shoe; while she (but only in extreme cases) would retaliate by taking off his legs, and leaving him exposed to the derision of those urchins who delight in mischief. (734; ch. the last)

The text subverts the notion that the result of patriarchy is two happy individuals (a male and female) who, combined in marriage, will produce a happy couple in which the woman will sweetly submit to her husband's "prerogatives." John Reed articulates a similar concern:

It is, in fact, surprising to discover how very much of nineteenth-century English literature, despite its praise of home and family, really depicts broken homes and contentious families; how often young people in the narratives of the time find themselves in a world hostile to their noblest instincts, a world governed by their implacable parents and infiltrated by seditious siblings. (476)

Dickens is not setting up Miggs as a model alternative to Dolly or Emma, or her life-style (as a prison turnkey) as an alternative to family. However, since the text has ascribed masculine qualities to Miggs and has given her power at least not to have to submit to masculine power, she is somewhat a cross between a man and a woman. This bisexuality (implied throughout the text) yields a vantage from which Miggs challenges the ideology behind domesticity. From her viewpoint—thus the text's—men and women who adhere to gender expectations and roles are in prison, and only women like her who do not (anymore) are free—or at least hold the key to that prison. Where the locksmith—who used to be her master—possessed the power of a key, that key could only lock prisons. After the locksmith refused to unlock Newgate Prison, the rioters set the doors on fire. The effect of this effort was that the entire prison caught on fire, cruelly killing entrapped multitudes (according to Dickens' account).

Even though Miggs possesses a key that locks and unlocks women, she is no savior. After all, she unlocks the doors only so that she can enter the prison, but she alone can leave it. She does nothing to eliminate the prison. She functions in *Barnaby Rudge* as an index to the multiple problems that domesticity as an ideology actually posed. Even as the text seems to run a course intended to culminate in marriage (rooted in domesticity) as the ultimate, positive enclosure, all along it also runs counter to that aim, constantly undermining, questioning, and challenging.

No wonder Varden thought of Miggs as a damper!

NOTES

1. According to the 1851 Registrar, there were 1,248,000 women in England and Wales between the prime ages of twenty and forty who were unmarried (qtd. in Greg 283).

2. See John Ruskin's lecture *(The Ethics of the Dust)* to young ladies on this very topic, urging them to keep their hearts clean and pure. Karen Halttunen's analysis also helps place the concept of appearance as revealing character in its historical context. See especially 1–89.

3. Michael Slater discusses "frights" in *Dickens and Women*, especially in defining Miggs (233).

4. In chapter 19, Dolly emerges from her house, and Tappertit contrives to abduct her. In chapter 59 she is in imminent danger of being raped by Hugh, Dennis, and Tappertit.

5. See Slater's discussion regarding the necessity for trials to purify women (244).

6. Actually, by the time of the Gordon Riots (1780), reformers had demanded abolition of these whippings. By the 1800s, the prison came to provide short detentions for pickpockets and beggars. It was finally closed in 1850 (Cowie 358).

7. Walter W. Crotch investigates the recurring references to prisons as a dominating image throughout Dickens' work, including in *Barnaby Rudge*.

PART II

Little Women, She-Dragons, and Misfits

Sex is a complicated thing.

Sex in the Victorian Age is a conundrum.

It seems the more sexually repressed people are, the more their sexual behavior deviates from social norms. Take, for instance, John Ruskin, referred to a number of times in this study. If ever there was an advocate of home and hearth with woman as angel firmly in place, it was Ruskin. Yet he married Effie Gray, a woman with whom he fell in love reportedly when she was a mere thirteen. Once married, he could not consummate the marriage. She left him to marry one of his closest friends. Later he fell in love with nine-year-old Rose LaTouche and at age forty-six proposed to her.[1]

That creator of stories and poems enjoyed by generations of children, Lewis Carroll, enjoyed photographing unclothed little girls (Carter 141).

George Henry Lewes, at twenty-five, communally resided with five married couples and two unmarried sisters. Lewes' wife bore two children to his best friend, Thornton Hunt. Because divorce was prohibitively expensive, Lewes continued to support his wife and all of the children while living with the famous novelist George Eliot for twenty-four years. Two years after his death, Eliot at sixty-one married a forty-one-year-old, J. W. Cross.

William Thackeray committed his wife to a mental asylum and fell in love with Mrs. William Brookfield—a married woman (Goldfarb 53). Edward Bulwer-Lytton, frustrated in his marriage, also committed his wife to an insane asylum; by most accounts she was both sane and furious (Showalter, "Insanity" 319). Mary Braddon lived with her editor while his wife lived in a Dublin mental asylum (Uglow xii). John Stuart Mills had an affair with the married Harriet Taylor for eighteen years (Johnson 26–35), and Thomas Carlyle had an

affair with the also-married Lady Harriet Baring (Goldfarb 50). George Mere-
dith's wife bore a child to the painter Henry Wallis (Johnson 52–55).

Dickens was married sixteen years to Catherine, who bore him ten children
and suffered at least two miscarriages. Enamored of eighteen-year-old Ellen
Ternan, he forced a separation from his wife. Ellen, according to her son,
was Dickens' mistress until his death.

All of these writers were expected to promote a certain code of sexual
ethics and moral imperatives. In view of the inherently rebellious nature of
writers and artists, it should not be surprising, though, that a little digging
into their works would uncover a number of ideological conflicts.

The purpose of this study is the excavation of Dickens' text. The first part
closely investigated the representation of women in two novels: David Copperfield
and Barnaby Rudge. Part II surveys dissenting women throughout Dickens' novels who index the sort of conflict with domestic ideology and sexual complexity mentioned. On the basis of the narrative's attempt to contain these
characters and the ways it reflects or deflects domestic ideology, these women
are considered in three different classifications: little women, she-dragons,
and misfits.

Many Victorian patriarchs saw women as lambs entrusted to their keeping.
It was a relationship reinforced by many a church sermon, that a man was
to see to his lamb in the same way that Christ was to tend his bride, the
church. This ideology is imaged in Dante Gabriel Rossetti's painting Found. In
the foreground crouches a woman whose illicit activity has obviously been
"found out" by a young man who is probably her brother or betrothed. Her
face is one of abject sorrow; in another minute she may die of shame and
despair. The face of the young man does not indicate censorship, only pity
and sorrow. In the background is a cart on which stands a bleating pure
white lamb that is not only significantly tethered, but also retained by a net.
Those restraints symbolize patriarchal control, out of which the woman has
slipped.

Certainly a reader can find evidence in Dickens' writing of this belief in
patriarchal shepherding. Therefore, in reference to Rossetti's painting, this
study categorizes the dissenting women by whether they are inside or outside
the fold. Of the latter, the women are further categorized by whether their
own rebellion places them outside or the characterization of the narrative
makes them unable to fit the fold because of some freakish defect. In all three
categories the narrative operates through the women with disrupting implications about gender issues. All of these females are dissenters, even if the
text does not depict them as consciously acting thus. Their presence and force
raise a number of revealing questions about Victorian womanhood and perceptions of sexuality.

NOTE

1. See Wendell Stacy Johnson (74–75), Bullough (539), Goldfarb (54–55), and
   Kirchhoff (18–19, 198).

5

The Women inside the Fold: Dickens' Little Women

A prime example of how convoluted matters can become is Dickens' little women. This chapter will focus on those novels with important characters who are child-women. It explores the novels and not just the women, because as argued earlier, one cannot remove any character from her fictive milieu and expect to identify her accurately. This is even more true in the first novel to be examined, where doubling of characters is such an important dynamic in manifesting the otherwise hidden part of an individual's psyche (Showalter, "Guilt" 31–39).

THE LITTLE WOMEN OF MARTIN CHUZZLEWIT

Geoffrey Carter has observed that Dickens does not develop any passages that deal with what can be considered healthy sexual relationships. The reader never learns anything about the romantic sexual liaison between Lady Dedlock and Nemo, for example. Instead Dickens dramatizes deviant sexual behavior (148). This is no more true than in *Martin Chuzzlewit*, but the behavior seems to be condoned or comically depicted as long as it is commanded by a patriarch. In question is whether the text is really sanctioning or critiquing such behavior.

Numerous scenes throughout Dickens' novel exude eroticism through male domination of the female. The first occurs at the hearth, that icon of domesticity. One of Dickens' most superb caricatures of a patriarch, Mr. Pecksniff, sits comfortably in front of a fire, having just had some brandy and water. His daughters are serving tea and ham and eggs. Both of them assume their proper position. Cherry plays the role of the mother, and Merry, the child, "took up her station on a low stool at his feet: thereby bringing her eyes on a level with the tea-board" (10; ch. 2). The Merry close-up is fraught with sexual suggestion:

It must not be inferred from this position of humility, that the youngest Miss Pecksniff was so young as to be, as one may say, forced to sit upon a stool, because of her simplicity and innocence, which were very great. Miss Pecksniff sat upon a stool, because she was all girlishness, and playfulness, and wildness, and kittenish buoyancy. She was the most arch and at the same time the most artless creature, was the youngest Miss Pecksniff, that you can possibly imagine. It was her great charm. (10)

Besides being rendered as a little girl, Merry is sitting on a stool as if being punished. The details are erotic:

She was too fresh and guileless, and too full of childlike vivacity, was the youngest Miss Pecksniff, to wear combs in her hair, or to turn it up, or to frizzle it, or braid it. She wore it in a crop, a loosely flowing crop, which had so many rows of curl in it, that the top row was only one curl. Moderately buxom was her shape, and quite womanly too; but sometimes—yes, sometimes—she even wore a pinafore; and how charming *that* was! (10)

In her unmarried state Dickens constantly ascribes little girl qualities to her. Lest there be any doubt that these descriptions are not meant to be alluring, consider: "sitting upon her stool [again], tying on the—oh good gracious!—the petticoat of a large doll that she was dressing for a neighbor's child: really, quite a *grown-up doll*, which made it *more confusing*: and had its little bonnet dangling by the ribbon from one of her fair curls, to which she had fastened it, lest it should be lost, or sat upon" (71; ch. 5; emphasis added). For a Victorian audience, Dickens cannot undress or dress Merry, but he can have her do this to a doll to suggest what the reader can do to Merry. This understanding has been cued by the references that have already been noted. The doll is large, not the size that one might assume a child would play with. It is a "grown-up" doll; it is Merry. The deliberate vague antecedent for the confusing "it" connotes sexual stimulation. The implications are further signaled by the little bonnet that dangles by the ribbon from the curls, like virginity that can be "lost or sat upon." The details are sexual signifiers that require little strain to appreciate their metaphorical allusions.

Merry is such a provocative little thing that, to add to this brand of eroticism, she is beaten by Jonas. Michael Slater suggests that Dickens is simply allowing his text to discipline women like Merry: "Here is Dickens apparently preoccupied with women as the insulted and injured of mid-Victorian England yet voicing no general condemnation of prevailing patriarchal beliefs and attitudes; rather, he seems to see the social and sexual trials of his heroines as a sort of tragic nurture which serves to bring them to their full 'womanly' (or spiritually superior) potential" (244). The text seems to support this theory, because over time, after abusive discipline, Merry matures into Mercy, now truly deserving of that name because she is in great need of mercy. She now shows mercy too, as well as kindness and consideration to others. Regardless of the outcome—eroticism and/or transformation—Merry has been conquered.

This is not an unusual text by any means. Many domestic novels by women and sensational novels by men follow this paradigm: an ingenue is either charmed or economically compelled or forced under dastardly duress into marriage to a fiend. If it is not known that he is a fiend prior to his wedding day, at least to his betrothed, it is soon apparent. Rape, debauchery, inebriety, womanizing, squandering of the family money, abuse of both wife and child: his deeds reflect an unredeemably dissipated nature. All is not hopeless for the woman, however. This sort of baptism by matrimonial fire will transform her into a more angelic creature who looks only heavenward for comfort. The coy burns away, and selfless attention to other people's needs consumes her.

One has to notice that in an age when marriage and the nuclear family were paramount social constructs and strict adherence to gender codes was prescribed, so many novels portrayed marriage as a form of oppression. In the Dickens canon, many more espoused men are oppressed than are women; nevertheless, the point is the same: marriage is a trap and a worldly source of suffering. Whether or not good can come from such an ordeal certainly cannot be much of a selling point for the institution.

Moreover, the *Martin Chuzzlewit* text seems particularly solicitous toward women, not only regarding the problems with matrimony, but specifically regarding women's powerlessness in a patriarchally privileged society. Even more remarkable is that the text impugns the Victorian mentality that women should suffer in silence. In pity and understanding, Mrs. Todgers confides to Tom that Mercy "never makes the least complaint to me, or utters a single word of explanation or reproach" (502; ch. 37). In short, Mercy suffers in silence as was expected of a good Victorian woman. She definitely has been initiated into the sisterhood of woman, and Mrs. Todgers recognizes it as such: "But in some odd nook of Mrs. Todger's breast, up a great many steps, and in a corner easy to be overlooked, there was a secret door, with 'woman' written on the spring, which at a touch from Mercy's hand had flown wide open, and admitted her for shelter" (502). This passage gives voice to otherwise silent women who are powerless pawns in a patriarchal game. Like Dickens' other silent sufferers (Nell [OCS], Flo [D&S], and Amy [LD], to list just a few), Mercy accuses no one for her wretched existence and tirelessly works all the more to please her oppressor. Natalie McKnight notes an inconstancy in Dickens' novels when reinforcing the suffer-in-silence attitude: "Dickens, therefore, serves out silence to punish his overly forceful female characters, while he partially affirms the silence in his docile women; yet, he seems to recognize at least occasionally in these characterizations the dangers of women's silence, no matter how attractive it might be to him" (54). The inconstancies are in keeping with the inherent inconstancies of working out an ideology that is supposed to be beneficial to all when it incapacitates one sex and entitles the other to dominate arbitrarily.

One didactic message that this novel is giving is that a woman who acts as coquette is not cultivating inner qualities. Because she overrates the superficial, she may very well attract someone who does likewise—like the brute, Jonas, who also has not cultivated his inner qualities and does not respect them in others. Jonas' attraction increases when Merry plays at dominating him through feminine guiles. It then becomes absolutely essential for the Dickens male to force her into submission.

The stance of the text is to frown on Merry's behavior and ensure that she is chastised. All women must stay within the confines of domestic ideology, and if they do not, either the father, the husband, the brother, or the Dickens plot will make sure that they will. Jonas has been given a "church-ordained right" to rule Mercy. If the husband should turn into a tyrant, the text warns with Judeo-Christian fervor, "Oh woman, God beloved in old Jerusalem! The best among us need deal lightly with thy faults, if only for the punishment thy nature will endure, in bearing heavy evidence against us, on the Day of Judgment!" (396; ch. 28). The text does chastise Jonas as well.

Such a system seems to deal neatly with all violators. All the while, the text underscores the lack of power women have to avoid sexual and aggressive abuse. Mary Graham is no coquette and does not need to become a better woman through more suffering. She has already experienced patriarchal domination in being a companion to Old Martin. She is a little woman, "young; apparently not more than seventeen; timid and shrinking in her manner, and yet with a greater share of self-possession and controul over her emotions than usually belongs to a far more advanced period of female life." By tending to the sick man and by being so pale, she fits the angel-in-the-house profile. By being "short in stature; and her figure [being] slight, as became her years" with all of the charms of her maidenhood including that very erotic wayward curl that hangs upon her neck (26; ch. 3), she is also the typical Dickens little woman. The text adds sexual tension to her relationship with an old man, through the landlady's embarrassment in learning that Mary is neither daughter nor niece nor wife to the elderly gentleman. The text is teasing us into thinking about Mary in sexual terms. This is acceptable as long as she does not start acting like a sexual creature, having needs and desires of her own.

With her innocence, goodness, and artless girlishness established, then the scene in the garden with Mr. Pecksniff is highly erotic, especially when he plays with her fingers, tracing "the course of one delicate blue vein with his fat thumb," and offers to bite her little finger (414–17; ch. 30). The text, from Pecksniff's point of view, calls his lovemaking "that chaste patriarchal touch." The text, from Mary's point of view, realizes that he has the "superior strength" and the power and cowardice to exercise it. One text would have the reader be aroused by a scene in which an innocent little woman is sexually dominated by a patriarch. The other would have the reader disgusted by the same situation. The garden scene illustrates the bifurcation of point of view toward the submission/domination mechanics of domestic ideology.

The bifurcation emerges from another sexual dynamic, and that is the December/May relationships that often occur in Dickens' novels. Usually the text depicts the father as a good patriarch and the young woman a true beneficiary. Marrying a father figure facilitates transfer of patriarchal power. The female is to respect not only gender, but age as well. Having submitted to the authority of her father since birth, she also will submit to a man who reminds her of her father. Although perhaps fortifying the bastions of patriarchy, such a practice blisters with incestuous implications. The problem with incest, besides its social taboo, is that it negatively reduces the genetic pool and introduces otherwise preventable maladies. Even if the text does not allude to physical incest, the psychological and sociological are damaging in much the same way. The idea behind inbreeding is to preserve desirable traits and eliminate the undesirable. History has proved that the opposite occurs in humans.

The incest theme is more apparent and complex in the brother/sister team of Tom and Ruth Pinch. Ruth is portrayed in the same way the other little women are: "a pretty little figure—slight and short, but remarkable for its neatness" (119; ch. 9). She is just as objectified and encoded with an uneven sexuality. This point can be illustrated by the narrative's references to gravy. Mrs. Todgers observes that "there is no such passion in human nature, as the passion for gravy among commercial gentlemen" (116; ch. 9). Merry giggles in recalling that they never gave any gravy to Mr. Pinch. Much later, John expresses his regard for Little Ruth: "Surely she was the best sauce for chops ever invented" (504; ch. 37). In these three passages, one may conclude that gravy symbolizes female sexuality and becomes the signifier for Ruth.

Besides this metaphorical signification, the sexual interaction between Tom and Ruth is discernible especially during the scene when Ruth prepares the famous beefsteak pudding:

Tom's attention wandered from his writing, every moment. . . . [Ruth] didn't put [the apron] on up stairs, but came dancing down with it in her hand; and being one of those little women to whom an apron is a most becoming little vanity, it took an immense time to arrange; having to be carefully smoothed down beneath—Oh, Heaven, what a wicked little stomacher!—and to be gathered up into little plaits by the strings before it could be tied, and to be tapped, rebuked, and wheedled, at the pockets, before it would set right, which at last it did, and when it did—but never mind; this is a sober chronicle; Oh, never mind! (516; ch. 39)

This narrative is supposed to be a "sober chronicle," one that can be read by the most puritanical Victorian audience, yet the details are charged with sexual allusions and teases. Ruth is coy with her own brother, and he is enamored by her: "And during the whole of these preparations she [looks] demurely every now and then at Tom, from under her dark eyelashes." This is his response: "For the life and soul of him, Tom could get no further in his writing than, 'A respectable young man aged thirty-five.' " He cannot take his eyes off her rosy lips (516–17).

Does the text mean, through Tom, voyeuristically to arouse readers toward Ruth? If so, why does it attempt to do so through a brother, unless the incestuous taboo is to heighten the sexual allure? Since John falls in love with her too because she is the "brightest and purest-hearted little woman in the world" (586; ch. 45), one might assume that Ruth is simply and asexually the Victorian ideal, who has been first appreciated by her family (in this case, a brother) and ultimately valued by a suitor. Frances Armstrong reads the text this way, that Ruth, in tending to her brother, is just preparing for marriage (55). But the love between Tom and John with its own sexual implications makes the triangle anything but simple and asexual.

Instead of or besides having an incestuous relationship, perhaps Ruth and Tom are the anima and the animus of the same person, in much the same way that one might argue that Helena and Neville Landless represent the female and male of the same person. In *The Mystery of Edwin Drood*, Helena, turning into Neville, assumes a male role (including an actual male disguise), but the text does not severely deal with her in typical Dickensian fashion for stepping over gender boundaries.[1] The difference between Helena and Dickens' "she-dragons" is that she wears a male disguise. She acts like a man and appropriately so when she assumes a male identity. As long as she can shed those garments and return to her naturally feminine self, she is doing nothing more than reaffirming that her identity is cloaked by a masculine signifier.

Gender is inverted in a similar and covert way in *Martin Chuzzlewit*, except that the differences dividing gender virtually disappear. Stereotypically, Ruth is a female angel-in-the-house. Not stereotypically, Tom is also an angel-in-the-house, a unique male angel:[2] "He was perhaps about thirty, but he might have been almost any age between sixteen and sixty; being one of those strange creatures who never decline into an ancient appearance, but look their oldest when they are very young, and get it over at once" (17; ch. 2). This passage inscribes him with ethereal qualities. Besides frequent allusions to goodness radiating from him, and children and adults flocking to him as if he were a Christ figure, his music lifts him heavenward. Tom appears to be a celestial creature in much the same way as are the female angels Agnes Wickfield *(DC)* and Madeline Bray *(NN)*.

Besides being an angel, he is not handsome, he is not a gentleman, he is not a man of the world. When he hands a basket packed by Mrs. Lupin to the coachman, he emphasizes that it is a platonic basket. Tom appears to be neuter—until the scene when he plays the organ for Mary: "When she spoke, Tom held his breath, so eagerly he listened; when she sang, he sat like one entranced. She *touched his organ*, and from that bright epoch even it, the old companion of his happiest hours, incapable as he had thought of elevation, began a new and deified existence" (340; ch. 24; emphasis added). If he had been forced into an emasculated role as self-denying angel, he has just been rescued. It is not difficult to interpret the organ as phallic (Houston 80). However, Tom's leap into manhood is short-lived for he soon has to give up Mary as if she were only a dream. He will continue to love her "with such a self-denying love as woman seldom wins" (424; ch. 31). Tom can be self-denying only as an emasculated male, as if no true patriarch would assume this role traditionally relegated to women.

Further indicators of his femininity is that he is as timid and trustful as is Mary. He takes Merry's place on the stool (82; ch. 6). His life is "more spiritual in self-denying thoughts" (167; ch. 12)—a female ideal. He is also depicted as possessing childlike innocence and purity. Similarly to masculinizing Helena *(ED)*, the text seems to emasculate Tom. The ideological strains are warping here, and the distinctions between male and female are so obscure as to challenge gender distinctions.

The plot wants to make John Ruth's lover; indeed they do marry. Tom regards John as a father to Ruth (651; ch. 50). Of course, the attraction of older male to the little woman is redundant in Dickens' novels, but the fixture of Tom forms a ménage à trois, unless one thinks of Ruth and Tom as forming an androgynous whole. Complicating matters further, the text marginalizes John. As with every other healthy, stable, masculine male in the Dickens novel, the reader does not get to know much about him other than how he functions in relation to a heroine.[3] He becomes substantial enough, nonetheless, when Tom forms the object of his desire—and Ruth, too. She vanishes into John: "Looking into [Ruth's eyes] for but a moment, when you [(John)] took her hand, you saw such a capital miniature of yourself, representing you as such a restless, flashing, eager, brilliant little fellow" (527; ch. 39). When John looks into Ruth's eyes, he sees only himself, his happy self. Granted, the man is in love, and being in love is often a narcissistic experience. However, the narrative does not tell us that *her* image is reflected in *his* eyes. This gap seems to signify that if one were to look into Ruth's eyes, one would not find Ruth, but, John. She has lost her identity; he has found his in her.

She also loses her identity in Tom: "There was something of her brother, much of him indeed, in a certain gentleness of manner, and in her look of timid trustfulness" (119; ch. 9); later, "Ruth . . . was the very moral and image of Tom." One might read these passages as if Ruth can only be signified by a male, but then the reader will still have to factor the emasculate Tom and the marginalized John into the equation. The result is a perplexing aggregate of gender perspectives.

THE LITTLE WOMEN OF THE OLD CURIOSITY SHOP

The Old Curiosity Shop also contains fascinating contortions of Victorian gender ideology. The little women in this novel are not much different from those already considered except to the degree to which they are sexually abused and exploited and except for the narrative strategy that constructs them. Mrs. Quilp is in much the same predicament as is Mercy except that Quilp is much more fiendish than is Jonas. Another little woman is a helpless and valueless girl-child starved and abused by a mother who neither has been served well by gender politics nor has served those politics well and by a father who exploits gender politics to its tyrannical, but legitimate limits. The key figure of this novel, Little Nell, mothers her grandfather and is sexually pursued by men even though she is still a child—but both forms of exploitation actually kill her.

The fourth chapter introduces the "pretty little, mild-spoken, blue-eyed" Mrs. Quilp. She has been "left to pine the absence of her lord." What a satire this is on those passages of advice novels that exhorted women to tend to the hearth while the husband is away, to arrange all things for his comfort and care, so that upon his return, the home will restore the complacency of his being, for

there is much in the lives of men, and particularly where business engages their attention, to lower and degrade their mind. . . . [H]e consequently needs a companion who will be supremely solicitous for the advancement of his intellectual, moral, and spiritual nature; a companion who will raise the tone of his mind from the low anxieties, and vulgar cares which necessarily occupy so large a portion of his existence and lead his thoughts to expatiate or repose on those subjects which convey a feeling of identity with a higher state of existence beyond this present life. (Ellis, *Wives* 35)

Betsy's husband is a patriarchal gargoyle: no crossing over of gender lines here. Quilp is definitely devoted to his business, and the world has definitely lowered and degraded his mind, but there is no hope that any angel-in-the-house, even an Agnes Wickfield, can lift him to a "higher state of existence beyond this present life," short of murdering him. As if that is exactly what Quilp supposes to be his wife's thought, he stages his disappearance and then spies on her to discover her reaction to his presumed death. All of her submission and sweetness never shame him to repent his cruel ways; instead, they are seen as a weakness that rouses the patriarch to even greater cruelty. Even though to an extreme, this scenario challenges the suitability, merit, and justice in subscribing to the angel-in-the-house practice of waiting on the master.

Earlier, Mrs. Quilp is joined—through no invitation of her own—by lady friends of her mother, in that it is "extremely natural that the discourse should turn upon the propensity of mankind to tyrannize over the weaker sex, and the duty that developed upon the weaker sex to resist that tyranny and assert their rights and dignity" (74; ch. 4). The bevy of feminine gab and complaint is meant to be satirical, but of whom? The women? Or men like Quilp who are given power to tyrannize? These women have something definite to anguish about, and efforts to reclaim their "rights and dignity" certainly are in order. Mrs. Jiniwin, Mrs. Quilp's mother, vows that had her husband ever said a cross word to her, she cannot say what she would have done but indicates what her actions would have been by twisting off the head of a shrimp. Suffering in silence is not her credo.

Those ladies accuse Mrs. Quilp of being untrue to herself. By compromising and showing meekness, she shows no respect for other women. Again, though the narrative delivers this scene for the reader's amusement, without the levity the language offers a considerable subversive impulse. What gives the license to remove the levity is the entire text that places Quilp in the center of patriarchal power and his wife's victimization. The logic in what these ladies say forms the syllogism: if a woman denies her self, she believes that she has no worth because she believes that no woman has worth. Mrs. Quilp's complicity adds more weight to the belief that women are inferior and need to be ruled. She contributes not only to her own subjugation, but that for all women. The result very easily could be the malicious abuse of a man like Quilp.

Another casualty of domestic ideology is the Marchioness. Quilp is her father.[4] Besides his despotic behavior, he also enjoys the patriarchal privilege of not having to acknowledge or care for his illegitimate daughter. Approximately thirteen when Dick Swiveller first meets her, she has been starved, beaten, and overworked by her mother, Sally Brass. As discussed in fuller detail in Chapter 6, Miss Brass is one of those Victorian women never cut out for motherhood. More to the point, her acumen favors the law, but women were not allowed to practice it. Miss Brass is not a nice person, but her bitterness is rooted in injustice that prevents her from doing what she is capable of and forces her to do what she is incapable of. The restriction affects not only her, but a score of people who feel the brunt of her anger. Of course, it works the greatest destruction on her child. The

Marchioness, starved, locked up, and narrowly defined without a name, is the manifestation of her mother's deprived inner self.

One additional point to be made about the Marchioness concerns the suggestion that she will enjoy a happy ending. And perhaps she will. However, the text has been busily colonizing the reader into thinking well of a patriarch like Swiveller who spends six years reinventing the young girl so that she will become a suitable wife for him. Granted, rescuing her from the horrid environment of her childhood and sending her to school are admirable. Also granted, the text would have the reader not take Swiveller too seriously but applaud his heroic actions. Yet he is the same man who connives to marry innocent Little Nell in order for his friend, Nell's brother, to get the grandfather's money. Swiveller is a duplicitous, shady fellow who does improve, perhaps touched by the vulnerability of the Marchioness and perhaps transformed by her feminine nursing efforts. But the young woman apparently is quite intelligent, judging from her amazingly rapid progress at school. Why is she not given other options than marriage to her benefactor? And she never names herself. And she appears inside a fictive milieu between two other little women: a Mrs. Quilp whose lack of power to define herself has already been discussed and Little Nell, whose similar helplessness results in her death. The happiness of the Marchioness' marriage, or any like hers, is dubious.

Little Nell's ending is more certain. Barely fourteen, she is often in flight from what Ingham describes "male illicit desire" (35). This would include that of Quilp and Dick Swiveller, who want to marry her. Quilp's intentions are more sinister as he greedily lusts for her. He and Nell are at the opposite ends of sexuality (Morgan 49–54). Kit, although innocuous, sets her to flight for reasons of which she may be unconscious. His body language and "uncommonly wide mouth" suggest sexual appetite (Houston 79). Her problems also include the grandfather and Nell's brother, Trent, who both try to use her to get money. As Houston puts it, she is "self-starved and sexually repressed. Nell is the center round which male sexual appetite circulates; though Nell seeks total cessation of appetite, almost every male character in the novel hovers greedily and sensually around her" (64).

Such sexual considerations of the little woman and ways they subvert gender ideology are similar to those already discussed. What is more complicated in this novel is that the sexual implications apply to a female who is more a child than a woman; in fact, she is referred to, time and again, as a child. Many critics have identified *The Old Curiosity Shop*, with its death of Little Nell, as characteristic of sentimental literature that allowed Victorians to grieve for their own dead children, in that the rate of infant mortality was quite high. Notwithstanding that interpretation, because of Nell's prepubescent state, the sexuality focused on her seems pedophilic. The point is not whether Dickens was a pedophile; the text is pedophilic in ways that were only hinted in the desire for the other little women. "Nice" men as well as villains have sexual intent toward this child, and those men do not receive overt scrutiny for any deviant behavior. Albeit gendered acceptable, their actions and attitudes prove fatal; Little Nell does die. This is an ideological crisis that runs as an undercurrent throughout the novel.

Hence in *The Old Curiosity Shop*, the story of a little woman reaches the emphatic consequence of woman's powerlessness, self-starvation, hopeless resistance, and sexual vulnerability. The death of Little Nell, no matter how sentimental and spiritually uplifting, epitomizes the fate of women crushed under the weight of oppression by gender definition.

THE LITTLE WOMEN OF LITTLE DORRIT

Insofar as *Little Dorrit* is the only Dickens novel named for a female protagonist and its title emphasizes her diminutive statue, it is germane to this chapter's study. Known as the little mother, Amy has maternal tendencies that are the more pronounced in their sharp contrast to Mrs. Clennam's lack of the same. She is the perfect Dickensian daughter, devoted to the exclusion of all else to the care of her father. The daughter acts as a mother and a wife to her father; and a mother to his other children, who are both older than she; and a mother to her sister's children.

These little women usually are expected to assume the role of surrogate mother. They cannot be sexual beings, in the sense that mothers, from a Victorian perspective, could not be thought of in that way. In reality, most of them had to be sexual beings in order to become mothers. Somewhat of a compromise to that dilemma, the Dickensian text has created young women who act as mothers but have tiny, prepubescent bodies. The diminutive signifies repressed sexual appetite (Houston 156). The small body also signals lack of personal nutrition; the tiny woman is supposed to be providing food and satisfying sexual appetites for others instead of for herself (McKnight 118). Perhaps James Marlow is right regarding women, such as Nell and the Marchioness, as tiny because they are starved for love (83); they give but they do not get. And perhaps this is what makes such a woman most alluring to Dickens—that she can sexually arouse, but sex with her cannot be consummated, so that the man is always in a state of arousal.

Little Dorrit duplicates the Euphrasia woman: the daughter who kept her father alive in prison through feeding him with her breasts (273–74; I: ch. 19). The reference becomes loaded with symbolism as applied to *Little Dorrit*. By assuming the mother's role and by literally providing his food, Amy does bear her breast to her father, who is in prison. Because it is a grown man she nurses, the image is highly sexual as well, and because it is her father, an Electra complex.

Legally, like Euphrasia, Little Dorrit is free to come and go; she is not an inmate because of debt or reckless speculation. This apparent mobility would support Alison Milbank's theory that the novel's women freely choose their captivity, but the men are inmates by force (118). She interprets Mr. Dorrit as representative of many Victorian men in sociosexual crisis brought on not by the limitations of domestic ideology but by an unstable world that puts stress on people who are conforming to domestic ideology. Mr. Dorrit has failed in the working world, his prescribed sphere of gender; therefore, his daughter is forced to earn money outside the home in order to provide for him and the rest of the family, an inversion of gendered responsibilities (107). If one agrees with Elaine Showalter that the novel's prison paralyzes and emasculates ("Guilt" 39), one has to own that the prison represents a much larger one, and add that it entraps women as well. Mr. Dorrit is an effeminate man (98; bk 1, ch. 6), but he was this way when he first entered the Marshalsea. He lost his manhood through an inability to provide for his family. In prison, however, he still enjoys the privilege of a patriarch, largely as a result of Amy's dual roles as breadwinner and bread server. Sarah Winter explains the perception this way: "Feminine domestic labor and emotional management provide the deferential capital needed to 'liberate' the emotional debtor from the 'prisons' of diminished patriarchal power and fallen families. . . . [Little Dorrit's] emotional management allows men to be reinstated to their positions of conventional masculine authority" (245–47). Little Dorrit is just as confined to the prison as her father. If she wants to sustain a "normal" family relationship, she cannot do it outside the prison; it must be "in there" where the patriarch resides; she must stay within domestic ideology, which, in this novel, is taking on all of the characteristics of a prison.

Little Dorrit supposedly perfectly satisfies the Victorian's patriarch's fantasy: through a close father–daughter relationship, the father can enjoy all of the benefits of having a wife without being disturbed by sex (Holbrook 10). This is where the text twists with inconsistency. "Little Dorrit is virtuous but fetishly sexual," David Suchoff insists (59). And so she is, along with all the other diminutive women in the Dickens' archives. Now Kimberley Reynolds and Nicola Humble argue that the Victorian novel presents prenubile girls as highly sexualized and, as such, on their way to matrimony (15). However, Arthur does not seem sexually responsive or sexually interested in Little Dorrit. Instead, he seems to look to her as the mother he has never had. Nevertheless, although twenty-two years old, Amy is one of Dickens' little girl creations and in that childish state, a sexually provocative creature, even if she does not appear to be so to Arthur. Yet, the text imprisons her, expecting her perpetually to be prenubile. She is sexually arousing, yes; sexually self-gratifying, never.

Dickens' little women are complicated representations of sexual turmoil.

If the reader could create a composite portrait of them with all of the ambiguities and implied sexual deviance, one would find Maggy: a twenty-eight-year old woman who stopped growing at age ten. But Maggy is not sexually alluring; in fact, she is monstrously unappealing. Paired with Little Dorrit, she is the hyperbole of that little lady. Voracious, the extreme opposite of Little Dorrit, who never needs to eat, she is the manifestation of a woman who is starved with womanly needs but must be satisfied with only a child's fare of milk and cookies. She is the gargoyle image of Little Dorrit, who was born in a prison and whose growth into a woman was perverted as a result.

THE LITTLE WOMEN OF OUR MUTUAL FRIEND

If *Great Expectations* is a bildungsroman about a boy maturing into manhood and all of the women in that novel seem to be subservient to the preservation of power in patriarchy, then *Our Mutual Friend* is a bildungsroman about a girl maturing into womanhood.

Jenni Calder and Michael Slater both consider Bella to be one of Dickens' more fully realized female characters.[5] She may not turn into a self-defined woman, but the reader is offered considerable narrative in order to get to know her. Also, she is, as Schroeder and Schroeder point out, one of the few women in the Dickensian archives to undergo change (268–69). Such feminine growth is not, by any means, revolutionary in a Victorian novel, for true to paradigm, Bella changes not for her own sake but in order to become a suitable wife for John. Nevertheless, she is more than an ornament, and the narrative seems to make a point of this through recurring allusions to dolls. The characterization of Bella, therefore, cannot be discussed without consideration of the dolls' dressmaker, Jenny Wren.[6]

Eugene Wrayburn says, "I think of setting up a doll, Miss Jenny" (268; bk. 2, ch. 19). Her admonition, that he will surely break it, follows. They, of course, are referring to Lizzie. Much later he asks Jenny once more to dress a doll for him, and she replies, "If you want one, go and buy one at the shop" (586; bk. 3, ch. 43). With his money he can purchase an acceptable wife. Lizzie has been dressed from the scraps of the lower class. Besides class disparity, the hardships that she was born into have molded her into a woman of quality. Eugene is Lizzie's superior by class, but inferior by character. By admission, he calls himself an idle dog. When Jenny asks why he does not reform, he replies that he needs someone "who makes it worth my while." Wrayburn expects to find a mother figure to inspire him to be a good man. Indeed, both Lizzie and Jenny are daughters/mothers to their fathers, but neither father changes his life for the better. Why then should Lizzie's influence on Wrayburn promise any other result? Ultimately, he needs Lizzie, but the narrative does not convince that Lizzie needs Wrayburn. Despite the economic security that Lizzie might have were she married to Eugene, she would suffer because of the inequity in his maturity and her ability to love selflessly.

This mirrors what the Boffins are trying to teach Bella, that money is not as important in a relationship as quality of character. Like that of Eugene, Bella's spoiled nature must be dealt with. Her maturation is complete as indicated by the metaphor of her living in a doll house (743; bk. 4, ch. 55) and her making doll's dresses for her own baby (812; bk. 4, ch. 61).

Lizzie's transformation is social. At the beginning of the novel she participates in her father's occupation of dredging the Thames for bodies to rob; afterward she sends her brother off to school so that he can support himself better. She works at an industrial job so that she can support herself honorably, and she and Jenny get training to become school teachers. Even if she does not marry Eugene Wrayburn, Lizzie has raised herself and her brother out of the sewers in which they were born.

However, overtly this novel is not Lizzie's story. The changes that she goes through only shadow those that Bella undergoes. Lizzie is like a doppelgänger whose nexus with Bella becomes obvious when they meet in chapter 42 of book 3. Here they are attracted to each other and merge into one unit, for it is at this time that they both undergo their most complete metamorphoses. Seeing how good and humble Lizzie is leads Bella to a full comprehension of her own shortcomings. After her visit with Lizzie, she tells John that she feels as if years had passed during that meeting; she grows up.

In articulating her fear of Headstone and her desire for Wrayburn, Lizzie indicates that she has come into full womanhood, and that means that she can be violated by one and won by the other. Another reality she has to contend with is that the man she loves lives in mortal danger. The gravity of the relationships with these two men convinces Bella of the carelessness with which she has handled her relationship with John.

Even though the novel continually returns to Bella, through its continual reference to Lizzie, it also suggests some significant subversive notions about women in general. Lizzie easily rows on the river; she is as strong as any man. Even though Old Betty calls her a "boofer" (beautiful) lady as she does Bella, Lizzie is strong enough to rescue Eugene from drowning. Lizzie, in other words, does not mimic a type, but she is womanly enough to be a strong influence on Eugene, to make him want to change his profligate ways. An obedient and loyal daughter to her father, devoted sister to Charley, and tender mother to Jenny and an equal to the womanly Bella, Lizzie is also independent, earning her own money and providing for Charley. She has the emotional strength to resist two suitors, one who terrifies her and the other who seduces her. This is no weak, brainless, spineless female. The text sets her up as a complicated ideal, not a typical angel-in-the-house. By an obvious Bella bildungsroman structure, it suggests that all women learn from a woman who diverges from the norm.

THE LITTLE WOMAN OF THE MYSTERY OF EDWIN DROOD

Before ending this consideration of Dickens' little women, a few comments about Miss Rosa Bud should be made. The very real danger of patriarchal power has been fairly evident in the novels discussed thus far. In the event, however, the reader doubts the accuracy of such an interpretation (as if, for example, the death of Little Nell [OCS] signifies some other theme paramount to that novel), then I would ask the reader to contextualize this danger in the entire Dickens canon. What may have been subtle in the former accounts of this study becomes blatant in *Edwin Drood*.

The name, Miss Rosa Bud, immediately signals that the text will not be metaphorically obscure or complex in her gender depiction. From the onset, the text tries to master her. She is "wonderfully pretty, wonderfully childish, wonderfully whimsical" (18; ch. 3), and is short, overly fond of the Lumps-of-Delight shop, after a visit to which one finds her "putting her little pink fingers to her rosy lips, to cleanse them from the Dust of Delight that comes off the lumps" (20). As was so with the host of little women who have preceded her, the text obviously makes Miss Rosa's juvenescence sybaritic and the male response to it lascivious.

In the following scene, the text invites the reader into voyeurism in much the same way already discussed:

Mr. Jasper was seated at the piano as they came into his drawing-room, and was accompanying Miss Rosebud while she sang. It was a consequence of his playing the accompaniment without notes, and of her being a heedless little creature, very apt to go wrong, that he followed her lips most attentively, with his eyes as well as hands; carefully and softly hinting the key-note from time to time. (50; ch. 7)

As a man, Jasper is naturally fulfilling his obligation to guide the erring, brainless female. That domination socially granted license to sexual domination. However, as the scene develops, the reader is no longer expected to be a participant in Miss Rosa's seduction, but to judge Mr. Jasper as the incarnation of patriarchal evil and become aware of the terror that the little woman feels at being lustfully objectified:

The song went on. It was a sorrowful strain of parting, and the fresh young voice was very plaintive and tender. As Jasper watched the pretty lips, and ever and again hinted the one note, as though it were a low whisper from himself, the voice became less steady, until all at once the singer broke into a burst of tears, and shrieked out, with her hands over her eyes: "I can't bear this! I am frightened! Take me away!" (50; ch. 7)

In Dickens' last novel the evil of uncontrollable patriarchal domination and its menace to both men (Jasper murders Drood) and women are prominent themes. Miss Rosa Bud courageously avoids a marriage to Drood that might follow the same disastrous course as Dora Copperfield's. The horrible ordeal with Jasper teaches her to put aside all coyness, lest it attract a wolf instead of a ram. By not acting as a pet or a plaything, she eventually will marry a young man and not a father type who will treat her like a toy. Finally, at the end of the Dickens canon, the reader will find text that severely censures gender ideologies that in earlier texts were only covertly resisted. Even though Dickens had not lived long enough to finish this novel, the narrative had already developed characters who were overcoming gender shackles and beginning to create happy relationships of men and women, the likes of which are not seen in previous Dickens novels.

NOTES

1. Such as is the case with the widow of a deceased brother of Martin. She is a "strong-minded woman"; therefore, she has a "bony figure and a masculine voice" (MC: 50; ch. 4).

2. This observation was made by Professor Anne Wallace of the University of Southern Mississippi. Although she did not include Tom in her list, Frances Armstrong identifies other male angels, such as Newman Noggs (NN), Gabriel Varden (BR), and Mark Tapley (MC) (71–73). Varden's angelic traits are discussed in Chapter 3.

3. Recall Allan Woodcourt (BH). Whatever Esther saw in him, the text is not telling. Nor does it tell much about Arthur Clennam (LD) and Eugene Wrayburn (OMF), but they are worthy suitors supposedly. Sam Weller (PP) and Mark Tapley (MC) are exceptions; they are strongly depicted, but they do not count in Dickens' economy because they are lower-class servants. As for David Copperfield (DC), Nicholas Nickleby (NN), and Pip (GE), their novels are bildungsromans, and therefore the reader is intricately aware of the characters' weaknesses.

4. For arguments from the narrative and Dickens' earlier manuscripts identifying Quilp as the father and Sally Brass as the girl's mother, see Grubb, Bennett, and Easson.

5. Several critics have noted the maturation of Dickens' perception of women, which they attribute to his relationship with Ellen Ternan. They identify Bella, Estella, and Helena as "Ellen" women, as indicated by similarities of name and by complexity of characterization. See Manheim 197, Alexander 125–28, and Stone (Night) 380–84, 413–14. Slater also perceives these three women in their complexities but disagrees about their prototype (196–97, 212–13).

6. Because Jenny, for reasons explained later, does not fit into the little women category, she is discussed more fully in Chapter 7.

6

The Women outside the Fold: Dickens' She-Dragons

Division of gender formed the foundation of domestic ideology. Social and legal agents reinforced the lines: men were supposed to work outside the home and woman inside; the two should never cross. Dickens' novels overtly confirmed this perspective. Women who transgressed patriarchal boundaries and exhibited unfeminine behavior and capabilities were not to be tolerated. Consequently, a host of Dickensian she-dragons are severely dealt with throughout the canon. At the same time, the text fails to align itself consistently with this aspect of ideology. Bobbing to the surface are disputes of arbitrary definitions based on gender, based on premises not founded on fact. Or perhaps another way to put it is that Dickensian characters, mimetic of all human beings, are more complex than simply two polarized types, man or woman, and as such, they "struggle (if only to come to terms) with the encompassing network that defines and controls them, no matter how conditional such struggle may be, no matter how necessarily it may backfire" (Langbauer 129). Rigid Victorian definition of man and woman cannot be sustained by the Dickensian text although a conscientious effort to do otherwise seems apparent. Instead, it is strained, challenged, questioned, criticized, and sometimes redefined, albeit often covertly.

THE SHE-DRAGON OF THE OLD CURIOSITY SHOP

Richard Swiveller in *The Old Curiosity Shop* creates an entirely new taxonomy of females. According to him, there are women who comply with social norms and those who do not. Of this latter there are two types:

mermaids and dragons, both marked by scales (350; ch. 36), meaning that their actions and attitudes are abrasive. According to his impeccable logic, mermaids, unlike dragons, look into mirrors and comb their hair. These are probably dissenting women who do not appear to be dissenters. They would include the haughty and elegant Lady Dedlock *(BH)* or the haughty and beautiful Edith Granger *(D&S)*. As for the other kind, Mr. Swiveller determines that Sally Brass is definitely one of those "She-dragons in the business, conducting themselves like professional gentlemen" (334; ch. 34). She will be the first she-dragon that this chapter will study.

The novel introduces her with praises of her abilities in the law until it tacks on this epithet: "a kind of amazon at common law" (320; ch. 33). Interested in the law at an early age, she eventually becomes the "prop and pillar" of her father's business. So far, she seems to be providing an excellent feminine service to a patriarch; after all, it is still the father's business and his success through her efforts. Instead of encouraging her to develop domestic skills, he encourages her to master the law. When she is unable to gain an attorney's certificate simply because she is a woman, the father gives her to his son "as an invaluable auxiliary" (348; ch. 36). In other words, he makes it possible for her to continue in the law by working for her brother, who can be certified. The text never censures the father for doing this, and Sally complies with domesticity by submitting to her father. But then Sally becomes too good at her nondomestic job and fails to subordinate her talents to patriarchal management.

She becomes so proficient in dealing with the complicated, male-dominated British legal system, she knows the law and all of its "slippery and eel-like [phallic] crawlings in which it commonly pursues its way" (321; ch. 33). Minus the blatantly obvious negative tone toward her, the text depicts her as an intelligent, knowledgeable, and talented person— person, but not woman. She does not excel in the "gentler and softer arts" peculiar to women (348; ch. 36). In fact, because she has crossed gender lines, the text has masculinized her. It compares her to a man:

In face she bore a striking resemblance to her brother, Sampson—so exact, indeed, was the likeness between them, that had it consorted with Miss Brass's maiden modesty and gentle womanhood to have assumed her brother's clothes in a frolic and sat down beside him, it would have been difficult for the oldest friend of the family to determine which was Sampson and which Sally. (320; ch. 33)

She is not being compared to just any man, but to the biblical prototype of masculinity, Samson, a comparison that makes her that more virile. On the other hand, the text may be conveying that the reason Sally has been able to seize gendered power is that her brother has surrendered it just as Samson did, when outsmarted by Delilah.

If that allusion to her masculine resemblance is not clear enough, Sally has a beard (320–21). And her voice is "deep and rich." Seemingly comfortable in her masculine identity, Sally taunts her brother about his own masculinity. When asked whether he has any man in him, the narrative supplies the answer: " 'He, he!' simper[s] Brass, who in his deep debasement really seemed to have changed sexes with his sister, and to have made over to her any spark of manliness he might have possessed" (608–9; ch. 66).

More to the point, Sally does not act like a woman. Instead of being a maternal care giver, she starves and abuses the little servant, who is actually her daughter.[1] She knows too much of the law for any man to risk marrying her for she would always have a legal advantage, which so few women enjoyed (321). Demonstrating superiority over men and intimidating all of them, she relishes being called a rascal when she should prefer being called an angel (322). Her preference registers an aversion to the angel role and her acceptance of a male designation to take its place.

Close to the end of Sally's story in the novel, some folks rumor that in order for her to escape reproach in her share of wrongdoings, Sally might "have gone down to the docks in male attire, and had become a female sailor; others darkly whispered that she had enlisted as a private in the second regiment of the Foot Guards" (665; ch. 73). Despite her facile efforts to pass as a man, society will not privilege her as a man. She must suffer for her defiance of gender. And so must Sampson for his abdication of manhood. The two are described now as homeless and hungry. People who do not conform to domesticity do not reap the benefits of domesticity. The text warns that they will have no home at all.

Nonetheless, the text, through Sally, has represented the plight of all women who are capable of and interested in pursuits outside domesticity. Is the text really trying to convey that a woman who takes on a man's job will lose her femininity as well as her happiness? Why should not society (even Victorian) admire and make a place for a woman who is sharper, more knowledgeable, and more capable than the men around her? Why should it condemn her for not loving and taking care of a child who reminds her at every instant that the father is Quilp? What if the child had been conceived through rape? If so, without abortion and without help in dealing with a rape, Sally's dilemma is more understandable. If there had been no rape, one might still sympathize with a woman who has never been trained to be a mother and has no desire to be one.

The reader is never told Sally's side of her story. But we are given enough details to know that the text has not judged her and women like her impartially. In that verdict, then, the text is revealing more than is apparent.

THE SHE-DRAGON OF HARD TIMES

Another woman whose story is difficult to glean is Mrs. Sparsit. She represents a different dissenter than the female who has been masculinized because of assuming a masculine role. Sparsit is the cast-off widow no one wants to support. Being a woman who does not venture across gender boundaries, she has no employable skills. Although hired to be a house-keeper to Bounderby, she seems qualified only to pour tea and spy on people. Boasting a descent from aristocracy, she adds status to the Boun-derby household, and that is why the manufacturer from the rising breed of nouveau riche keeps her.

When Bounderby tells Mrs. Sparsit that he is going to marry Louisa Gradgrind and that he has made arrangements for the housekeeper to take up residence in an apartment at the bank, he is flabbergasted that she does not fly into a rage or swoon. Bounderby knows that she must have expected always to be his partner at the hearth for she has been acting "correctly" like an angel-in-the-house. The hearth should be her reward. The news of his marriage to Louisa should have infuriated her. But Mrs. Sparsit is a woman of self-possession, and she has more worldly wisdom than most Victorian female characters. Biding her time, she knows that the Bounderby marriage will not work because, for one reason, it is an arranged marriage without love. Telling him that he has acted like a father to Louisa not only reinforces the age disparity (another reason she assumes that the marriage will fail) but also suggests an incestuous relationship (38; ch. 7). She also reacts against his calling the girl "little puss" as if women deserve to be regarded in a more dignified manner. Indeed Bounderby's objectification of Louisa is his crucial trait that dooms his marriage to failure.

Later she suspects that Louisa is having an affair with the handsome James Harthouse. Such speculations, let alone her detective work, are in-appropriate to a domestic angel-in-the-house. Actually, Mrs. Sparsit exag-gerates the angel role—or through her the text satirizes that role—by obsequious submission and worshipful adoration of her master. The house-keeper feeds his ego, so that when his wife fails to do likewise, Bounderby is all the more aware of Louisa's noncompliance to wifely behavior. All the while, Mrs. Sparsit is using her domestic power to manipulate him.

Diane Belcher has this to say about Mrs. Sparsit: "In all her stereotypical maliciousness Mrs. Sparsit is nevertheless a portrait of a woman determined to take control of her life and to alter the condition in a world that presents her with few options. She is one of the cleverest women Dickens created, and, not surprisingly, one of the most repulsive" (93). Even if what Belcher says is true, the text is ambivalent in its treatment of her, mainly because her dissenting behavior seems justified by her relationship with such a bully as Bounderby, the "personification of masculine power and boorishness" (97). When Sparsit exploits gender roles to the maximum, she does not violate domestic ideology; the text that barely communicates her story ex-poses the inadequacy of domesticity as a government over sexual behavior. Women like Sparsit do live in a world ruled by patriarchs, many of them unresponsive to the needs of women who are not little pusses. These Spar-sits must find pockets of power inside or outside gender-restricted spheres that will enable them to survive.

THE SHE-DRAGONS OF GREAT EXPECTATIONS

Three women are depicted as veritable she-dragons in *Great Expectations*: Mrs. Joe, Miss Havisham, and her protegé, Estella. Through Pip's point of view, Mrs. Joe is the quintessential bad mother and wife; Miss Havisham, the woman who never became a wife but did become a bad mother; and Estella, a warning to young ladies that they can end up as one or the other with very unhappy consequences.

Beneath the surface of text, the reader can find another point of view regarding Mrs. Joe. She was only eighteen when she became an orphan. Additionally she was forced to raise a child who was not hers in a time when women could not support themselves, much less dependents. Two years later she married a man who was not her intellectual equal (Barickman et al. 16).

The reader is never told her Christian name. When a Victorian woman marries, she loses her name and is to assume the signification of her husband. So why not call her Mrs. Joe? Actually, this is not what the text is overtly attempting with her epithet. Instead, it facetiously calls her Mrs. Joe to convey that the woman has stolen masculine power. Her theft is also symbolized by the cane with which she beats Pip. If the cane, referred to as the Tickler, isn't phallic enough, then Mrs. Joe seizes another by throwing Pip "as a connubial missile," or penis child, at Joe.

Alison Milbank does not interpret Mrs. Joe as a thief of masculine power, but as an abuser of feminine power. Mrs. Joe is a woman who uses her domestic space "either as a reformatory for punishment of male misdeeds, or as a weapon in some sexual power game" (122). However, the text does not regard her as feminine. Far from being described as buxom, or maternal,[2] she is "tall and bony" (6; ch. 2). Other than this description, the text does not attach masculine qualities to her. Significantly, she "almost always [wears] a coarse apron, fastened over her figure behind two loops, and having a square impregnable bib in front, that was stuck full of pins and needles" (6). In other novels wearing an apron is an indication that a woman is appropriately functioning in a domestic sphere.[3] Instead of assuming a male disguise, as Sally Brass does, Mrs. Joe is seen to be more treacherous. She hides behind an apron and concentrates all of her domestic power to dominate the men in her household: "She made [the apron] a powerful merit in herself, and a strong reproach against Joe, that she wore this apron so much. Though I really see no reason why she should have worn it at all; or why, if she did wear it at all, she should not have taken it off every day of her life" (6; ch. 2). Obviously she is not happy having to play the role of a housewife and mother, and her husband and adopted son are not happy about her having to do so either. The text does not provide her an alternative, though, and that misfortune ought to justify somewhat her hostility.

Richard Barickman et al. observe that the text has converted many usual instruments of domesticity in the Gargery household into instruments of aggression (68), as illustrated in the following scene: "My sister had a trenchant way of cutting our bread-and-butter for us, that never varied. First, with her left hand she jammed the loaf hard and fast against her bib—where it sometimes got a pin into it, and sometimes a needle, which we afterwards got into our mouths" (8; ch. 2). Barickman's team understands from the narrative that Mrs. Joe's rage is justified. What was a woman to do if she possessed talent and intelligence and hungered for an avenue of expression outside the home (74)? Such a question is subversive. The novelist Mrs. Dinah Craik preempts it: "The hierarchies of the soul's dominion belong only to a man, and it is right they should. Nature, which gave to man dominion over the intellect, gave to her that of the heart and . . . there scarcely ever lived the woman who would rather sit meekly by her own hearth, with her husband at her side, and her children on her knees, than be crowned Corinne of the Capital."[4]

When Mrs. Joe extends her influence into the male sphere of business, the text retaliates. Mrs. Joe tries to tell her husband how he should run his shop. Orlick beats her with a hammer, a masculine instrument and signifier. Milbank regards this act of violence as beating Mrs. Joe into submission. She even loses power in the house. She can no longer write, so she ceases to be superior to the illiterate Joe (125–26). For attempting to steal power from her husband, she has been tamed (Ingham 83). But the text has done more than that. It has chastised her, forced her to suffer and repent of her ways, and then die, freeing Joe to marry a truly good domestic woman, Biddy. All the while, the reader is not to question the rightness of these consequences for a woman who happened to have more "masculine" sense than did her husband; nor to consider that the woman was married to a man who was more maternal than she; nor to question, then, whether gender expectations are unrealistic and unfair to both men and women. Instead, the Victorians were to believe what John Ruskin said in his famous *The Ethics of Dust* (1890); "You must either be house-Wives or house-Moths; remember that. In the deep sense, you must either weave men's fortunes, and embroider them; or feed upon, and bring them to decay" (200). The text seems to support this ideology in its treatment of Mrs. Joe, but not in the context of the entire novel. Pip thinks that he has won his fortune through Miss Havisham. The truth is that neither Mrs. Joe nor Miss Havisham, as a woman, has the power to ensure her own fortune, much less his, nor does she have the power to prevent his prospering, as Ruskin suggests. Pip is made a gentleman by no one within a domestic fold, but by a male convict.

The reader must remember that this novel focuses on Pip—his deprivations and expectations. From his perspective, Mrs. Joe is an unloving mother surrogate, in contrast to her husband. The novel never focuses on Mrs. Joe's deprivations and expectations although they are there in underlying text. Seemingly not sensitive to this exclusion of information, the critic Carl Hartog has concluded that Mrs. Joe's major sin is that she does not love: "At the center of Dickens's portrayal of women in *Great Expectations* lies a stark and melodramatic image: women, lacking the capacity to love, become destructive to themselves and to men" (248). Perhaps she does not love because she is not loved for who she is. Perhaps she does not love because it is not always so that women naturally become maternal to orphan brothers and subordinate to men they marry in order not to starve. What of her dreams? Why does society not allow her to have any great expectations?

Unlike with Mrs. Joe, the text has clearly indicated that Miss Havisham was once in the bloom of her youth, placing all of her hopes and expectations in marriage—as any good Victorian girl should do. After she has been forsaken at the alter, her subsequent despair and freezing of time are not only a psychological prison; they are social. Without marriage, women simply had very few options of how to survive in this society. Miss Havisham's cumbersome and putrid gown constantly reminds her and the reader that she wears the cloak of womanhood. The gown calls to mind that wonderful line from Elizabeth Barrett Browning's *Aurora Leigh*: "This vile woman's way of trailing garments shall not trip me up." The gown is killing Havisham and nearly does so by catching on fire.

Strangely, then, Estella seems to play a greater role in the novel than a young girl preparing or not preparing for marriage. In fact, she and Pip do not marry each other, and the novel does not end in a wedding ceremony in the way that many of the other Dickens novels do. Of course, this deemphasis of marriage may be the result of Miss Havisham's embittered training. But most of the marriages in this novel are unhappy ones. If Miss Havisham had married Compeyson, she would have been a battered wife, insofar as he did marry later and abuse his wife. With her yellowed, tattered bridal gown and rotting veil, Havisham is the outward manifestation of the inward psyche that exists in women like Mrs. Rudge *(BR)*, who marry only to become abused and broken in spirit. On this inconsistency about marriage in Victorian literature, Barbara Weiss writes, "There has perhaps never been an age (or a literature) as relentlessly *pro* marriage as the Victorian period, in which a loving marriage is generally seen as the resolution to every social ill in the novel." And yet, "time and again, married union is envisioned as an insecure and tormenting state, susceptible to the same upheavals which are breaking down the traditional social values everywhere" (67).

Although she does not use her freedom from marriage well, Miss Havisham is free of patriarchal constraints. She has the liberty to define herself, even if she chooses to be a macabre bride ghost and angry matriarch. Her character circumvents patriarchy, and she reproduces herself in Estella. When Victorian literary conventions would have a man seduce the woman, thus ruining her forever, this novel allows a woman to destroy its hero (Ingham 38). Miss Havisham effects this through Estella. However, the text counterattacks by marrying Estella to a man who will abuse her.

The question remains whether the text understands the reason for Miss Havisham's hate. She is not the personification of an old maid, after all, for she is dressed as a bride. She has paid the price to marry but has reaped no benefits for doing so. What through her is the text then saying about the merits of domestic ideology for women?

And is Estella only the manifestation of her hate? Rather, as Gail Houston so perceptively understands, is she not the archetype of "woman" bred to be desired but able to have no desire herself (159)? Why then should she be regarded as an anomaly when she is so perfectly the product of Victorian ideology, unless the text means to suggest that very point?

Estella is the exact opposite of an angel-in-the-house. Instead of submissive, she is willful and domineering. Instead of gentle, kind, and tender, she is calculating, malicious, and hard. Instead of reserved, she is acrimonious. Instead of internalizing her suffering, as was expected of a good Victorian woman, she inflicts suffering on men. Instead of using her beauty and her inner qualities of strength to attract men for their own good, she attracts men for her own purpose. This is not to imply that Estella is a healthy, assertive prototype of the twentieth-century woman. She is, nonetheless, a woman who has been trained to garner agencies of female power and to use them to balance the scales.

Thwarted expectations is the theme of this novel, but they are not just the expectations of a young man. The three major female characters, like Pip, operate within a sexual ideological framework, with expectations that bring them only bitter disappointment and severe brutalization.

THE SHE-DRAGON OF LITTLE DORRIT

Like Miss Havisham, *Little Dorrit*'s Miss Wade violates gender codes in her intentional reproduction of self in another woman. Unlike Miss Havisham, Miss Wade would never wear a wedding gown. Definitely a dissenter is this Miss Wade, who refuses to be imprisoned by ideological constraints. Insisting upon the right to assert her own selfhood, not only does she define herself in the way she lives her life, but her deportment communicates her defiance: "I am self-contained and self-reliant; your opinion is nothing to me; I have no interest in you, care nothing for you, and see and hear you with indifference" (62; bk. 1, ch. 2). Pet Meagles is so concerned about Miss Wade's traveling alone, she volunteers the protection of her father, only to be told plainly that the latter has no use for a patriarch.

Wade considers people, and especially people who conform to domestic ideology, fools. An orphan, she was raised by a single woman who called herself a grandmother who took care of ten children in all. As a member of that non-nuclear-type family, Wade was never likely to be anything but a woman dissenter. Always passionate (a definite non-angel-in-the-house trait), she has a volatile involvement with another girl, a relationship many critics have understood to be homosexual. Whether or not this is so, Wade is in constant conflict between who she is naturally and who society thinks she should be. The object of her love is a young girl who is pretty and knows how to practice the "feminine" habits of smiles and tears to get what she wants. Wade measures the girl as "despicable and false"; Charlotte is the embodiment of what the Victorian ideal of a little girl should be. At the same time attracted to and repulsed by Charlotte, Wade struggles until she rejects the model of domesticity. From this point on, she refuses to conform to "feminine behavior." Neither does she allow any man and his family to buy her, "body and soul," merely because she falls in love and agrees to an engagement. At great price she purchases her independence.

Even as the text seems to censure her nonconformity and mercilessly attack her for her attempt to reproduce herself in a young girl (Tattycoram), it also reveals that had she married Henry Goram, she would have entered into a marriage as wretched as the one that Pet Meagles does experience with him. Pet is just the opposite of Miss Wade; she is like the Charlotte of Miss Wade's youth. Or another way to say it is that Pet's twin sister who died in early childhood represents that part of a woman that yearns to hold on to her own self but cannot possibly do that and at the same time hold on to familial relationships that require her to deny herself. This is the same dilemma with which Tattycoram has to come to terms. She is exactly like Miss Wade in temperament and strong selfhood, but if she wants to live within the only intact family unit within the novel, the Meagles, she has to commit suicide of the self.

The title of Miss Wade's chapter, "The History of a Self-Tormentor," is significantly ambiguous. Does Wade torment herself because she has an "unhappy temper," one that she cannot but should control? Or does the text, albeit veiled, justify her unhappiness and anger? Is she tormented by living in a society that refuses to grant selfhood to women? Although Miss Wade seems to have been released from an ideological prison defined by domesticity, she does not enjoy her freedom because almost everyone else is inside that prison.

Since Tattycoram is received by the Meagles as a returning prodigal daughter, the text ultimately tries to subdue Miss Wade but not without ambivalence: a young woman would do well to control her temper and surrender her will to the patriarchally driven family. Otherwise she might end up alone like the willful, independent, free-to-travel-and-do-as-she-pleases Miss Wade.

THE SHE-DRAGON OF *A TALE OF TWO CITIES*

One cannot leave this chapter on viragoes without considering the extreme of all mean women in the Dickens canon: Madame Defarge. Based upon the famous knitting women who kept a record of those condemned to the guillotine, she is the antithesis of the ideal woman. Instead of being a part of the birthing process, she oversees death. Instead of being the delicate creature who faints at the first sight of the unbearable, Defarge stoically regards blood and gore and human suffering. Instead of submissively attending to the needs of her master in the domestic sphere, Defarge deftly hews off the head of men beneath her feet. Another female revolutionary calls her an angel (317; bk. 3, ch. 12). If she is, she is the angel of death.

There are a few holes in this picture, however. For one, Madame Defarge is a participant in what has often been considered a noble fight to overthrow aristocratic oppression. Along with her countryman, she means to end poverty and disease among the lower class and win freedom and justice for all. Her husband treats her as an equal, and she heads up an army of women who have just as much at stake as men in winning their independence. This is a revolutionary war, and the text demonstrates that women have as great a capacity to fight as do men. When men wage war, it is glorious; when women wage war, what is it? Yet the French Revolution was won by both sexes.

There is another hole in the picture, and Madame Defarge tries to fill it by her declaration in chapter 12 of the last book. When she was a girl, her family was severely taxed, forced to work without pay, and could not keep enough of the fruit of their own labor to prevent starvation. The marquis de St. Evrémonde (Darnay's uncle) desired her sister, who was at that time married and pregnant. He raped her. Their brother was killed in trying to avenge her. One week later, the sister died with her unborn babe. Therefore, by the time Defarge is depicted as a woman of evil in a fight with that woman of love (Miss Pross) and then is shot in the struggle, the reader is to know that the Briton defeated the French, and that good triumphed over evil. If this is the text's corrective to a revolution that overthrew a system of class boundaries, a revolution that seemed to threaten many an Englishman, then the injustice that Defarge experiences is even more glaring. The novel may have wanted not to narrate a sympathetic story about Defarge, and definitely not to create a sympathetic ending to her; nevertheless, her story is embedded within that novel, and when exhumed, deserves sympathy and reassessment.

NOTES

1. See the discussion of the Marchioness in Chapter 5.
2. See Chapter 3.
3. For example, Ruth Pinch and her apron *(MC)*, referred to in Chapter 5.
4. Quoted in Kennard (17) from Craik's *Olive* (London: Chapman and Hall, 1850, 166–67).

7

The Women Who Don't Fit into the Fold: Dickens' Misfits

Previously, this study has mostly considered stereotypical behavior and how it subverts domestic ideology. Women either fit inside or outside the ideological structure through their conformity or their rebellion, respectively. This chapter will analyze women who are not inside the fold because they do not "fit"; they are perceived as being atypical or "aggerawayters," like Jerry Cruncher's wife in *A Tale of Two Cities* (49; bk. 2, ch. 1). In many cases this is so because domestic ideology has warped them; they are freakish in some way. Regardless of how they comply or do not comply with gender prescription, from the male point of view in the novel, they are—to borrow a term from Ellen Moers—"agitating women": they agitate because they are figures that distort domestic ideology. As caricatures, they embody aspects of domesticity to an extreme. The satire does not point to their extreme personalities, however, but through them to diverse aspects of domesticity.

RELIGIOUS ZEALOTS

The first type of "aggerawayters" appears throughout the Dickens canon. These are the religious zealots. Susan Weller *(PP)* and Mrs. Snagsby *(BH)* are devoted servants to the apostles of the Lord. Here they are submitting themselves to what many believe to be the highest male authority on earth, and the text satirizes them. Or does the text satirize the patriarchal structure of Christianity, which taught women total self-abnegation and submission to male authority?

Two more religious women, for whom the text does not enlist sympathy, are Mrs. Jellyby and Mrs. Pardiggle *(BH)*. Women were supposed to perform good works and visit the sick and poor. Because Mrs. Jellyby takes advantage of one of the few opportunities allowed her within domestic ideology to utilize well her administrative skills, and that opportunity carries her beyond the domestic sphere, she falls under terrible censorship. And so does Mrs. Pardiggle, who, to the opposite extreme, does not do charity work well. As a woman, she is expected to visit the poor and the sick as if all women have a natural aptitude for charity. On the other hand, the text calls her the "inexorable moral policeman." Insofar as this was exactly the duty expected of every woman, it is ironic that the text mocks Mrs. Pardiggle when she performs hers. If a woman shows too much aptitude and devotion for "the Lord's work," she must be contained. This is an irrational position for domestic ideology to assume.

"Powerful women are sexually threatening," Elaine Showalter observes in Dickens' portrayal of strong women like *Little Dorrit*'s Mrs. Clennam. She assumes this is why Arthur cannot regard Amy as anything but a non-threatening, asexual child. This attitude is the result of his upbringing by the overbearing Mrs. Clennam ("Guilt" 34). Good women cannot be sexual in the Dickens' creed; otherwise, through sex they are able to attack men where they are vulnerable. This is a castration fear: an anxiety about losing power.[1] But David Suchoff pairs Mrs. Clennam with Little Dorrit as two women whose right to their own sexuality have been denied by patriarchs (73). Regardless, their sexuality does seep through the text. For example, Mrs. Clennam does have an appetite for wine (an uninhibitor) and oysters (believed by many Victorians to be an aphrodisiac). Nonetheless, Arthur's mother is just as incarcerated as is Dorrit and is physically and psychologically paralyzed.

Even if the text treats Arthur's mother with utter disdain, a different regard can be evinced from subtext, which contains her story. She was brought up by a repressive father and then forced to marry a man who had been married before and produced a son. To ensure that the son will not grow up in the same sinful ways as the father, Mrs. Clennam insists upon raising the boy by herself in strict Calvinistic fashion. She in no way violates domestic ideology by doing so. She, as did many Victorians, holds that it is her job as a female to force out the weakness of the father, whose transgressions were believed to be passed down to succeeding generations. Through "bondage and hardship" Arthur will be able to work out his "release" (859; bk. 2, ch. 31). This is not a practice based on cruelty, yet the text depicts Mrs. Clennam as a cruel woman.

Mrs. Clennam walks for the first time in twelve years and leaves the prison of her room in order to stand up to Mr. Flintwinch and Rigaud, two men who have been conspiring to blackmail her. Flintwinch is the quintessential patriarchal dictator, crazed by the power he is able to impose upon his wife, Affery, and his "mistress," Mrs. Clennam. In fact, he is more interested in holding power over the women than in blackmailing for money (853; ch. 30). Rigaud is a diabolical villain complete with dastardly moustache. His demise occurs with the literal collapse of the Clennam home upon him, appropriately because he was instrumental in the family's sociological and psychological collapse.

This happens at the same time that Mrs. Clennam experiences her miraculous recovery and goes to the prison to ask Little Dorrit for forgiveness. When she returns to her home, she witnesses its collapse and is saved from its destruction through Little Dorrit. Each woman finds the strength to save the other miraculously from destruction. Neither, however, can save the other from imprisonment. Little Dorrit, through first her love for her father and later her love for Arthur, might have spent her entire life in a literal prison. After the desolation of her home and for the next three years, Mrs. Clennam is unable to move and does not have "the power to speak one word" (862; ch. 31). She is the passionate and religious woman who has been both immobilized and silenced.

The text does not satirize Mrs. Cruncher *(TT)* because she is already immobile and silent, except for her frequent "flopping." In much the same way that the text mocks Mrs. Clennam, Mr. Cruncher mocks his wife. The result, however, is that the reader feels sorry for her. Mrs. Cruncher is not sanctimonious like Mrs. Varden *(BR)*. Nor is she as severe as Mrs. Chadband *(BH)* and Mrs. Clennam *(LD)*. She is a humble woman who beseeches God to save her husband, who definitely needs to be saved from his malicious self. Cruncher believes in woman's piety and her connection with the spiritual forces, so that when things go amiss with his moonlight profession, he blames her for setting God against him.

Here is a woman acting as a good angel, complying with gender expectations. Her husband beats her for it, and his son follows suit.

The Cruncher scenario falls into what A. O. J. Cockshut describes as Dickensian humor:

It is derived largely from idiosyncrasies of language, showing forth impossible eccentricity. It lacks the morality, the good sense, the analysis of the typical follies and inconsistences of human nature, which is the main strength of comic tradition. Instead it reveals new abysses of absurdity, fantastic and yet hypnotically real to the reader, in characters who fall outside normal canons of judgment. (18)

Cockshut is right: the text does not analyze nor make a moral issue of how Jerry has the freedom to abuse his wife. Regardless of their comic effect and intent, the idiosyncrasies, eccentricities, follies, inconsistences, and absurdities in characters mimic the same inconsistencies in real human beings, not stereotypes, when and because they try to behave according to an ideology. The distortions that surround some of the most comic women and women in comic situations provide revealing satire about the Victorian ideological pressure to conform to unrealistic expectations of gender decorum.

WOMEN THINKERS

This satire is most apparent when the Dickens novel takes on women's rights advocates and bluestockings. The satire glares from the black of the page, but the grounds for these women to be dissenters can be found in the white space. For example, Victorian men were expected to go off and nobly fight wars, but women, like Mrs. Leo Hunter *(PP)*, wrote odes to expiring frogs. Nothing that women were involved with outside the sphere of domesticity was to be taken seriously. The female intellectuals of America in *Martin Chuzzlewit* are not even worth mentioning by name. They are likely to thrive in that tobacco-spitting, swamp-infested country just like mosquitoes.

Dickens makes his stand with Miss Wisk in *Bleak House*: "Miss Wisk's mission, my guardian said, was to show the world that woman's mission was man's mission and that the only genuine mission of both man and woman was to be always moving declaratory resolutions about things in general at public meetings" (431; ch. 30). Feminists were regarded as women who wanted to be men. In a way, the text is subversively true: women wanted and still do want the same privilege and power that men have. The implication, however, is that these women were denying their own womanhood and perceiving men as tyrants. This was supposed to be a terrible thing, but one could interpret the text as making a straightforward declaration about what women did want: that is, to reinvent womanhood according to their own terms and understandings, as well as to free themselves from the tyranny of patriarchal control. This is one Dickens joke that not everyone would find amusing.

The text of *Nicholas Nickleby* also reveals much about the prevailing notion of women who thought. About his wife, Mr. Wititterly sincerely bemoans: "Your soul is too large for your body. . . . Your intellect wears you out; all the medical men say so; you know there is not a physician who is not proud of being called in to you" (274; ch. 21). One is not to believe that her intellectual sensitivities have literally made her sick (although intellectual efforts by women were believed not only to make them sick but to produce defective offspring[2]), for she obviously lacks genuine intellectual acumen if all she has to say about Shakespeare is that he was a "delicious creature" (355; ch. 27). The text mocks women who consider themselves intellectual when all Victorians know that women cannot think.

Mr. Wititterly continues his praise of his wife by repeating what he understands doctors have advised him: "Be proud of that woman; make much of her; she is an ornament to the fashionable world, and to you. Her complaint is soul. It swells, expands, dilates—the flood fires, the pulse quickens, the excitement increases—Whew!" (274; ch. 21). The next thing he does is "[flourish] his right hand to within something less than an inch of Mrs. Nickleby's bonnet, [draw] it back again, and [blow] his nose as fiercely as if it had been done by some violent machinery." He has reached nothing short of orgasm. What has aroused him is the intensive consideration of his wife's passion. Now, women were not supposed to be passionate, just as they were not supposed to be intellectual. Either Mr. Wititterly fantasizes about his wife—a commentary itself on what some men really want in a woman—or else, through him, the Dickensian narrative satirizes a social system that denies women the right to passion and intellect, treating them as invalids if they are in possession of these unladylike virtues.

WIDOWS

Not an intellectual but a very wise woman and often considered the most comic female creation of Dickens' career is Mrs. Sarah Gamp *(MC)*. She has often been the center of the most serious analysis of how the Dickensian text treats women. For Barickman et al., she represents everything that a Victorian wife should not be, for example, observing that Sarah's husband has probably left her because she drove him away. She has no children (her son either is dead or is an illusion, as is Mrs. Harris). She is economically independent of men; she earns her own living. And she is emotionally independent of men; she does not need them, but they need her when they are sick (106–7).

This inverted power structure is represented through Mrs. Gamp as the "ubiquitous Femme Fatale . . . a clear literary expression of a dread of the female." What Michael Slater means by this statement is that Sairey represents men's exaggerated fear of female power. She is the nurse and the overseer of birth and death (224). The threat is clear in chapter 25 when Mrs. Gamp is attending to the young Lewsome, who has a fever: she pins his arms against his sides "to see how he would look if laid out as a dead man" (354; ch. 25). Ironically, earlier in that chapter, the undertaker, Mr. Mould, remarked upon how shrewd Mrs. Gamp is and said that he would like to bury her for nothing (351). Her womanly ability to deal with both ends of life seems to be exasperating to men who are used to being in control.

I do not see her as exercising much power. Her fantasy friend, Mrs. Harris, evidences that. The mythical friend and the world that she and Mrs. Gamp traverse are a support system for an unhappy woman who cannot find any other channel to express her unhappiness and anger (McKnight 63). Her dialogue with Mrs. Harris subverts important gender expectations:

"Mrs. Harris," I says, at the very last case as ever I acted in, which it was but a young person; "Mrs. Harris," I says, "leave the bottle on the chimley-piece, and don't ask me to take none, but let me put my lips to it when I am so dispoged, and then I will do what I'm engaged to do, according the best of my ability." "Mrs. Gamp," she says, in answer, "if ever there was a sober creeture to be got at eighteenpence a day for working people, and three-and-six for gentlefolks—night-watching," said Mrs. Gamp with emphasis, "being a extra charge—you are that inwallable person." (270; ch. 19)

Several things are happening here. Insofar as women were to suffer in silence, Mrs. Gamp has created an alter ego that expresses her suffering in a permissible way. A good woman should be humble and self-denying. So Mrs. Gamp is; it is Mrs. Harris who sings her praises. A woman should not drink, but it is Mrs. Harris who leaves the bottle, and it is to be understood that Mrs. Gamp would rather not touch the evil stuff, but might need to do so in order to do her job. Through Mrs. Harris, Mrs. Gamp denies that she has a drinking problem but indicates that domestic responsibilities (tending to the sick and dying) can be so stressful as to drive a woman to drink. Also, a woman should not discuss with a gentleman financial matters, but Mrs. Harris can conduct that necessary part of the business. Mrs. Gamp makes it clear to Mrs. Harris that she would gladly perform such services without charge (insofar as female labor has no monetary value). But Mrs. Harris is like a business manager and has no choice but to collect funds. This is a subversive text insisting that domestic labor must be valued because it deserves to be and because women without husbands taking care of them have to earn a living in order to survive.

In the next scene when Mrs. Gamp makes her appearance as a nurse to Mr. Lewsome, she comes to relieve her colleague, Mrs. Prig. Mrs. Gamp does not attend to the patient until she makes sure of all the personal amenities, including removing the patient's pillow for her own use. Probably such demonstrations as these have convinced Leonard Manheim that Dickens vents his most severe anger toward his own mother through the representation of the wicked mother surrogate, Mrs. Gamp (184). However, Mrs. Harris assures that her friend is the most self-sacrificing and self-denying woman one could meet. Of course, this is what Mrs. Gamp knows society expects her to be. After all, she is a woman. But the text reveals that all women are not natural care givers, and when, given no choice, being thrown into a care-giving occupation can be oppressive. Furthermore, the novel does give a woman voice to present her viewpoint, even if it is done through the doubling of an invisible woman. But women who do use their voice, like Mrs. Prig, are given a beard and a deepened voice, as if it is unwomanly to want a different life. Yet the novel gives plenty of reasons why these women might want such a life.

Another widow who seems to be the brunt of a Dickensian joke on women is Mrs. Nickleby. Slater concludes that she is one of the "endlessly entertaining embodiments of certain traditional masculine attitudes toward women" (223). He observes that she is the receptacle of

all the time-honoured causes of men's serio-comic exasperation with women—their supposed butterfly-mindedness, illogicality, vanity, garrulousness, preoccupation with pretty things, impracticality, sentimentality, proneness to romantic daydream-ing, exaggerated respect for social rank and social conventions, and a complacent pride in the superiority of "feminine intuition" over reason and common sense. (223)

Truly, if Mrs. Nickleby were one's mother, she would be insufferable. However, all that she is and does is perfectly in line with gender parameters. Mrs. Nickleby is not a subversive character, but in portraying her as the end product of breeding women to be charmingly desirable and nonthrea-tening to men, the text is subversive.

McKnight additionally contextualizes Mrs. Nickleby: "Her husband dies, she loses her social and economic position, her son leaves home and her daughter goes to work. She no longer has a fixed habitation or position" (78–79). When all parties are not in place within the ideological framework of gender, then a woman certainly can become as anxiety-ridden as is Mrs. Nickleby. More can be said too about her situation: free of nuptial re-straints and patriarchal overseer, Mrs. Nickleby enjoys incredible freedom. She can flirt (79) and enjoy the benefits of courtship with whomever she wants in the guise of securing another husband without seriously intending to marry again. Why should she? Her children are taking care of her, and she never has to answer to them.

Little Dorrit's Mrs. General, a dangerous widow on the prowl for a second husband, is the colossus of Victorian womanhood. She is the "model of accurate dressing, and whose manner [is] perfect, considered a piece of machinery" (486; bk. 2, ch. 1), a woman without opinions who trains women in her charge to be likewise, and her eyes hold no expression because they have nothing to express. A delicate lady, she must not be told anything shocking. The perfect Dickensian woman who tolerates no pas-sion and varnishes everything about herself (503; bk. 1, ch. 2), she is the brunt of Dickens' satire. At this, the reader must wonder why. Constance Harsh figures that Mrs. General is an "archetypal embodiment of patriar-chal forms of oppression" (163). After all, she is the brainless and passion-less ornament males seemed to consider the womanly ideal.[3] The magnification of these "feminine attributes," as if under a microscope, calls into question whether the text actually advocates them.

Another woman in this novel who paradoxically conforms to the do-mestic ideal but is at the same time ridiculed by the text is Flora. As de-lectable as a child-woman might be, especially if she is playful like Dora

Copperfield and survives her eighteenth birthday in a Dickens novel, she's bound to grow into a Flora Finching. Much that has been written on the women in Dickens' life[4] helps explain why he idealized the young and vilified the older woman. And much has been written about the Victorian propensity for child–brides whom older husbands could finish molding into ideal wives.[5] Rather, this study wants to identify the eruptions in text due to inevitable irreconcilable notions of womanhood, and Flora Finching is a definite eruption.

She is introduced in a chapter notably titled "Patriarchal." The centerpiece of this text, she is described strictly through a patriarch's point of view: Arthur "had ardently loved this woman, and had heaped upon her all the locked-up wealth of his affection and imagination" (191; bk. 1, ch. 13). Their marriage was prevented by his mother. Now, more than twenty years later, Arthur returns from China and anxiously visits the beloved of his youth, only to discover that she, who had once been a "lily," has become a "peony." She is a middle-aged, silly, overweight flirt with delusions that she is still an object of desire. Why would she think otherwise? The middle-aged Mr. Clennam is not required to change his expectations and behavior in courtship. Besides, Flora had been trained to practice such "feminine behavior" and learned that it got her not one marriage proposal but two. Why would she think that because she is in her forties courtship behavior has changed? After all, Pet Meagles acts very much this way and attracts Mr. Clennam. The difference, of course, is that Pet is twenty. But this is the only difference; Pet is the Flora of twenty years prior:

A fair girl with rich brown hair hanging free in natural ringlets. A lovely girl, with a frank face, and wonderful eyes; so large, so soft, so bright, set to such perfection in her kind good head. She was round and fresh and dimpled and spoilt, and there was in Pet an air of timidity and dependence which was the best weakness in the world, and gave her the only crowning charm a girl so pretty and pleasant could have been without. (54–55; bk. 1, ch. 2)

Pet is the second generation of women of this type who have learned from their mothers (like Flora) what a woman needs to do to charm a father and a suitor.

Now this novel's subtext does not treat the coquette with favor: coyness can lead both men and women into troublesome marriages. When Arthur meets the now ripened Flora, he realizes that he had once come close to marrying her. Had he done so, he would now find himself in the same crisis that the middle-aged Dickens experienced when he decided to separate from his wife. Despite his realization, Arthur is attracted to Pet with thoughts of marriage to her. Where the text seems to be charmed with the likes of her, just as Arthur is, the Flora text seems to warn against such attractions. The Pet and Affery subtexts echo this warning: Miss Meagles attracts and marries a villain who holds every promise of making her life even more miserable than the tortured life of that abused wife Affery. Narrowly escaping imprisonment with Flora and then Pet, Arthur does eventually become attached to a child–woman, Little Dorrit. She is so much the opposite of the coquette, she seems to have no life in her, and yet this is the text's advocacy of a feminine ideal. If the text would not have offered us any more information about Flora after the "Patriarchal" chapter, one might assume that in comparison, Little Dorrit is indeed the preferred mate for Arthur (although the text does not describe him as a Romeo). Since the text did make room for Flora to become a more fully realized character, it renders a more complex portrait of the Dickens little woman.

Depicted as a female who eats and drinks and talks too much, and talks incoherently, Flora is portrayed as a buffoon. Examining the text around her, though, the reader ought to perceive her in a more sympathetic light. Left only with memories, she lives with two impossible relatives. Her father is "the Patriarch," who appears to be benevolent but who extorts from his poor tenants. The other is a leftover from her marriage to Mr. F, an aunt who seems suspicious of and bitter toward all patriarchs. The aunt's favorite expression seems to be "Bring him for'ward, and I'll chuck him out o' winder!" Sandwiched between the two, Flora is the embodiment of the Victorian woman who has been robbed of her sexuality. Remarkably, however, of all of the men and women in this novel, she is the most effectual and seems to be the most healthy. No longer dependent upon feminine guiles to get what she wants or needs from a patriarch, she is able to reach within herself to perform good works, demonstrating a strength of gentleness and kindness. She acts like an angel-in-the-house—although she is quite corporeal. Dickens does not represent her by any one body part, such as her bosom; she does not seem to be a mother type, but she is as tender as any mother to Maggy and Little Dorrit. The narrative pokes fun at her: she is the plump little Maria who has grown into the obese Catherine Dickens. Regardless of the narrative's initial depiction of her, Flora soon breaks out of its prison. She emerges as the most substantial character in the novel as if her entire being has broadened into kindness. Her source of power lies within her, and the beneficiaries of that power are men and women alike.

SPINSTERS

One woman whose love also is not requited but who does not seem to mature well without a man is Rosa Dartle *(DC)*. Her scar puts her into this chapter instead of the she-dragon chapter, along with her other sisters who seem to be freakish in some fashion or another. The facial scar was inflicted by a hammer that Steerforth threw at her. In one sense, she is scarred because she has the misfortune to love him. It is not that she is crossing over gender lines in her behavior, for in the text's introduction of her, she appeared to wish to be married. She is also described as "a little dilapidated—like a house—with having been so long to let" (251; ch. 20). The house is a significant indicator of her subscription to domesticity, but the ideology has not only failed her but exploited and damaged her as well.

Overtly, the scar signifies passion, which, as discussed, was considered to be threatening and to demand subduing. As the scar reddens during her backgammon game with Steerforth, one could assume the description is sexual, as if Rosa becomes aroused when challenged by a male. Instead, one might read her passion as rage. When she plays the harp like an angel one moment and strikes Steerforth like a cat the next (369; ch. 29), she is the betrayed woman. Her passion is a bitterness in having been used by Steerforth, in having been charmed and petted by him and then carelessly discarded in the same way he would later discard Little Em'ly. The scar is the visible evidence of what men can do to women; it represents the invisible scar on Little Em'ly's reputation. It signifies the liberty and power that men had in this society to initiate relationships and the inability of women to do the same.

The lack of power that women could muster in Victorian society would have been most crucial and evident in the pursuit of marital bliss. Despite their depiction as seductresses, flirts, and manipulators, women still felt most severely the bonds of domesticity as they defined them either as Miss or Mrs. This point is most pronounced in *The Pickwick Papers*.

Mr. Pickwick's mission is to travel with three other men for the purpose of broadening their minds and observing the manners and characters of their compatriots. He is enjoying mobility with all of its advantages in a way that women were not allowed. Surely, he and his partners have not taken to the road to seek brides; nevertheless, husband-seeking women seem to line their path. Doreen Roberts views the novel similarly: "The women want to capture the men and anchor them in one place, and the plot's function is to rescue them and keep them moving" (299). What else could these men expect? This is Victorian England, where men could engage in nondomestic pursuits, but women could not. With that kind of arrangement, of course a bachelor's journey would eventually take him down the aisle, for what else was the purpose of domesticity if not to transform women into wives to ensure that they would stay home and that their men could be free for pursuits away from home?

Pickwick's journey leads him first into the country to stay with the Wardles. The brother introduces Rachel as a Miss who is not a Miss (89; ch. 4). In other words, she is an unmarried woman who is past marrying age. Another time he refers to her as the "single relative," as if marital status is her sole signifier. Sensible to the "spinster aunt" stigma, Rachel plays the coquette even as she berates her nieces for doing likewise. What else is she supposed to do when she finds herself in the company of several bachelors and she lives in a society that ostracizes her for not being married? Her flirtation enchants Mr. Tupman. Watching her efforts to catch a man, the villainous Jingle conspires to elope with her in order to win her money. He is bought off by her brother. Then, in shame, Rachel goes to visit some relations "far enough off."

Angus Wilson has said that Rachel Wardle is Dickens' "joke on spinsters" (*World* 119). The novel does not do anything but what Dickens' society did to "redundant women."[6] The narrative does treat her as a joke. But there are some serious underlying statements that this novel is making about marriage through her. One of the few chapters that tells us something about Rachel also contains a story entitled "The Convict's Return." This is a tale about a woman who is terribly beaten and abused by her husband. She is the angel ideal who bears all, hopes all, turns heavenward for strength, and remains meek and tender, especially to her son. When the boy grows up and becomes an outlaw, he breaks his mother's heart, and she dies under the burden. In this context, perhaps the novel is suggesting that Rachel is better off unmarried.

Regardless, her reality is that she is surrounded by people who are either married or working at getting married. Even though she is financially well off and beloved by a family, the text describes her as "gunpowder" surrounded by lighted gas just waiting for an explosion (142; ch. 8). Apparently having nothing else to occupy her and under social duress, she focuses her passions on acquiring a man. This is why she is so easily duped by Jingle. However, as all of her male friends and relatives "come to her rescue," she insists that she does not want to be rescued. She has no choice in the matter and can only faint away throughout the proceedings of patriarchs' taking charge.

Rachel stands in sharp contrast to Pickwick; she lacks the mobility to go off on adventures as he does. She is deprived of the right to define herself outside marriage. And she lacks the liberty to determine whether to be married or not. She does appear to be a foolish and desperate woman. That the text would depict her in this way, granting her no dignity nor sympathy for the social pressure that bears down upon her, is a warped criticism on society that did perceive unmarried women that way.

Through Rachel the text also calls in question the social pressure on all parties to marry. "If the novel begins with unlimited freedom," observes Gail Turley Houston, "it ends in the bonds of matrimony" (39). Pickwick's men start out on a male-bonding journey, charged with nondomestic goals and aspirations, but they cannot avoid the pitfalls of domesticity. Is this the message of the novel to men?

DWARFS

Miss Mowcher *(DC)*, a great knower of sex, discerns how such liberty and power allow men to be recklessly inconstant in their dealings with women. She accuses David: "Is he fickle? oh, for shame! Did he sip every flower, and change every hour until Polly his passion requited?—is her name Polly?" (285; ch. 22). She is short, and as already discussed, shortness is usually desirable in a female. However, now at age forty or forty-five, she is so fat that she has no throat, no waist, no legs. This is what happens to the dimpled diminutive who does not marry. The burden of a society unkind to spinsters bears down so hard that Miss Mowcher is like a comic-strip character that has been physically compressed.

Another dwarfian, as opposed to diminutive, woman is Jenny Wren *(OMF)*. With her bad back and "queer" legs, she is dwarfian because she does perform her duties like a devoted, loving daughter, complying with gender expectations, but the burden of taking care of a drunkard father has crippled her.

Filial devotion, even to the extent of a daughter's taking care of a father who should be taking care of her, runs throughout Dickens' novels. The text attributes angelic qualities to all of them as if their particular service to patriarchy is the epitome of womanhood. However, like Jenny, these daughters do not fare well under the burden. Little Dorrit spends most of her childhood in prison with her father *(LD)*. Little Nell dies while in flight with her grandfather *(OCS)*. Dolly is almost raped by Hugh *(BR)*. Lizzie has to help her father rob bodies on the Thames for a living *(OMF)*. Madeline's father tries to marry her off to the knave Sir Mulberry Hawk *(NN)*. Agnes is pursued by the ruthless Uriah Heep *(DC)*. Pecksniff allows his daughter to marry a man who will beat her *(MC)*. Mr. Dombey disowns his daughter for no other reason than because she is a girl *(D&S)*. And Lucie is almost sent to the guillotine by Madame Defarge, who desires revenge on Lucie's father *(TT)*. One might deduce these things happen when the father does not meet the requirements of domestic ideology, and that failure seems all the more tragic when the daughter conforms so well to the Victorian ideal.

But here is Jenny with her abrasive tongue, who chastises her father and other males and labors in order to support herself and her father. Although Jenny is little, she does not fit into the fold. Cheated of her childhood as Lavinia has been cheated of her daughterhood, she is as saucy as Lavinia, if not more. With her threats to force scalding liquid down her future husband's throat if he turns out to be a drunkard and her independent decision to change her name, Jenny is much more her own person than Bella will ever be. She does not fit the stereotype. Her broken body is an emblem of domestic ideology gone awry. Instead of the text's idealizing the girl-child, and even making her sexually desirable because of her vulnerability, here in *Our Mutual Friend* is a more realistic picture of what happens to a Victorian girl victimized and beaten by a drinking father who has power over her. She is forced to help earn the family's living when she is not even a full-grown woman. When dolls ought to be her playthings, they are her employment; she is a dolls' dressmaker and she takes care of her father, called by Wrayburn Mr. Dolls. Even if she were older, Jenny would be hard-pressed to find any other than the paltry-paying labor allowed women: sewing, cooking, cleaning, child rearing, and the like. It is no wonder that she declares that when she marries, she will have to be hard on her husband and force him to accept responsibility. The amazing subversive element of this is that the text is sympathetic to her unladylike behavior and attitudes. On the other hand, she will always be a cripple. A woman cannot be as competent and authoritative over men as is she and remain intact. Women like Rose Dartle *(DC)* and Miss Wade *(LD)* do not get happy endings, and Jenny is a miniature version of both. But this novel does give her closure: the promise of a happy marriage. The differences between Jenny and these other viragoes are the love that she has for her father; the response she shows to her good angel, Lizzie; and the kindness shown to her by another misfit, Mr. Riah. For these redeeming womanly virtues, and in consideration of her wretched childhood, the text will overlook her bossiness.

Two other Dickens daughters are worn and aged beyond their years because of similar domestic burdens. Both can be found in the novel with a title that bears a telling indictment of domesticity: *Bleak House.*

Charley is really Charlotte Neckett, but how different she is from the nasty Charlottes of *Oliver Twist* and *Little Dorrit.* Paradoxically, she is what those Charlottes should be: kind, gentle, hard-working, honest, but an angel whose house has been very bleak. It consists of a young brother and sister for whom she is solely responsible. Yet her name is the masculine form, which is appropriate in one way. Like a patriarch, she has had to be independent enough to act as both parents to her siblings after her father dies. And she has had to find employment outside the home in order to provide for herself and them. Although she stays within the confines of domesticity by washing and housekeeping, and then becoming Esther's maid, it is curious that Dickens gives her an affectionate male name (his own) without giving her masculine qualities. This is a high honor given by a patriarch to one he esteems to represent the best that is "inherently female" in the female when forced to assume a role vacated by another patriarch. Because she is a nondissenter, Dickens puts aright her world by having the benevolent Mr. Jarndyce fend for her family. She does not remain a dwarf, but grows up to marry a well-to-do miller. But it must be remembered that domesticity, the "bleak house," is what dwarfed her in the first place.

Similarly Judy Smallweed, who apparently is as small as a monkey, has managed the household in the absence of parents. Unlike Charley, she is no sweet child, but like Charley, she has never played with dolls nor heard of Cinderella (300; ch. 21). Although Dickens did not give her a masculine name, he did make her a twin to a brother. He will enter law; she will continue work in the flower business. Hence she will confine herself to domesticity and take care of her grandparents. But she is not submissive nor does she control her passions. She rules her house and all of the men who live in it and who visit it with a terrifying "weazen forefinger." Mr. George and Grandfather Smallweed rely heavily on her worldly knowledge, the sort of which a proper Victorian daughter would have very little of, and offer even less. She is more like a twin to her grandfather; they are constantly of the same mind and behavior or are terribly at odds with each other. The text seems to be ambivalent about how to respond to this perverted example of a dissenting/nondissenting woman.

Not so in the last chapter: three little women who were orphans who assumed domestic responsibility at an early age are rewarded with more domestic responsibility but this time with what is to be understood as bliss in their own marriage. These are Caddy, Charley, and of course Esther. No mention is made of Judy. One of the last symbolic acts that can indicate her prospects is found in chapter 33. The grandfather throws her at his shrunken wife; she is the "young virgin" butted against "the old lady" (474). Most likely, this is to be her fate: forever a "small weed" who grows and sells flowers that are thorny. She one day will become an old lady like her grandmother and then live perpetually in a childish state. Her patriarchal grandfather grew her that way.

THE GYPSY

The last misfit considered here is Helena Landless in *The Mystery of Edwin Drood*. As suggested earlier, although the text presents she and her brother as actual twins, metaphorically they signify male/female sides of the same person. This section explores how Helena complicates sexual ideology in a somewhat different manner.

In the scene in which Jasper is dominating Miss Rosebud as she plays the piano, Helena intensely watches Jasper and exchanges knowing looks with her twin (50: ch. 7). Several complicated exchanges are going on here. First, Helena is protective of Rosebud against the power wielded by Jasper in his aggression toward the singer. Second, Helena, who possesses a powerful passion similar to Jasper's, challenges Jasper for control over Rosebud. Third, her identity is closely entwined with her brother's, so that she feels the same kind of love that he feels for Rosebud. Fourth, Helena, so identical to her brother and often assuming a male disguise, desires Rosebud as a male would.

When Rosebud passes out, Helena comes to her defense, like a man, and carries her effortlessly to a sofa. She searches the "lovely little face with her dark, fiery eyes, and tenderly caressing the small figure." Rosebud remarks, "O, I am such a mite of a thing, and you are so womanly and handsome." Sylvia Manning claims that even though Helena often acts like a man, this line proves that she is "utterly feminine" (74). I think not, at least, not in the way that the Victorians had been defining the feminine up until this point. The rest of the passage awards power to Helena that most Victorian women were not allowed: "You seem to have resolution and power enough to crush me. I shrink into nothing by the side of your presence even" (52; ch. 7). There are at least three astonishing aspects of Helena's passion. The first is that it often arises in response to and is directed to another woman, as evidenced in the foregoing passage. Second, Dickens' text often chastised and subdued women of passion; not so in *Edwin Drood*, although the passions of Neville and Jasper destroy them both. Third, her passion is very much like that of Jasper, and she is depicted nearly as darkly. Nevertheless Helena, a definite non-angel type, becomes the heroine and wins the key figure of masculine good, Mr. Crisparkle.[7]

The relationship between Rosa and Helena is so very "un-Victorian" in that, as same sex, it seems more agreeable than heterosexual. After Rosebud's declaration, Helena replies, "My pretty one, can I help it? There is a fascination in you" (53), and later she addresses Rosebud as her *own* Rosebud. Caresses, kisses, hugs, intimate care for and attention to each other, declarations of love, terms of endearment—these all seem to demonstrate a depth of bonding between the two women. The issue is not whether what they feel for each other is lesbian in nature. The text is constructing an intricate relationship outside domestic ideology that seems more real than the succeeding relationships that the women will have with the men they will marry.

There is another context in which to question the novel's ideological stance. Rosa tells her affianced Eddy that for her birthday she was given a ball. At an all-girls seminary, the ladies had only each other with which to dance. Some of them pretended to be their brothers. One affected to be Edwin, but Rosa refused to dance, professing to be tired of him and vice versa.

Through recounting the scene, she insinuates that in their relationship they are tired of each other. She does not seem happy about marrying Edwin or getting married in general. When they agree to go for a walk, Rosa suggests they pretend that he is engaged to someone else and that Rosa is not engaged at all (19–20; ch. 3).

Although one might argue that the point of this passage is to show Rosa as too young for a serious relationship or as merely trying to gain reassurance of her fiancé's love, one cannot dispute the tension evident between the genders. Regardless of the reasons, getting married is not Rosa's woman's dream; it is her dread.

One might argue that the text gives Helena a twin's identity and allows her to dress as a male to legitimatize the love between Helena and Rosa. As long as Helena passes as Neville, she may also pass as a lover of Rosa. The problem with this interpretation is that Helena is not Neville; she is a woman with dual sexuality and gender. She is just as capable of loving

Rosa as she is capable of loving Mr. Crisparkle. She is able to "break" Jasper and cause him to divulge his murderous deed. She is a dark gypsy who learns how to tame the same sort of darkness that makes a man like Jasper capable of murder. That a woman could contain such darkness defies the angel-in-the-house stereotype. That a woman could control such darkness challenges the notion of woman as the weaker sex who needs to be protected from such things. That a woman could bring down a man who has murdered two men concedes courage and power to all women. And after all this, that a woman deserves to marry a good-hearted and wise clergyman like the Reverend Crisparkle is an outstanding departure from formulaic plots committed to perpetuating rigid gender codes.

NOTES

1. Patricia Ingham also argues that the Dickens text constantly works to suppress female sexuality and passion. Three novels that Ingham cites illustrate how powerful and threatening the uncontrolled woman is to socially powerful men: she decimates Dombey's house *(D&S)* and Bounderby's empire *(HT)*, and she causes Sir Dedlock to have a stroke *(BH)* (110).

2. It was believed that the uterus was attached to the nervous system. Intellectual stimulation could cause women to produce "weak and degenerative offspring"—according to the research by Carroll Smith-Rosenberg and Charles Rosenberg (335–40).

3. At least this is Mary Wollstonecraft's famous complaint in "A Vindication of the Rights of Women."

4. Like his mother, by whom he felt betrayed because she sent him to work in the blacking factory; and like Mary Hogarth, his beloved sister-in-law who died in his arms when she was only seventeen; and like Maria Beadnell, who rejected him in his youth and who at age forty-four had become a giggling "elephantine creature" (qtd. in Du Cann 55); and like his wife, Catherine, from whom he separated; and like Ellen Ternan, with whom he had an affair. For an in-depth treatment, see Michael Slater's *Dickens and Women*. For more information on Dickens' changing attitudes to Maria Beadnell, the prototype of Flora, see George Baker (81–102) and C. G. L. Du Cann (19–60).

5. See Jenni Calder (98–117) and Deborah Gorham (38–46), two of many who speak on this subject.

6. This was the term that W. R. Greg used in discussing the problem of England's unmarried women. See his "Why Are Women Redundant?" (1876).

7. Forster claimed that Dickens had intended this ending before he died.

PART III

Brass, a Ring and a Handkerchief, and a Woman's Story

"Dickens lived in an age when shaded feminine virtue was not the thing. Women had to be white, or they had to be black," surmised Audrey Lucas in the 1940s (706). Unfortunately many readers perceive the Victorians in much the same simplistic terms perhaps as a result of what may seem to be stereotypical depictions of people and a rigid barometer of morality throughout the nineteenth-century novel. It is just this sort of generalization about Victorian literary conventions that George Levine attacks forty years later: "Nineteenth-century realism, far from apologizing for what is, deliberately subverts judgments based on dogma, convention, or limited perception and imagination. . . . What seems clear becomes cloudy as we see more and from different perspectives. Even as they articulate the social codes, these novels complicate them, engaging our sympathy with lost women, tyrannical husbands, murderers, revolutionaries, moral weaklings, rebellious girls, spendthrifts, and dilettantes" (20). Such complexity is apparent in *Oliver Twist* and *Bleak House*, especially in regard to a number of conflicted notions that the text perpetuates about women.

In Part III, as in Part I, the gender dynamics in two novels are closely investigated. The extensive warping found in *Oliver Twist* warrants two different focuses. Chapter 8 considers the problems of perceiving Rose Maylie as an angel-in-the-house. As in *David Copperfield*, the narrative conflicts by demonstrating a bias in favor of a non-angel type, the prostitute Nancy, depicting her strength in character and moral rectitude in contrast to the weak, insipid ineffectiveness of the angel Rose. The text seems to challenge the power of the angel to overcome evil with good, to protect a helpless child dependent on her, or to lead a fallen woman to repentance—all tasks to which an angel should be equal.

Chapter 9 continues the study of *Oliver Twist*, focusing on the text's treatment of fallen women. Because *Oliver Twist* deals with two fallen women (Nancy and Agnes) and one tainted woman (Rose, as a sister to Agnes), this analysis distills how the Dickensian text complies with and departs from Victorian literary conventions in its assessment of these women.

The final chapter analyzes Dickens' attempt to write a woman's story in *Bleak House*. A Victorian woman searches for identity throughout the text only to be constantly veiled, defaced, negated, and denied power to signify self. The text illustrates her inner conflicts with ideal womanhood all the while she is trying to conceal and deny them. By the novel's closing, the conflicts are not resolved. The tension and agony that have characterized Esther's search for contentment reflect the text's own frustrations with the assertions of domestic ideology.

Hence this project ends with a study of articulation as well as of repressed articulation of woman's voice present in one of Dickens' best-known works. Esther's narrative conveys the struggle to accept domesticity as a hegemonic ideology. Containing gaps, conflicts, questions, and sometimes contradictions, the novel undermines and countermines the concurrent effort it has made to promote an absolute and essential schema for gender relations. The text unravels as it weaves ideological patterns, thereby perhaps more closely approximating the complexities of gender issues.

8

The True Heroine of *Oliver Twist*: "Brass Can Do Better Than Gold"

This chapter investigates the complication of social codes intertwined with the ideological operations of *Oliver Twist*. In particular it focuses on the fluctuating social lines that divide such women as Agnes (a fallen woman) from Rose (an ideal woman) and from Nancy (a prostitute). The similarities as well as the peculiar differences between these women that appear in the text confound Dickens' idealized image of the domestic woman. When a wise housemaid comments about Nancy, "Brass can do better than the gold what has stood the fire" (266; ch. 39), the text is putting forth a set of values that radically complicates a domestic ideological construction of womanhood. Where gold usually represents a higher value than brass, and the angel-in-the-house is estimated of greater social worth than a prostitute, the text in *Oliver Twist* sometimes inverts those values and, at other times, simply throws them into question. This subversion of a supposedly hegemonic domestic ideology becomes apparent through a study of Agnes, Rose, and Nancy, three women who dissent in varying degrees from the angel prototypes, while the text modulates in its estimation of them.

Complicating an investigation of Dickens' women is the nineteenth-century idea that women should remain in the background, their goodness and influence felt in the foreground but never acknowledged. Closely studying a Dickens' woman, then, requires digging deeply into text, where information about her is often submerged. Once having located this information, the reader is well advised not to separate the female character from the text that has interred her, for a burial ground often has much to reveal about a person's character and society's regard of that person.

The composition of Agnes is a case in point, beginning with how the text portrays her from the onset. She is introduced only by implication in the headnote to the first chapter:

TREATS OF THE PLACE WHERE OLIVER TWIST WAS
BORN, AND OF THE CIRCUMSTANCE
ATTENDING HIS BIRTH

The *Oxford English Dictionary* defines "to treat" (as it is probably used here), "to deal with some matter in speech or writing," and specifically to deal with that matter "in the way of literary art." The headnote promises a literary discourse on the peculiarities of Oliver's birth. However, the details surrounding his parentage will be deliberately obscure, and the first scene will introduce a woman whose presence and later absence will carry a lingering significance throughout the novel.

The first paragraph that follows the headnote comments satirically on itself by referring to the "item of mortality whose name is prefixed to the head of this chapter." "Mortality" carries a double-entendre: because the only name in the prelude is Oliver's, the reader might assume that he's the mortal in the allusion, but "mortality" is more often used to mean "fatality." Then the "item" refers to the name "prefixed to the head of this chapter," Oliver Twist, but "mortality," from which the "item" came, refers to the significantly missing mother. Details of this birth are not soon forthcoming, nor is any information about the mother's death shortly afterward. The text does not tell the name of the town, the name of the workhouse, the date, or, most strikingly, the woman's name. In fact her name does not appear until chapter 38. Besides textual repercussions, the gap may be read as society's willful indifference to an unwed mother: she is a mere statistic, a liability to the economy. She is a nonperson who exists outside the construct of a socially acceptable family.

The text represents the nameless woman as a symbol for all unwed mothers, apparent by the reference to hers as the "old story." A dozen years after *Oliver Twist* was first serialized, Dr. William Acton listed a figure of forty-two thousand illegitimate Britons born in 1851 alone: "One in twelve of the unmarried females in the country above the age of puberty have strayed from the path of virtue" (qtd. in Goldfarb 49). Agnes, referred to by Brownlow as an "erring child" (328; ch. 49), was the mistress to Edwin Leeford, who had been long separated from a wife. Because of this scandal, Brownlow recounts: "Goaded by shame and dishonour [Agnes' father] fled with his children into a remote corner of Wales" (344; ch. 51). The poor cottagers, who took in her sister on their father's death, were told of Agnes' "shame" and told that the sister "came of bad blood" (347). Agnes suffered the same ignominy as prostitutes. As such, she is linked to Nancy, and both, in a company of other wronged women, are portrayed by frequent intrusions and gaps in text as victims.

Brownlow, as a Dickens mouthpiece, exposes such injustices and challenges the mores (regulated by patriarchy) that govern love and marriage. Although he refers to Oliver as the "offspring of a guilty and miserable love" (330; ch. 49), Brownlow does not express disapproval of the extramarital liaison that produced the child; in fact, he deems the first marriage to have been a mistake, criticizing the Leeford family for forcing Edwin to marry out of "family pride, and the most sordid and narrowest of ambitions" (326). Yet Edwin did what an obedient son should do; he married for the good of the family. Agnes, on the other hand, followed the dictates of her heart and pursued an affair that brought shame to her family. Brownlow's judgments do not support traditional patriarchal ordering meant to secure economic and social soundness in family formations.

Further, Brownlow calls Monks (alias Edward Leeford) "the most unnatural issue," which Monks says is a "hard name" (326—an interesting response that bears on patriarchal privilege in naming discussed later in this chapter). Brownlow obviously prefers Oliver as if he were the legitimate issue of a preordained relationship. After all, Oliver resembles Edwin's sister, who was Brownlow's fiancé, and Oliver obviously possesses the "gentle heart and noble nature" of his mother (344; ch. 41). This is the matrilinear inheritance that Brownlow so esteems. In contrast, Monks has turned out to be a disreputable coward.

Finally, Brownlow judges society's value system regarding the two sets of relationships; he mocks it as a "feeble censure," suggesting that there is a higher judgment that sanctions the Agnes/Edwin love.

Nevertheless, Agnes dies in disgrace, and her family suffers the stigma. Edwin contracts a fatal disease in Rome, but the text does not suggest that his death is punishment for his affair with Agnes. Rather, the connection implied is that the pursuit of money (for the sake of his family) kills him (327–28; ch. 49). Only the woman is considered fallen. Indeed, the very last words of the story are "she was weak and erring," with no mention at all of Edwin's culpability.

Before Agnes dies, she prays "the day might come when [Oliver] would not feel so much disgraced to hear its poor young mother named" (165; ch. 24). The text will have much work to do to accomplish this alteration to social codes for, in support of patriarchal privilege and especially in light of inheritance laws, the text should not have a child–especially a boy–named after the mother. If patrimony is not established, then, ironically, the child must get its identity from patriarchal society; Mr. Bumble calls him Oliver Twist, an act by a patriarch who is a source of power but who, at the same time, is no source of nurturing. Such an identity proves inadequate and causes Oliver to search for an alternate, which is not found until he learns who his mother was.

Agnes' name has additional potential that the text denies her and her son and, in that denial, indexes the mother as a suppressed source of power to her son. If those industrious workers of charity Mr. Bumble and Mrs. Corney had known her name during Oliver's birth, that discovery would have told them that Agnes was well connected; they certainly would have tried to locate the relatives in order to gain a reward. Oliver would not have had to suffer the deprivation caused by life at the workhouse.

The potency of a name is further articulated when Brownlow judges Monks unworthy to bear the name of Leeford, and Monks replies, "What has the name to do with it? . . . What is the name to me?" Brownlow's response paradoxically empowers the female with matrilinear privilege. He says, "But it was *hers*" (326; ch. 49), and because Monks inherited it from her (and not specifically from Edwin Leeford), Brownlow will show him mercy.

The conspicuous absence of names registers the lack of power that women have to signify themselves. Agnes does not get a name until the novel's end, and even then on her marble slab there is no surname. Charlotte has no last name until she marries. Neither has Nancy a last name, nor will she gain one because she never marries. In contrast, Oliver, a male orphan who searches for identity throughout the novel, has been awarded at least a cursory patronymic name. When Brownlow appears in chapter 10, as Arnold Kettle astutely recognizes, Oliver takes on substantial character. Earlier he was mostly portrayed as a symbol (qtd. in Raina 30). Throughout the next ten chapters, Oliver's name appears 285 times, and more than 400 epithets characterize him (Raina 30). In addition, several other males exercise the power of changing their own names (Monks, Mr. Fleming, Jack Dawkins, and Noah Claypole). The power to hold onto one's name and to name one's self and others is a powerful privilege denied to every female in this novel except Rose (discussed later).

There is another important nameless (and faceless) woman in this story. The narrative relates only that she is the first wife of Mr. Leeford and the mother to Monks—it does not reveal her name. Nor does it provide any details suggesting that she had been a termagant or any other type of Dickensian unpreferred woman. All it relays is that Edwin had been forced into a marriage with an older woman. This is one of the gaps referred to earlier. What is her story? She too was forced into the marriage. The bitterness and gambling habits in later years may have stemmed from her own marital unhappiness, making her as much a victim as Edwin. Her unvoiced story is a subtext flagged by a conspicuous absence of representation in the text. She is just as much a victim as are Agnes and Nancy, who are unable to overthrow the male forces that ultimately destroy them. Arnold Kettle is right to perceive *Oliver Twist* as being more than an orphan's tale; he suggests that it is also about "a wronged woman" (259), a phrase that can stand as a universal designation for all the wronged women in *Oliver Twist*, Agnes, Mrs. Leeford, Rose, Nancy, and perhaps even some of the minor characters such as Mrs. Bumble, Mrs. Sowerberry, and Charlotte.

In terms of the bias with which these last three characters are presented, the notable absence of their stories in the text indicates women's lack of power in a manner that Laurie Langbauer describes: "[Dickens'] novels construct as male the very englobing system of power that these errant women attempt to unsettle or escape" (131). These are women, as Langbauer defines them, "carried away by transgressive desires" (130); they are regarded as socially dysfunctional because they introduce so much disorder to a world that normally enjoys order constructed by men. On the surface it would appear that these three female tyrants deserve our disdain or laughter. Villainous females in Dickens' novels, who mistreat orphans and bully their gentler mates, are monstrous caricatures, similar to the hideous types identified in Dickens' text by Ellen Moers ("Agitating Women" 17–18). The text means for the reader to judge them as violators of sexual ideology and traitors to their own gender. The exaggerated features of stereotypical caricatures signal those qualities that threatened the very core of domestic ideology. Such protrusions are representations of feminine independence, resourcefulness, and aggression. These three women possess dominant personalities, and their capabilities challenge masculine power, even more than Miggs *(BR)* and Sally Brass *(OCS)*, because the former reside within the ideologically correct sphere for women: they are married (including Charlotte, who acts like a wife in the early chapters and later does marry Noah Claypole). To the degree that the women are not portrayed favorably in the Dickens text, one can measure the threat that such women posed to a domestic order legislated and reinforced by patriarchy.

Of course, the converse is usually true: if Dickens portrays a woman favorably, it is because she performs her "woman's work" well, acting properly within the enclosure of domesticity. Despite that rule of thumb, Dickens' portrayal of Rose and Nancy raises some perplexing challenges to domestic ideology.

For example, the text subverts the patronymic code of naming with regard to Rose by having a widow adopt her, giving Rose her last name. The child's identity will develop from the nurturing of the kind widow. Rose also has the power and wherewithal to resist marriage, and when she does marry, she will not have to lose her name or her relationship with her female mentor. What a contradiction she is in the Dickens novel, in which female power—the kind through which a woman defines and rules herself—is usually regarded as a threat to domesticity.[1] In *Oliver Twist* Dickens portrays Rose favorably as a conforming angel-in-the-house. Clearly she is the Victorian ideal:

The younger lady was in the lovely bloom and spring-time of womanhood; at that age, when, if ever angels be for God's good purposes enthroned in mortal forms, they may be, without impiety, supposed to abide in such as hers.

She was not past seventeen. Cast in so slight and exquisite a mould; so mild and gentle; so pure and beautiful; that earth seemed not her element, nor its rough creatures her fit companions. The very intelligence that shone in her deep blue eye, and was stamped upon her noble head, seemed scarcely of her age, or of the world; and yet the changing expression of sweetness and good humour; the thousand lights that played about the face, and left no shadow there; above all, the smile, the cheerful, happy smile, were made for Home, for fireside peace and happiness.

She was busily engaged in the little offices of the table. Chancing to raise her eyes as the elder lady was regarding her, she playfully put back her hair, which was simply braided on her forehead; and threw into one beaming look, such a gush of affection and artless loveliness, that blessed spirits might have smiled to look upon her. (194; ch. 29)

She exemplifies all the attributes of the "mould": she is young, beautiful, frail, mild, gentle, pure, ethereal, intelligent, sweet, pleasant, charming, coy, and blessed. She even possesses the right physiognomy ("intelligence . . . stamped on her noble head"), and she is performing domestic tasks, adorning both table and self for the gratification of others. The "blessed spirits" give her their approval. Even Nancy calls her the angel lady.

Yet, though Dickens depicts Rose as an angel woman, she is blemished in a way that nineteenth-century literary conventions would highlight. Perhaps this is why Dickens, after creating a woman more wonderful than would be deemed prudent for a character with a social blot, originally decided to kill her. Rose falls deathly sick but fantastically recovers. According to the biographer Edgar Johnson, Dickens had intended to have Rose die but "could not bear to describe the fair young creature breathing her last amid the blossoms of May."[2] Obviously, if Dickens changed his mind about her death, then he had to devise a reason for the illness. The narrative can support this plot development. First, Rose's brush with death makes her that much more angelic; if she was not "good" before (because of the family scandal), she is now. Second, the near loss intensifies Harry's efforts to win her as a wife, and that, in turn, hastens the plot to reveal the mystery of her heritage. Third, the punitive fingers of death cannot claim Rose even if literary convention would have her die because she is a tainted woman. Although Rose's shame is not due to her own sexual straying, the story implies that such behavior runs in the family. Regardless of the reason, Rose thinks of herself as unworthy of Harry and a potential threat to his reputation. Margaret Lane, in her preface to Mrs. Gaskell's *Ruth* (1853), concludes that Victorian literary conventions determined only three choices for a seduced woman: "emigration, prostitution, or death— and . . . on the whole, the Victorian public preferred death" (vi).[3] The text conflicts: Nancy and Agnes must die—even if the text treats them sympathetically as victims—but Rose can live happily ever after. Further, Harry accommodates her—rather than she, him—by taking a vocation that would lower him in class so that they can be social equals.

Before the text reaches this blissful conclusion, the social problem between Harry and Rose is defined. Though guileless, Rose poses a real threat to Harry, and that is why she refuses to marry him. Resolved to do her duty, she says:

I owe it to myself, that I, a friendless, portionless girl, with a blight upon my name, should not give your friends reason to suspect that I had sordidly yielded to your first passion, and fastened myself, a clog, on all your hopes and projects. I owe it to you and yours, to prevent you from opposing, in the warmth of your generous nature, this great obstacle to your progress in the world. (235; ch. 35)

By the time Harry proposes, Rose believes that she carries latent moral malignancy. She also knows how important a reputation is for a young man just starting in public life. The people who can help him be successful have power, but she adds, "Those connexions are proud; and I will neither mingle with such as hold in scorn the mother who gave me life; nor bring disgrace or failure on the son of her who has so well supplied that mother's place" (236; ch. 35).

Harry, on the other hand, poses a real threat to Rose, similar to the one that her sister experienced. Mrs. Maylie voices her reservations about her son's marriage: Rose "deserves the best and purest love the heart of man can offer," but Harry is just a young man with "many generous impulses which do not last; and . . . among them are some, which, being gratified, become only the more fleeting" (226; ch. 34). In other words, she fears that Harry may "one day repent of the connexion he formed in early life" (226) because of the reputation of Rose's family. This consequence would destroy Rose much as Leeford's misadventure destroyed Agnes. Mrs. Maylie's concern for Rose reflects a radically different perspective: Rose is not the "seductive Eve"—the proverbial reason that man sins and suffers. Instead she is the pure and innocent, the prelapsarian Eve who shares the garden with a fallen Adam. Man is the beguiler.

After being refused, Harry asks if he were "poor, sick, helpless," would she turn away from him? She replies that if he had been lower in class, closer to her station and not susceptible to a tainted reputation by being married to her, they would be very happy (236; ch. 35). So Harry gets rid of his wealth and chooses a humble church life. Instead of affecting Harry adversely, Rose proves to be a blessing, for he assumes a pastorate at a village church. This commitment shows that he is willing to give up his life to the service of others: a noble, rather feminine calling, but one that is to bring contentment and self-fulfillment. The text seems to outline woman as victim while alluding to woman as a powerful agent that not only can

define herself, but also transform men into better people. Instead of reproducing a woman's sin (as did Agnes in birthing an illegitimate child who
has to suffer for her "weak and erring" ways), Rose reproduces an abundance of legitimate "joyous little faces that [cluster] round her knee."

Angelic virtues and power notwithstanding, Rose is not the heroine of
this story. When Nancy tells Rose that Oliver has a brother who aims to
kill him, Rose helplessly cries, "But what can I do?" and "What am I do?"
and "Of what use, then, is the communication you have made?" (269–70;
ch. 40). As for Nancy, she does not need a man to escort her through a
crowd even though she is on a dangerous mission. However, she does understand the mechanics of the middle-class system and advises the damsel
in distress (Rose) to get a man to help. Nancy knows exactly what needs
to be done in order to protect Oliver and her efforts save him.

The text is not advocating that women become prostitutes in order to
develop character and fortitude. Rather, it is setting aside judgment of
Nancy's caste in order to identify value in the individual. Instead of her
being a mere item and nonentity, as Oliver's mother was considered, and
instead of being a celestial nonentity as is Rose, Nancy has the brass to do
some good. In response to the criticism leveled against Dickens that Nancy
is not credible because she does not talk realistically and appropriately to
her life experience,[4] John Lucas theorizes: "What she *is* differs from what
she is seen to be. That is why, I think, she is given a manner of speech that
belies her outer appearance" (28).[5] On the surface of Dickens' text is an
attempt to break through preconceptions about people and exterior appearances. Society values gold and underrates brass, but brass has much
more strength and practical use than does gold. Translated, this means that
society values the angel-in-the-house, but a woman like Nancy is much
stronger of character and provides more practical service.

However, the text never successfully moves past external appearances to
get to the heart of a woman like Nancy. It fails to break through the
barriers that enclose Nancy. Her goodness is a gendered goodness. She
becomes a good person only when she helps Oliver or nurses her "husband." Nancy Armstrong considers her as "the antithesis as well as a surrogate for that mother" (182). This perception could be plausible because
there is a conspicuous lack of mothers in this novel and an abundance of
orphans, and Nancy tries to protect Oliver. Regardless, there are many
women, who, more than Nancy, fit the Dickens image of nurturing mothers
who serve as surrogates, such as Mrs. Maylie and Mrs. Bedwin. Nancy
falls outside patriarchal confines because she is not a wife or mother, but
the text dispenses angelic qualities to her as long as she acts like a wife and
a mother. She is, as a streetwalker—as Laurie Langbauer argues—no different from the Dickens homebodies (like Rose). Both kinds of women are
imprisoned inside a gendered enclosure where they can be managed and
dominated, and their usefulness to society prescribed (131–32).

Dickens further emphasizes that Nancy has womanly virtue. She bleeds when struck and faints as often as Rose does. With a "woman's tenderness" and wifely attentions, she nurses the man she loves (256; ch. 39). Nancy will do what she can to prevent Oliver from being lured into a life of crime, but only under the condition she does not endanger her man (an admirable angel-in-the-house priority). Nancy will not let Rose save her soul nor will she flee England in order to start over abroad without Sikes. In her love for a man, therefore, Nancy is just as self-denying as is Rose.

Dickens invests his prostitute with heroic virtues. He demonstrates this idealism in chapter 39 when Nancy hastens through a crowd to meet Rose for the first time. The activity is flushed with meticulous and metaphorical detail:

Many of the shops were already closing in the back lanes and avenues through which she tracked her way, in making from Spitalfields towards the West-End of London. The clock struck ten, increasing her impatience. She tore along the narrow pavement: elbowing the passengers from side to side; and darting almost under the horses' heads, crossed crowded streets, where clusters of persons were eagerly watching their opportunity to do the like.

"The woman is mad!" said the people, turning to look after her as she rushed away.

When she reached the more wealthy quarter of the town, the streets were comparatively deserted; and here her headlong progress excited a still greater curiosity in the stragglers whom she hurried past. Some quickened their pace behind, as though to see whither she was hastening at such an unusual rate; and a few made head upon her, and looked back: surprised at her undiminished speed; but they fell off one by one; and when she neared her place of destination, she was alone. (264)

This is London's night life; it is ten o'clock, but the streets are still busy. Nancy aggressively elbows through the crowd; figuratively, she makes her way through an unaccommodating life. The spectators think that she's mad, but the "stragglers"—the fringe of society—watch on with "greater curiosity." Some quicken their pace in order to keep her in view. Others try to catch up, but she outdistances them all, until by the time she reaches her destination, "she [is] alone."

There is too much going on in this passage to assume that Dickens is describing only a city scene, even if he typically does paint such settings with vivid and imaginative strokes. These three paragraphs form a nested allegory defining a hierarchy of culture according to reactions to Nancy. Those who think she is mad represent that prim, prudish segment of the British population who superciliously and indignantly snub the nonconformist. Some of these types may demonstrate, in addition to those attitudes mentioned, curiosity; amongst these, some admire her. Others, who are not so priggish, would dissent if they could follow a leader, which is what Nancy represents. But Nancy succeeds when they cannot, implying that dissent must be an individual conviction and demonstration if change in society is to be realized.[6]

The dissent that this scene exemplifies, of course, is not Nancy's thievery and prostitution. By rising above her station and defying her misapplied but admirable code of loyalty, Nancy does the right thing literally at a cost to her life. It also saves her soul. Thackeray generously supposes, after having read *Oliver Twist*, that prostitutes "have, no doubt, virtues like other human creatures; nay, their position engenders virtues that are not called into exercise among other women" (qtd. in Collins 46). It is easy enough for the angel Rose Maylie to provide a nice home for Oliver, but it is costly for Nancy to see that he gets it.

Applicable in this comparison of Nancy with Rose and Agnes (three women who win varying degrees of social acceptance throughout the text regardless of their questionable moral standing) is the metaphor mentioned earlier: "Brass can do better than the gold what has stood the fire." Nancy, of the three, transgresses most by being a practicing thief and prostitute. The text represents her as brass. Rose is valued more like gold because of her angelic qualities. Similarly, because Agnes surrenders her life through loving a man and then giving birth to a male child, the text awards her approbation. However, Agnes could have not only saved her own life but protected her child by pawning her gold locket. The woman who attended Agnes stole her jewelry. This woman confesses on her deathbed: "The only thing she had. She wanted clothes to keep her warm, and food to eat; but she had kept it safe, and had it in her bosom. It was gold, I tell you! Rich gold, that might have saved her life!" (165; ch. 24). The gold piece, as it passed from Bumble's hands into Monks', only put Oliver's life in increasing danger. His mother, who was "good as gold," could not save him. Had she relinquished a sentimental trinket for practical good, she and Oliver might have survived. Although Rose and Agnes are valued as gold, they are ineffective in saving Oliver. Only Nancy, made of brass that has "stood the fire," succeeds in performing this high maternal duty.

Oliver Twist has produced some rather radical statements that subvert the Victorian ideology of womanhood: there is no difference between the best woman in society (the angelic Rose) and the worst (Nancy)—other than what is defined by social circumstances. The point is emphasized through the following dialogue between Nancy and Rose. Nancy cries to Rose: "Thank Heaven upon your knees, dear lady . . . that you had friends to care for and keep you in your childhood, and that you were never in the midst of cold and hunger, and riot and drunkenness, and—and—something worse than all—as I have been from my cradle. I may use the word, for the alley and the gutter were mine, as they will be my deathbed" (267; ch. 40). From Nancy's perspective, the only difference between women like her and Rose is entirely arbitrary and circumstantial. Rose could easily turn into a Nancy; the middle ground is Agnes. What really distinguishes these women from each other, what determines how the text portrays them, is passion, a subject discussed in the next chapter. Because Nancy is a passionate woman, the text will cause her to be passionately murdered. Because Agnes was not disciplined and participated in a relationship outside domestic sanction, she also died. Because Rose controls her passion, demonstrated by her decline of Harry's proposal, she will live and be happy. Nevertheless, to Harry Stone the Rose and Harry love story "is pale, anemic, substanceless, conventional. . . . The relationship lacks the slightest hint of physicality or personality, much less passion; it is all bloodless spirituality and disembodied harmony, a union redolent of heaven rather than earth" (*Night* 348). Exactly. Although Stone negatively perceives the development of this couple, and perhaps the contemporary reader does likewise, the Victorian text has been headed in this direction all along. The passionless and ethereal were the nineteenth-century ideal. Whether the Victorians really preferred such relationships or could even achieve, much less, sustain them, may be a different matter. In this novel all but the Rose/ Harry relationship are a deadly combination of bad patriarchs and passionate women. The only happy marriage will be the Maylie couple, but it is a problematic one. The people truly capable of producing "a little society, whose condition approached as nearly to one of perfect happiness as can ever be known in this changing world" (357; ch. 53), lie outside the nuclear family: Mr. Brownlow and Mrs. Maylie.

Such observations muddle what the Dickens text covertly promotes in ideology. Perhaps even a fictitious text controlled by a Victorian who believed in domestic ideology cannot translate the ideal into a real matrix, much as one may surmise that the Victorian in daily life could not. The problems may lie with the unrealistic goals of the ideology or most likely lie with the players who, like Dickens, were in conflict about gender roles and expectations.

Still, what drives *Oliver Twist* is the contrast between the gendered ideal and the socially unacceptable: Rose versus Nancy. Dickens creates much distance between the two women by making Rose a ministering angel. Nancy tells Rose, "If there was more like you, there would be fewer like me,—there would—there would" (267; ch. 40). The text comes full circle— encompassing domestic ideology—by eliminating the women (Agnes and Nancy) who stood outside its circumference and by forming Rose into an angel-in-the-house. Covertly the text notes the deletion of the women who were victims: Agnes, because a patriarchal system branded her a fallen woman as a result of her pregnancy, and Nancy, who had been brought up by a patriarch to steal and prostitute herself, and who later loved with undying loyalty a patriarch who did nothing but abuse her. The text also notes a woman (Rose) who enjoyed autonomy from the patriarchal system until she also fell in love, and, as a result, slipped into her proper place as nurturer in the home.

This is the blessed scene that brings the novel to a close:

I *would show* Rose Maylie in all the bloom and grace of early womanhood, shedding on her secluded path in life, such soft and gentle light, as fell on all who trod it with her, and shone into their hearts. I *would paint* her the life and joy of the fire-side circle and the lively summer group; I *would follow* her through the sultry fields at noon, and hear the low tones of her sweet voice in the moonlit evening walk; I *would watch* her in all her goodness and charity abroad, and the smiling untiring discharge of domestic duties at home. (359; emphasis added)

The novel ends, then, with Dickens returning to the Victorian image of the ideal woman. Although Rose was unable to save Nancy and it was really Nancy who saved Oliver's life, Rose's goodness overflows and makes happy all of the already good people around her. More accurately, the good people surround her and contain her within a proper domestic sphere so that she will never be a social misfit like Nancy or Agnes. Notice the language in the passage. The narrative pulls in the "I": the narrative departs from its focus on the major character in this scene: Rose. The language emphasized is the language of obligation and desire. The verbs, "show," "paint," "follow," and "watch," convey voyeuristic activity as if the patriarch in the narrative would possess her. The language is tentative, though, as if implying that a patriarch does not have full power within domesticity either. Perhaps women like Rose are too angelic, and for a man to access her, he would have to turn angelic too as Harry does by entering the ministry.

As for Monks, who was the legitimate and thus socially acknowledged offspring of Edwin Leeford, he seizes the opportunity provided by Mr. Brownlow to start over his life in America, only to squander all of the money. He returns to "fraud and knavery" and dies in prison. Contrary to what must have been a commonly held belief, virtue, according to the Dickensian text, is not codified in the genes and propagated through the proper state of matrimony. Neither is virtue the monopoly of the socially conforming, church-sanctioned sexually correct. The text suggests that if Nancy had gone to America, she would have enjoyed a life comparable to Rose's, but in the New World. It appears that fallen women are to be considered victims of their environment and that, if given a chance to reform, they would, and society would stand to benefit from their reformation. They are the brass that "can do better than the gold" because they have "stood the fire." Suggested is that such opportunities are not possible in English society, which still has not learned that "all that glitters is not gold."

All in all, the text complicates what is to be considered the ideal woman.

Deviating from literary and social conventions, the novel values some of the qualities exhibited by two fallen women (Agnes and Nancy) and de-values some of the qualities exhibited by an angel-in-the-house (Rose). The text so undermines domesticity through these character portrayals that by the time the novel closes, this reader is unsure of whether the judgment on each woman is the novel's endorsement of domestic ideology or a challenge to the value system of a Victorian society that endorses domestic ideology.

NOTES

1. Compare the portrayal of Rose, for instance, to that of such self-defining women as Miggs *(BR)* and Sally Brass *(OCS)*.

2. (Vol. 1, 201). This outcome, John Lucas assumes, is the effect of Mary Hogarth's death just one year prior to Dickens' writing *Oliver Twist* (49). If he had had the power to rewrite Mary's life, he would have kept her alive, and this is what he does with Rose.

3. A more thorough discussion on the portrayal of the fallen woman can be found in Jean Kennard's *Victims of Convention* and Nina Auerbach's *Woman and the Demon*, two references that prove useful in the next chapter.

4. W. M. Thackeray criticizes the credibility of the Nancy character in an August 1840 article printed in *Fraser's Magazine*: "Boz, who knows life well, knows that his Miss Nancy is the most unreal fantastical personage possible; no more like a thief's mistress than one of the Gesner's shepherdesses resembles a real country wrench. He dare not tell the truth concerning such young ladies" (qtd. in Collins 46).

Philip Collins also includes an article that he believes was penned by G. H. Lewes, which comments on the "language which this uneducated workhouse-boy ordinarily uses" (qtd. in *National Magazine and Monthly Critic* [December 1837] 68).

5. Lucas continues, "The same tactic applies to Oliver. And to object that Dickens is being unrealistic in employing such a tactic would be absurdly trivial—especially when we remember that what he is doing here is something quite new in the English novel." Dickens' use of speech to sign a character's inner worth was a revolutionary technique in novels.

This theory, that gentle speech signs innate goodness, is also proffered by Arthur Adrian (79). Additionally, Angus Wilson argues that Oliver's standard dialect indicates his gentle birth (*World* 54).

6. Dickens develops this philosophy more fully in *Barnaby Rudge* in his treatment of the Gordon Riots.

9

The Passionate and the Contained Women of Oliver Twist: A Ring and a Handkerchief

When Oliver Twist dispatches a lusty wail in protest at having to enter a cold and friendless world, the surgeon who helps deliver him notices that the mother is not wearing a wedding ring. He shakes his head, saying, "The old story" (*OT* 19; ch. 1). From the onset Victorians know what kind of woman this mother is. The specifics about her (name, age, physical description, talents, dreams, goals, relations) are unimportant; she is a faceless type, bringing another bastard into the world. There is nothing new here, and because the adulteress expires in the first pages of the novel, one would expect that Dickens, indeed, will not add anything to the old story.

However, *Oliver Twist* rewrites the old story and through its complicated codes and perceptions about sexuality makes the fallen woman no cliché. Two symbols in particular codify female sexuality. The first is the ring, symbolizing the vagina; the second, the handkerchief, symbolizing the hymen. Through the recurrence of these emblems as they are developed through the characters of Agnes, Nancy, and Rose, Dickens' text contributes and distorts its rendition of female sexuality within its developing helix of domestic ideology.

Agnes, the first woman victim of the "old story," is considered first. Although not married, Agnes does possess a wedding ring given to her by Edwin Leeford (314; ch. 38). The ring is an outward sign of a sexual relationship sanctified and legalized by the public procedure of marriage. Agnes' ring cannot represent this social signification because Leeford did not marry her. The ring then represents Agnes' physical sexuality (her vagina) used by a man in exchange for gold (the ring) without social approbation. The exchange is an act equal to prostitution and causes as much disgrace.

Because old Sally is "the only woman about her" (165; ch. 24), Agnes entrusts the ring to the nurse, assuming that her sexuality (represented by the ring) would be safe in the hands of one of her own sex, who, as a nurse, is a care giver. Sally, however, steals it and the gold locket, with plans to exchange them for money. Clearly, a woman's sexuality is not her own. It is her most vulnerable area, the point at which her enclosure of self is most easily violated. This theme is symbolized by the gold locket, which "has the word 'Agnes' engraved on the inside. . . . There is a blank left for the surname" (253; ch. 38). She has lost her identity, having bartered it for a ring. Traditionally, when a woman marries, she loses her name and identity, becoming a blank to be filled in by her husband. For Agnes, that blank is not completed, and that which should have safeguarded her son's identity (the ring/her sexuality/she as baby producer) becomes lost, so that her son has to spend his youth in search of a surrogate mother.

Evident throughout *Oliver Twist* is the barter of woman's sexuality for social survival, a theme also predominant in *Dombey and Son*. However, close to the end of the novel, when Rose offers a reward for Nancy's information about Oliver, Nancy will not exchange her integrity and goodness for either money or a ring. Rose offers her first a purse, urging, "Take it for my sake, that you may have some resource in an hour of need or trouble" (311; ch. 46). Nancy's refusal signs her repentance and the turning point of the novel. She stops the sale of herself, and even more significantly, the text stops the barter of woman's sexuality, a commodity often exploited in the world of *Oliver Twist*.

Next, Nancy declines to take Rose's ring, unlike old Sally (and possibly Edwin Leeford), who stole Agnes'. She tells Rose: "I have not done this for money. Let me have that to think of. And yet—give me something that you have worn: I should like to have something—no, no, *not a ring*—your gloves or handkerchief—anything that *I can keep*, as having belonged to you" (311; emphasis added). By rejecting the ring, Nancy rejects patriarchally defined marriage and the use of sex for financial survival. By pressing, instead, for something that Rose has worn, Nancy is asking for something that is personally a woman's, not something given to her by a man. As the ring symbolizes the vagina violated by the male, so the handkerchief (an emblem discussed more fully later) symbolizes the maidenhead. Nancy wants from Rose the virginal purity that the prostitute had lost in her youth.

The ring also connects two characters whose projection as sexually active women could be seen as overtly threatening to domestic ideology, but the text frequently fluctuates regarding these women. Although Agnes, as an unwed mother, is a fallen woman, the text also portrays her as an angel type and, moreover, as a wronged woman whose purity has been defiled.

It seems that she is so good, she does not belong in this world. The illicit affair, although ratified by love, totally destroys her. The text also bestows angelic qualities on Nancy (although a prostitute) and emphasizes her moral strength of character. It would appear that the text—in its ideological construction of the angel women—does not remain consistent in defending domesticity because it also entertains a positive regard for two fallen women.

Agnes and Nancy, therefore, add to the ranks of Dickens' dissenting women; they fall outside patriarchal confines and their characterization subverts domestic ideology. They also form a special category of dissenters through the text's ambivalent portrayal of them as seduced or seductive women. Jean Kennard, who provides an insightful discussion on nineteenth-century literary conventions in regard to seduced women, infers from her reading of *Wuthering Heights*, that one should not expect the purpose of its plot is to bring a woman into maturity. She must die for her error (13), a paradigm that seems to be repeated in *Oliver Twist*. Both fallen women—Agnes and Nancy—do die. Kennard argues that such nineteenth-century novels, like Austen's, develop plot through having the female character learn how to choose a "right" suitor over a "wrong" suitor. Once the woman has matured enough (like Emma) to know who is the best man for her, her growth stops and the novel closes. Marriage is the end of her maturing process (10–18). Marriage, as a literary symbol, says Kennard, "indicates the adjustment of the protagonist to society's values, a condition which is equated with her maturity" (18).

Nancy already knows that Bill Sikes is not the best man for her. She tells Rose that she and hundreds like her "set our rotten hearts on any man and let him fill the place that has been a blank through all our wretched lives" (271; ch. 40). Note the word "blank" again, suggesting that without a man (husband or father) to give the woman an identity, she has no identity. Nevertheless, from the first, Nancy is already a mature woman. Many readers probably do not realize that she is only sixteen (calculated from information in chapter 16[1]), for she seems much older. She possesses the wisdom to recognize that the liaison with Sikes does not put her in a socially acceptable position. At this point, according to Kennard's paradigm, she should either repent and get another man or die. She has not developed maturity through moral schooling; the novel does not provide a world designed to mature her into a morally upright woman (as does Charlotte Brontë's *Villette*, for example). Instead, she has matured because of a hard street life, and every effort she makes toward moral uprightness is thwarted. Finally, after the text depicts her in several heroic episodes, she dies, but it is not just prostitution as an infraction of domestic ordering that kills Nancy; it is also her passion.

One cannot regard the text's endorsement of Nancy without reckoning her prostitution (which the text downplays) and her uncontrollable passion (on which the text makes critical judgment). Nancy is a curious mix of woman. More precisely, Dickens' portrayal of her is an amalgam that complicates his dissemination of domestic ideology. She *is*, first of all, a prostitute. Dickens' ambivalence toward her reflects the ambivalence Victorian society expressed in general toward prostitutes.[2] They were seen as a moral contaminant but at the same time a useful and necessary service that helped preserve the home—so argue E. M. Sigsworth and T. J. Wyke in their study of Victorian prostitution and venereal disease. They list three benefits that the prostitutes provided for middle-class society: they (1) safeguarded the virginity of the young ladies of the wealthier classes, (2) shielded married women from "grosser passions" of husbands, and (3) helped prevent divorce (87). The extent to which prostitution coincided with ideological management of women is evidenced from the estimated fifty thousand prostitutes in England and Scotland, more than nine thousand in London alone (Fernando 7). In 1840 there were one hundred prostitutes for the sixteen hundred undergraduates at Cambridge University (Calder 90). Their employment was in much demand in the home army; as a result, 260 of 1,000 soldiers were infected with venereal disease (Fernando 7). Russell Goldfarb indicates how widespread this profession was and what concerns it raised by identifying sixteen books and twenty-six articles written on prostitution (between 1840 and 1870) in England and Scotland (48). A *Westminster Review* article (1850) reasoned that the increase of prostitution was due to young men's using this service in order to postpone marriage until they could afford to live like gentlemen (qtd. in Houghton 366). Nancy, as a prostitute, is an essential agent in the preservation of the middle-class home, protecting the virginity of women (like Rose) while their men (like Harry) prepared financially and socially for marriage.

Regardless of its practical benefits to the middle class, prostitution was a major social matter. Marion Shaw regards Victorian prostitution as a subculture plagued by urban poverty, disease, and crime.[3] With a population of one million in London in 1801, doubling by 1841, and then adding another million by 1861 and yet another by 1871 (Boyle 212), the alarming increase in slum dwellers and the problems raised by slum conditions posed a real threat to the middle class. (This is the affliction theme vividly depicted in *Bleak House* by the infectious, pervasive fog that carried disease of the slums to Bleak House.)

Pam Morris identifies the prostitution link between the two classes in a different way. She concludes that the Victorian middle class wanted to believe in its own "respectability" as if it contrasted to the moral lassitude of the lower class, but Dickens exposes its hypocrisy. By dealing with seduction and prostitution, he uncovers an intimate connection between the two. This is what Morris considers to be Dickens' "social sub-plot": characters of diverse social orders come together through illicit love affairs; his text reveals the "hidden bonds of their shared humanity" (11).

Nina Auerbach suggests that the fallen woman became a centerpiece of Victorian literary typography. She identifies her in the poetry of Tennyson and Robert Browning as "the abased figurehead of a fallen culture," transmuting "a woman's fall from a personal to a national event, one that inspires and symbolizes Victorian England's epic portrait of its own doom" (157). The two poets, according to Auerbach, considered prostitution as an agent of moral decline, ruining first the home and then, by extension, the entire nation. The pervasiveness of the enterprise signals serious flaws in domestic ideology that would either allow or require a man to search outside domesticity for sexual gratification and to deny the same to women inside domesticity.

Dickens was aware of prostitution as a social issue and apparently perceived ways to diffuse it as a social menace. His ideas are well documented in a letter to the philanthropist Angela Burdett-Coutts. The baroness was seeking advice from Dickens in setting up a corrective facility for women arrested for prostitution. Dickens counseled that it should be explained to an inmate "that she has come there for *useful* repentance and reform, and means her past way of life has been dreadful in its nature and consequences, and full of affliction, misery, and despair to *herself*" (qtd. in Osborne 73). Without exception, all of the Dickensian prostitutes are ashamed of their unchastity and are portrayed as victims treated badly by men. Dickens just could not seem to think of women as being inherently bad. *Oliver Twist* illustrates that such women continue to harbor in their breast what Merryn Williams defines as "feminine goodness."[4] Nancy nurses Bill when he is sick "with a touch of woman's tenderness, which communicated something like sweetness of tone, even to her voice" (256; ch. 39). This is the same voice that can utter such blasphemies that Dickens dared not repeat them in print (behavior so unacceptable to Dickens that when he once heard a girl swear in the streets, he had her arrested[5]).

Believing that women were happiest at the hearth and that prostitutes would naturally want to be led into the domestic fold, Dickens became an avid supporter of Miss Coutts' project. In fact, he served as the chairman of the administrative committee for Urania Cottage from 1847 to 1858 and was often active in running this asylum for convicted prostitutes (Goldfarb 49). He expressed his confidence that women were able to turn their lives around: "She is degraded and fallen, but not lost, having this Shelter [Urania Cottage]; and . . . the means of Return to Happiness are now about to be put into her own hands, and trusted to her own keeping" (qtd. in Osborne 74). The very name of the shelter reinforced the advocacy of domesticity (associated with the coziness of "Cottage") as not only the ideal state for women but divinely ordered ("Urania" pertaining to the "celestial" or "heavenly").

This belief in the angel within the fallen woman is a theme of domestic ideology that is developed in the scene when Nancy meets with Rose to talk about Oliver's danger. Rose (the second time joined by Mr. Brownlow) seems to express more alarm and concern for Nancy than for Oliver. Dickens turns Rose and Brownlow into evangelical mouthpieces for the ministry of fallen women. When Mr. Brownlow suggests to Nancy that she can start her life over in "a quiet asylum, either in England, or, if you fear to remain here, in some foreign country" (310; ch. 46), he reflects Dickens' hope that a penitent woman would want to return to domesticity. In *David Copperfield*, the seduced and beguiled Little Em'ly is restored to her family, and they all relocate to Australia. The prostitute Martha likewise goes abroad, marries, and lives a productive life. Including Alice Marwood *(D&S)*, all three die a literal or metaphorical death but are born again through baptism of water (David prevents Martha from drowning; she and Little Em'ly cross the seas to Australia; Alice sickens in both a literal and a figurative storm).

However, the text forms a web of patriarchal attitudes toward female sexuality that are more malevolent and phallocentric than sympathetic in the ways identified previously. Dickens owns that prostitutes are victims of society, but this is the same patriarchal society that controls the woman at the hearth. He accuses Fagin (the surrogate father) of making Nancy into what she is, and Mrs. Brown, likewise, of turning her daughter into a prostitute in *Dombey and Son*. The 1846 letter to the baroness blames, not the girl, but society for her condition: "Never mind society while she is at that pass. Society has used her ill and turned away from her, and she cannot be expected to take much heed of its rights or wrongs" (qtd. in Osborne 74). Although Dickens considers Nancy's life immoral and criminal, he treats Nancy with pity. Nothing is said, remarkably, about the clients she services. Nancy would have no job if there were no market, and that market, composed of middle-class males. Michael Slater quite rightly concludes: "Here is Dickens apparently preoccupied with women as the insulted and injured of mid-Victorian England yet voicing no general condemnation of prevailing patriarchal beliefs and attitudes" (244). The text reaffirms domestic ideology with woman firmly situated within a family unit playing an angel-in-the-house role as does Rose. If she is outside this sphere, she cannot hope for any happiness for she deserves none. Yet Nancy is a prostitute *because* men are outside "their place within a family unit" and partake of her services, without repercussion. This lack of accountability (a male privilege) is a gap in the text that not only supports the portrayal of Nancy as a victim but also signals the sexual problems created by domestic ideology that affected both genders.

Dickens suggests another cause for prostitution through Nancy's telling Rose that if there were more women like Rose, there would be fewer women like Nancy (267; ch. 40). This is Dickens laying charge to women to uphold the moral well-being of society: it is the duty of good women and the natural power of their goodness to influence both men and women to behave morally.[6] This is the age-old story of Eve—if she had quit eating the apple in Eden, the serpent would have gone away. Ironically women are to prevent other women from becoming prostitutes to men when none of the women has the financial or legal means to survive without the trade of their sexuality or gender identities for economic sustenance. In *David Copperfield* Martha saves Little Em'ly; in *Dombey and Son* Harriet Carker saves Alice; and here in *Oliver Twist* Rose saves Nancy. At best, though, these women save each other's souls, and they minister healing. They must rely on men to make it possible for the fallen woman to secure an alternate life-style not dependent on the sale of her body. When this is not possible, as seems to be the case for Alice *(D&S)*, she must die.

Concerning Dickens, Walter Crotch finds "he always makes his appeal to our pathos, our humour, and our toleration in their behalf. . . . He assumed a new, a definite, and a *ministrant* attitude toward women and the particular urgencies of the changing position and outlook" (173; emphasis added). On the surface, Dickens' text seems full of compassion and redemptive hope for women like Nancy. However, note the stance that Dickens takes toward these fallen women in both the Coutts letters and *Oliver Twist*, and even the way he is perceived by Crotch. The posture is supercilious and promotes patriarchal domination. Dickens' text would guide the repentant woman, who has fallen out of domestic enclosure, back to the fold. As long as the woman submits to this form of domination, then all will be forgiven and she will be given another chance to serve her menfolk and children at the hearth, and, most important of all, to get her sexual appetite and behavior under patriarchal control. What is not overtly expressed is that Nancy's sexuality cannot be her own: not to give or withhold or enjoy at her choosing and at her price. Such lack of sexual and gender power lies undisclosed like the other side of a coin that lies face down. Its particulars can be assumed on the basis of the knowledge of what appears on the foreside.

Because women were told that a good woman could not like sex, Jenni Calder theorizes that prostitutes were able to take care of male needs that would not have been proper for women to enjoy at home (90–91). The image of a sexless woman was a part of domestic ideology based on illusion and not reality. After all, the Victorian adult woman spent much of her adult life being pregnant. Regardless, an expert on such matters, Henry Mayhew (1861), declared, "literally every woman who yields to her passions and loses her virtue is a prostitute" (vol. 2, 215). And the expert on sexuality Dr. William Acton (1865) assured the public that women did not naturally enjoy sex.[7] He wrote: "I should say that the majority of women (happily for them) are not very much troubled with sexual feeling of any kind" (*Functions* 112). Lest there be any doubt as to what women and to what passions he refers, the doctor added: "Many of the best mothers, wives, and managers of households, know little of or are careless about sexual indulgences. Love of home, children, and of domestic duties are the only passions they feel" (113).[8]

Nancy's true crime, therefore, is not that she's a prostitute—a situation that Dickens thought could be remedied. Rather, she is a prostitute whose—or because her—sexuality cannot be subdued.

Analyzing the Victorian perception regarding female passion through the study of Tennyson's *The Princess*, Marion Shaw has observed, "Uncontrolled, unlegalized female sexual desire both emasculates men and reduces their manly function" (122). Auerbach also reacts to the Victorian depiction of the passionate woman: "She seems to enlightened minds a pitiable monster, created by the neurosis of a culture that because it feared female sexuality and aggression enshrined a respectably sadistic cautionary tale punishing them both" (157). Obviously, one basis of such fear lies in the potential correlation between loss of masculine sexual dominance and similar loss of power in the social sphere.[9] Therefore, women like the fiery Nancy pose a threat to men intent upon holding their superior position of authority within domesticity. Nevertheless, to dominate a woman of such passion also poses an exciting challenge and a way to reassert masculine supremacy. The victor must explicitly feel power because he has had to flex it, whereas otherwise his power is assumed and unchallenged at the hearth.

In Dickens' text, dominating a woman, especially a strong woman, takes on erotic tones, as evident in the following scene. After having participated in the abduction of Oliver, Nancy regrets her complicity. When Oliver tries to escape and Bill wants to set the dog on him, Nancy assiduously protects the child. Bill flings her across the room, but she continues, undaunted, to defy him. After Fagin delivers a blow to Oliver's shoulders, Nancy wrests his club loose and threatens to kill any one of them who touches Oliver again. The narrator intervenes with a comment about her behavior: "There is something about a roused woman: especially if she add to all her other strong passions, the fierce impulses of recklessness and despair: which few men like to provoke" (115; ch. 16). A description of the "roused" Nancy intimidates the most ignoble of scoundrels and ruffians but also seems to excite Bill. The text seems to be ambiguous about Nancy's passion, sending out mixed signals of both repulsion and attraction. It seems even more ambiguous as to which reaction it would evoke from the reader. This is a revealing gap in didactic literature, especially when dealing with such a socially significant issue as woman's sexuality.

The scene continues with hints of multiple imprecations from Sikes and rising hysteria from Nancy. She becomes so overwrought that she bites her lip until the blood comes. This is not just extreme behavior; it is erotic. She tears her hair and dress "in a transport of passion," and then rushes on Fagin, but Sikes seizes her by the wrists and prevents any further struggle until she faints. Although it would appear that these destructive acts are being performed by Nancy to herself, in actuality they are results of her being subdued by Fagin and Sikes. With the violence done to her hair and dress and the flow of blood, Nancy is being raped, metaphorically.

In a much later chapter after another outburst of passion, she sits rocking herself, tossing her head, and then laughs hysterically (299; ch. 44). In the Victorian canon, passion and sex are closely related and they equate to insanity and animalism, so that Nancy's wild behavior would be understood as the natural result of failure to control her passion. A twentieth-century reader, however, might understand Nancy's hysteria and neurotic behavior as the reaction to violent domination of the male over the female. Sikes is referred to as the robber in this last scene and Nancy as the girl. He is stealing her right to anger and resistance to his power, and she is helpless to prevent the theft.

Nonetheless, the text charges not Sikes for passionate outbursts, but Nancy, and hers represents behavior that is unacceptable for an ideologically correct woman. As a prostitute, she had a chance in a Dickens novel to begin anew, but because she is also a woman of passion—thus a social aberrant—she is doomed to die a fitting violent death.

None of the Dickensian wild women ends up happy, and the text's indictment of them is clear in *Oliver Twist*. Charlotte seizes Oliver "with her utmost force, which was about equal to that of a moderately strong man in particularly good training," and then strikes Oliver with her fist (53; ch. 6). The language conveys her demonstration of passion in masculine terms. Later, when married to Noah Claypole and partner in his schemes, she uses a "feminine" demonstration of fainting to deceive men into treating her as a gentlewoman who is supportive and sympathetic of their problems. In this way she is able to extract the information that Claypole sells. By its negative stance toward Charlotte, the text judges her for exploiting what usually is considered an acceptable and expected trait of a true woman (fainting when shocked by something too impure or worldly for her delicate disposition). Charlotte's ploys are a betrayal to her own sex. Or perhaps the text is using Charlotte satirically to undermine a traditional image of woman as the weaker sex.

Likewise Mrs. Sowerberry displays her unfeminine passion by scratching Oliver (who is only a frail child) and then becomes hysterical and maliciously rails at his mother. But it is not until the undertaker's wife, like Charlotte, resorts to "feminine tactics" by bursting into tears that she is able to get her husband to do her bidding. The text also regards her as a traitor to her sex.

Tears do not work for Mr. Bumble's wife, who is referred to once again curiously as Mrs. Corney instead of Mrs. Bumble, indicating her refusal to occupy a submissive posture in relation to her current husband. Tears failing, she knocks off his hat and then, in a very unladylike manner, clasps "him tight round the throat with one hand" and inflicts "a shower of blows (dealt with singular vigour and dexterity) upon it with the other," followed by "scratching his face and tearing his hair off" and then pushing him over a chair (241; ch. 37). This tirade is her response to Mr. Bumble, who tried to inform her that the "prerogative of a man is to command." The text is meant to be humorous and to satirize both man and wife; however, it articulates the locus of domestic ideology (that a man should rule the woman) and then provides a rebellious response by a woman. In other words, within the Dickensian text sounds a woman's voice resisting domesticity. Although the text is critical of Mrs. Corney's passion, it also advocates her case, for in the very next scene, Mr. Bumble enters the laundry room, intent upon bullying the female paupers at work there, when he is once again assailed by his wife, who is referred to, this time, as Mrs. Bumble—emphatically noted as his wife. Even so, she makes it quite clear that she and her women will not submit to him. His degradation is complete, and the text does not ask the reader to feel sorry for him (as Dickens does with R. Wilfer in *OMF* and Gabriel Varden in *BR*). Dickens is allowing Mrs. Corney to use either feminine or unfeminine behavior—whichever will work—to chastise a powerful man, whom the text portrays as a patriarchal bully.

In fact, all four women (Nancy, Charlotte, Mrs. Sowerberry, and Mrs. Bumble) are not simply passionate women; they are angry women. They are capable women who have been taught to resort to faints and tears in order to get what they want. Dickens' text does not overtly support women's anger, but it does covertly provide reasons why women should be angry, and it inscribes their rebellion. After all, Nancy has submitted to the only father she has known (Fagin) and to the only "husband" she has known (Bill), demonstrating a prime virtue of womanhood through obedience to male authority, only to be abused and exploited. Regardless, the text would have her control her passion, like Rose, who controls not only her own passion, but Harry's (235; ch. 35). Through Rose, Nancy should be able to find salvation.

George Watt suggests that the transfer of virtue from Rose to Nancy is what Dickens means to symbolize through the white handkerchief in *Oliver Twist*. When Rose gives Nancy the handkerchief, Watt says that it serves as a "ritualistic means of passing purity from one soul to another" (17). Purity is something that can be conferred by one woman on another, in an act that arises from a sympathetic understanding and a mutual disdain for sexual violation. Among other things, then, the handkerchief symbolizes the maidenhead.[10]

The first reference to a handkerchief appears in chapter 3. In the previous chapter, when Oliver had the unlucky temerity to ask for more gruel, the "gentleman in the white waistcoat" predicts that Oliver "will come to be hung." Locked in solitary confinement, Oliver contemplates suicide by hanging himself with a pocket handkerchief—if he had one. Continuing with the handkerchief as a metaphor for the maidenhead, the meaning extends into this scene. What could strangle Oliver is his mother's unmarried status, symbolized by the handkerchief. The world treats him with utter scorn because he is a bastard. Born outside a family unit, he poses a threat to society.

The handkerchief was also considered an item of luxury not allowed to paupers "by express order of the board" (15). As if in retaliation, Fagin's poor boys steal handkerchiefs and train Oliver to do likewise. The silk handkerchief, then, is also a symbol for class status (Davidoff 397; Jordan 582–85; McMaster 47–49). Once in the possession of the poor, though, the handkerchief becomes an instrument of destruction—a possible hanging device for Oliver and an exchange between Rose and Nancy that ends in Nancy's brutal demise.

As a class symbol, the handkerchief connects to sexual signification through middle-class morality. This interpretation considers the handkerchief to represent sexual purity. Society would safeguard the sexuality of its middle-class women as long as women complied with morals regulating sexual behavior inside and outside marriage (like Rose but unlike Agnes). Lower-class women (like Nancy) often resorted to prostitution as the only means to secure earnings. Yet, as demonstrated by Fagin's underworld, handkerchiefs could be stolen and sold. The middle class saw its own sexuality as paradoxically virginal and passionless, as epitomized by Rose. The middle class saw lower-class sexuality as animalistic and violent, as demonstrated by Nancy. Hence, Nancy's murder serves as a significant statement of the inviolability of middle-class morality, supporting a theory that Nancy Armstrong proffers: "[Nancy's] mutilated body expresses intense hostility towards the working classes, even though Dickens represents them as victims who need to be rescued. One could say this body provided a field where two notions of the family confronted one another and the old gave way to the new" (183). The point of her murder seems to be that the middle class can subjugate the lower class (182). The handkerchief is a middle-class social symbol that cannot be, will not be, soiled by the lower class. Instead, some nebulous justice would be sure that the handkerchief would be destroyed first rather than allow middle-class values to be compromised. Perhaps a prostitute can be redeemed, but a woman's display of passion must be dealt with mercilessly. Appropriately, then, Nancy dies a bloody, passionate death.

The text may overtly perform the dynamics described, but the exchange between Nancy and Rose is more complicated and subtly critiques masculine domination of the female. Perhaps Rose is able to impart purity to Nancy and a chance for a new life—an angel-in-the-house should be able to enact such a reformation. When Nancy holds up Rose's handkerchief, it is spotted with Nancy's spilled blood. Sikes is called the "house-

breaker"—an epithet that holds some significance because of his defiance
of domestic mores. His violation of Nancy is also a violation of Rose because the handkerchief was Rose's purity transferred to Nancy. Hence,
Sikes' violent murder of Nancy is the ultimate rape possible because domestic ideology makes women vulnerable to sexual domination and an
overpowering that can result in death.

Recalling an earlier reference to the handkerchief as a hanging device,
covertly the text extends its metaphor to imply that middle-class morality
has the potential to be a strangling purity. One who possesses such purity
(even though it is a cardinal virtue of domesticity) seems unable to survive
on earth. This would include Agnes if one discounts her fallen state and
views her strictly as a pure woman who gives up her life so that her child
can live. Oliver and Nancy, regardless of appearances and social status, are
pure of heart. Oliver nearly dies frequently in the novel, and these brushes
with death make him all the more unearthly—as also happens with Rose.
Nancy does die. She might have had the chance to emigrate to America
and build a new life, but her love for Bill and her tenacious loyalty to
him—both pure motives—destroy her.

In her death scene she holds up Rose's handkerchief in folded hands to
heaven and prays "for mercy to her Maker." The club (like the club she
dared to use on the patriarch Fagin) falls upon her and silences her forever.
Her passion is finally subdued, but at what price? The text has become
embroiled with conflicts. Nancy has been portrayed as a good woman, and
her participation in prostitution regarded with sympathy and understanding. The text, at times, races inevitably toward her death as the only so-
lution to sexual passion. If female passion were given vent, it would
threaten an ideal of womanhood when some part of a woman could not
be ruled by a man. Or is Nancy too pure to survive in this world, especially
in that part of the underworld to which she is born? The narrative de-
nounces her murder as one of the "foulest and most cruel" deeds. Then is
Bill's club an instrument of judgment? And if so, is the judgment on Nancy
as an uncontrollable woman, or on a system that usurped patriarchal authority over her? Because the club (as a patriarchal symbol) destroys a good
woman, does it not judge itself through the very act of committing injustice? Patriarchal domination over a woman may be an ideology promoted
in the text of *Oliver Twist*—especially in regard to Nancy, who often transgresses the boundaries of gender restrictions. But it is, at the same time,
condemned—also especially in regard to Nancy, whose goodness transcends the boundaries of gender considerations.

One can read Nancy's murder in yet another way that follows the strand
of sexual symbolism traced in this chapter. If Rose's handkerchief represents the hymen and Rose transfers this virginity and class status to
Nancy—if such a transference were possible (and it could have been, had
Nancy emigrated to another country and started life afresh)—and if Sikes'

bloody murder of Nancy is also a bloody rape of Rose, then Brownlow, as a representative of the moral middle class, acts as the avenger. Much of this interpretation neatly places all of the characters under the omnipotent providence of middle-class morality, but the text closes with a number of irksome questions that challenge whether or not that morality is benevolent. If Nancy was so good that she could save Oliver, why could she not reform Sikes or Fagin or any of Fagin's gang? Why could Rose not save her? If Agnes had been the good woman Brownlow would have us believe that she had been, why did she not survive in order to be a good mother for Oliver?

Although Agnes, Nancy, and Rose exhibit domestic qualities, they are not to be empowered by that conformity. The novel acts as a form of domination. At the root of the identities of these women is their sexuality, sometimes represented by the ring and at other times by the handkerchief. At this arbitrary locus (sexuality) are the women subdued and domestic ideology championed, but not without a text that in order to accomplish this has to commit rape. All three women are subjugated in this way. And there is none to avenge them other than the text exposing itself.

NOTES

1. Nancy has been thieving for Fagin since "a child not half as old as this? pointing to Oliver," and she has been in the same trade for twelve years (116; ch. 16). In chapter 2 Oliver is nine (6). Thus Nancy must be about sixteen.

2. For more information concerning mid-Victorian prostitution, see William Acton's *Prostitution*, Judith R. Walkowitz's *Prostitution and Victorian Society*, Henry Mayhew's *Selections from* London Labour and the London Poor, Frances Finnigan's *Poverty and Prostitution*, Keith Nield's *Prostitution in the Victorian Age*, Stephen Marcus' *The Other Victorians*, Ronald Pearsall's *The Worm in the Bud*, Lynne Agress' *The Feminine Irony* (28–30), Jenni Calder's *Women and Marriage in Victorian Fiction* (90–99), Lloyd Fernando's *"New Women" in the Late Victorian Novel* (7), Russell M. Goldfarb's *Sexual Repression and Victorian Literature* (46–50), Walter E. Houghton's *The Victorian Frame of Mind: 1830–1870* (366), Martha Vicinus' *Suffer and Be Still* (77–89), and George Watt's *The Fallen Woman in the Nineteenth-Century English Novel*.

3. Marion Shaw, in his feminist reading of Alfred Lord Tennyson, includes a chapter on fallen women that may prove useful to the reader (125–26).

4. By studying the Dickens women who suffer a blighted life, Merryn Williams concludes that Dickens believed that all women are innately good and can overcome evil (76).

5. Michael Slater tells this story that Dickens himself recounted in "The Ruffian," published in *All the Year Round*, October 10, 1868 (qtd. in 138).

6. This belief that women were to be moral beacons is articulated by Mrs. Sarah Ellis in *Women of England* (1843).

7. Nancy Cott provides an informative study of the formation and promotion

of the Victorian ideology of "passionless women" in her article of the same title. See also Barbara Welter's *Dimity Convictions* (62–67).

8. For a survey of the medical theories concerning female sexuality during the Victorian period see Carroll Smith-Rosenberg and Charles Rosenberg's article.

9. Michael Slater sees this neurosis personally at work within Dickens himself: "Dickens's apparent nervousness about any manifestation of aggressive female passion (as opposed to passive female devotion) may be linked to an equally detectable nervousness about his own strong sexual responsiveness to women" (356).

Harry Stone has much to say on this score too (*Night* 274–414; 532–37).

10. For other possible interpretations see John Jordan's "The Purloined Handkerchief," in which he notes that *Oliver Twist* contains more than fifty references to this accessory (581).

10

The "Pattern" of Bleak House: A Woman's Story

In the past decade, *Bleak House* (of all of Dickens' novels) has received the most attention from critics—especially from those intrigued by Dickens' endeavor to write female narrative.[1] From Dickens' deliberate attempts to see things through women's eyes and to express them through a feminine discourse, one can chart how he worked out what he perceived to be a female definition of domestic ideology. More significant to this study is his conscious representation of gender, which has produced the most salient ruptures in domestic ideology that this study has explored thus far. A Victorian patriarch trying to write like a woman, Dickens labored to depict a credible character with a voice appropriate to her sex at a time when women were to be obscure and silent.[2] The result is Esther, a woman—as Alex Zwerdling puts it—"alienated from her true self and unable to acknowledge her deepest feelings" (101).

Esther, to Laurie Langbauer, is "Dickens's fullest representation of the inside of a woman's mind because it shows one so brainwashed by and intent on maintaining the male order" (153). All the while that the text constructs Esther as an exemplar of womanhood and a female advocate for domesticity, it also struggles to convey Dickens' understanding of women, and at the same time to convey a Victorian woman's attempt to understand herself. This is no easy task because Esther is constantly being either defined or effaced by other people.

Critics disagree as to Dickens' success in producing a credible female character and discourse. G. K. Chesterton considers Esther ("in some ways") a failure (157); George H. Lewes, a monstrous failure (qtd. in Zwerdling 94). Yet John Ward concludes that the character demonstrates "insight and perception rarely accorded a woman in Dickens's fiction" (38), though Mary Daehler Smith feels that Dickens sacrificed her to a thematic function: "She is a moral guide, not a rounded character" (11). Norman Page emphasizes that Esther's role is largely as an observer; therefore, her presence in the narrative is to be unobtrusive: "Dickens needed to create a character whose unassuming personality would enable her to mingle freely with a large variety of characters without determining the tone of the episode by the force of her own qualities" (176), a model that coincidentally mirrors the self-denying angel-in-the-house. Robert Donovan thinks that she is a good narrator because she is "as transparent as glass" (43). Is she? Donovan also finds her observations made "under a simple, traditional, and predictable system of moral values" (44), but the text reveals multiple conflicts in Esther's narrative as it overtly reaffirms those values. I am more inclined to agree with Zwerdling, who praises Dickens for his experiment: "Esther Summerson is Dickens' most ambitious attempt to allow a character who does not fully understand herself to tell her own story" (101).

Especially intriguing are Suzanne Graver's observations of Esther. Besides the split narrative, Graver hears two voices from Esther: "a dominant one that is cheerfully accepting and selflessly accommodating; and a muted one, itself double-edged, that is inquiring, critical, and discontented but also hesitant, self-disparaging, and defensive" (4). Graver's theory raises several provocative questions. Was Dickens so insightful a writer that he was able to create a woman who might have experienced the fissure within herself that was created by domestic ideology? Or does this fissure emerge because a male writer could not consistently conceive a feminine ideal pitted against harsh realities of the world? Does the male-driven text then demonstrate that the empirical awareness of "female" cannot reasonably sustain the ideological construct? If so, is the problem with the female model or with the patriarch who fabricates the model, or is it with harsh realities?

The Victorian might argue that the angel-in-the-house will operate fine as long as she stays within her domestic enclosure. It is only when she becomes mobile in the way Esther does that she runs into problems. Yet Esther's interests focus on the personal and the domestic; she gives herself to relationships within those parameters (Korg 16–17; Chase 114). If this is so, the text indicates that the nondomestic world, like the fog, cannot be kept out of the home. Bleak House is a fitting signifier for the home as Dickens must have perceived it. Perhaps Frances Armstrong is right in her judging that Dickens lost faith in the home as a retreat and center of strength (151–52). About *Bleak House* she concludes: "Heaven may be a home, but the universe is not; the best one can do is try to make it more home-like" (102).

Most recent criticism focuses on Dickens' feminine rhetoric in this novel rather than on his characterization or depiction of the home. Morton Dauwen Zabel applauds the novelist's effort: "Dickens achieves something new in his art in this book: a depth of focus, a third dimension in his perspective, a moral resonance and an implicit ambiguity of sympathy and insight" ("Undivided" 337). Esther's point of view has to be modest, reticent, and affectionate, whereas the third-person point of view conveys the unbridled Dickens with his "high-stilted irony, acerbity, harsh immediacy, and scathing contempt" (337). Page identifies Esther's tone as "quiet, conversational, confidential, intimate; her language is for the most part unaffected and even commonplace," with "little, great, beautiful, dear" as typical adjectives (175). The third-person narrator, however, carries a "rhetorical and emphatic style" through such diction as "implacable, elephantine, undistinguishable, haggard" (175). Graver describes the first-person narrative as "domestic, protective, personal, and affirmative." Esther's values are corrective to those values noticeably absent in *Bleak House*'s society. The third-person narrative is more "wide-ranging, public, probing, and dark" (3). Esther's discourse strikes Pam Morris as resembling confessionals written by women in religious magazines (90–91). Alison Milbank regards the third person as mobile and godlike, whereas the first person is circumlocutory, domestic, and subjective (83). All of these observations confirm that Dickens achieved a consistency in representing two distinct points of view divided by gender.

This study will investigate Dickens' narrative efforts to mimic the female and will track the gaps in and disturbance of domestic ideology that result. After all, with a title about a "house" the novel promises to operate on domestic ideology in one way or another. I find that the most disruptive conflicts that modify ideology are the actual articulation and creation of identity in the Esther narrative. Complications in the text emerge through three layers of this narrative: (1) Dickens' attempts to give a woman articulation through Esther, (2) that character's frequent and overt denial of articulation, and (3) implicit signs within the narrative that beg desperately for articulation, though only a telling silence ensues. The imagistic/thematic foci examined in this chapter derive from the multiple references to documents and the authority of textuality either to produce that articulation or to suppress it. The analysis also considers how mirrors give Esther the autonomy to define herself and what happens when they are either taken away from her or shattered. Such strategies attempt to open up the text to locate the gaps, conflicts, and refoldings that complicate its ideological posture.

The narrative takes a particular interest in its own discourse as well. Like a metafiction, *Bleak House* comments on itself.[3] It unfolds its narrative by constant review of its techniques. The allusions to letters in this novel number roughly thirty, not including the hundreds written by Mrs. Jellyby. For a novel that is not epistolary, much of the narrative progresses because of characters' careful observance of their own narrative construction and dependence on texts. Besides letters, there are countless documents of all kinds.[4] The first chapter mentions an "interminable brief," bills, cross-bills, answers, rejoinders, injunctions, affidavits, issues, references to masters, master's reports, mountains of costly nonsense, documents, folios, "eighteen hundred sheets," and "heavy charges of paper." In addition to paperwork, the text refers to various writers: shorthand writers, the reporters of the court, the reporters of the newspapers, and copying clerks. Such textuality might reveal Dickens' own tentativeness with his production of female text by alluding to "legal-type" documents and "professional" writers as if, through their "authority," to achieve verisimilitude for his novel. Or the structure might be Dickens' construction of the female as tentative, passive, unsure—a woman's telling her story in a nonlinear fashion, resorting to documentation and self-reflection to validate her experience and, in lacking the privilege of assertion, to articulate that experience in a nonforthright manner.

In chapter 2, the attention to writing becomes even more prevalent and significant. Lady Honoria Dedlock notices the handwriting of a legal copy sported by Tulkinghorn. Because she almost faints, the reader and Tulkinghorn know that there is something noteworthy about the document's writer. This copy, of course, signals the first secret of the novel's mystery, for the handwriting is that of Lady Dedlock's onetime lover, Captain Hawdon.

Esther's first correspondence is with Mr. Krenge, the solicitor who secures her as a companion to Jarndyce's two wards. Esther's letter is warm and sincere, thanking Mr. Krenge for the position. His letter is a cold, formal, formulaic response. These two styles contrast for the next six years of correspondence as Esther is being educated. All the while, the letters, ironically depersonalized, have been copied by her father (unknown to her).

Esther's father is a law writer but is unaware that he is corresponding with his own daughter. Besides, he is not composing letters; he only copies them. He seems to lack power to define himself in much the same way as his daughter (who is also a writer, as narrator of the story). His name is Latin for "nobody," which, as argued later, is exactly how Esther perceives herself. By defining a man who is unable to control the events in his life, in particular his domestic situation (by not being married to Honoria and not parenting his daughter), the text contributes to an undercutting of gender power in this novel. Not only are the women sometimes—but not always—powerless to travel their own courses, but so are the men.

The next important writer Esther meets is Caddy Jellyby, who is her mother's amanuensis, writing hundreds of letters regarding the Borioboola-Gha campaign. The four envelopes in the gravy signal Dickens' disapproval of women's participating in a male project (writing) to the neglect of their household duties (such as setting a good table). Ellen Moers perceives that Caddy is used "to dramatise Dickens's initial point: that the misdirection of female energies to social causes, at the cost of domestic responsibilities, brings havoc to marriage, home, family, indeed all society" (14). Esther is to repair this social damage. She is Dickens' ideal woman set against the wrong kind of woman (15). As Mrs. Jellyby converses with Mr. Quale about brotherhood (an illegitimate topic for a woman), Ada and Esther (clearly the "good" women present) sit in the corner and tell stories to the children (57; ch. 4), doing one of the things that women are supposed to be doing with stories. When Caddy charges Esther to disparage the domestic disarray of the Jellyby household, Caddy also warns her not to tell stories, but to tell the truth—in other words, to condemn Mrs. Jellyby's failure to live up to the domestic ideal. This has to be Esther's story, insists Caddy: a confirmation of the domestic sphere for women.

Esther, the "little housekeeper," keeps her disapproval to a minimum at this first meeting by sarcastically telling herself that she should be ashamed for being so concerned about Peepy and so little concerned about the more noble mission to Africa (54). By nearly halfway through the book, she (or Dickens) is much more indignant: "I thought of the one family so near us who were neither gone nor going to the left bank of the Niger, and wondered how [Mrs. Jellyby] could be so placid" (341; ch. 23). It's only natural, then, that this problem realizes its fullest dimensions when the African project fails and Mrs. Jellyby must engage in even heavier correspondence in support of women's rights (879; ch. 67). Thus Dickens vents not only disdain for women who write outside the acceptable patriarchal confines, but also for those who work to change the ideological system.

The text, however, will approve Caddy's writing to her mother and father about her engagement because this event indicates her intentions to set up her own domestic sphere. This is no loss to her mother, who (Caddy says) thinks of her only as pen and ink (201; ch. 14). Caddy is not to pursue writing as a career in itself, as does the mother and as the mother has tried to require of her daughter. Instead, writing is a legitimate tool for women only if they use it to reinforce or further domestic ideology without neglecting their domestic tasks. Caddy takes charge of the pen to repudiate Mrs. Jellyby's nondomestic life-style and to model herself instead on the domestic "pattern," Esther.

Later Esther will teach another motherless child how to write. This young woman, Charley, will struggle to write herself. Caddy and Charley are, in a way, Esther's children, who, like Esther, are pursuing the act of reproducing themselves in their writing. For all three, writing is painful labor. It is a form of self-expression and a process of self-definition, which throws a woman who strives to deny self into utter conflict. And the text demonstrates this conflict in the scene when Caddy falls asleep with her head on Esther's lap and Esther tries to cover them both with a shawl. After the fire goes out, Esther's narrative continues:

At first I was painfully awake and *vainly tried to lose myself*, with my eyes closed, among the scenes of the day. At length, by slow degrees, they became indistinct and mingled. *I began to lose the identity* of the sleeper resting on me. Now it was Ada, now one of my old Reading friends from whom I could not believe I had so recently parted. Now it was the little mad woman worn out with curtsying and smiling, now some one in authority at Bleak House. Lastly, it was no one, and *I was no one.* (60–61; ch. 4; emphasis added)

Notice the covert plot: Esther is not comfortable in this domestic scene. She dreams rather wistfully of her old school friends and the time when they used to read together and not bother about domestic responsibilities. Then she dreams that she is performing a domestic role required of her and because of such, she is "mad" and "worn out," compelled to appear pleasant and happy about doing her duty. Next she is the mistress of Bleak House, about which she tells us nothing. The house in the dream has been very bleak indeed. Finally, having reached the zenith of womanhood in her dream, she is a "no one," a nonentity.

The emphases highlight the changes in Esther's identity. Besides getting lost, her identity merges with another woman's and, along with hers, disappears altogether. This will not be the last time that a woman's identity merges with that of another. Later Jo confuses Mademoiselle Hortense with Lady Dedlock (325–26; ch. 22) and those two with Esther (439; ch. 31). Still later, everyone mistakes Jenny (the brickmaker's wife) for Lady Dedlock because the two have exchanged clothes (ch. 57). Lawrence Frank suggests that the purpose of the obfuscation of identities is to make Esther see that she is like Lady Dedlock and Mademoiselle Hortense, two very passionate women. He interprets Esther's narrative as a story of a woman who must accept sexual passion as a natural trait for a grown woman (64–83). The identity merger involves many more female characters than Lady Dedlock and Mademoiselle Hortense, though, as if incorporating women into a sisterhood in which their individualities are indistinct. Even as the text deals unfavorably with women outside domesticity, it also seems to expose domesticity as a dynamic that forces women to supplant their individual identities with one: domestic woman or the "pattern" (as Bucket calls Esther). The practice of self-denial as a domestic virtue results in a hopeless sense of nonexistence ("I was no one"), not at all celebrated by the text.

In chapter 36 the text—supposedly narrated by a woman—makes another emphatic attempt to deny woman's right to write her text. Esther writes a letter and draws a cottage scene (two acceptable domestic activities for a woman, especially if she is doing it for another woman). The letter and sketch are for an old lady to send to her grandson overseas. The whole village thinks that Esther's production is an incredible achievement. In fact, the sketch goes all the way to America, and a return letter praises her skill. But the ever humble Esther gives the credit to the post office (514).

If the ideological message to the reader is not clear enough, then it becomes so later in that same scene. Esther witnesses a bride, who Esther knows is able to write, marking an "x" on a register. Because the groom cannot write, the bride does not want to shame him by demonstrating that she can. At this act of modesty and female charity, Esther/Dickens exclaims: "Why, what had I to fear, I thought, when there was this nobility in the soul of a labouring man's daughter!" (514). Dickens contains Esther's writing with repeated and varied examples of women's writing as threat—as threat to male self-confidence and to marriage itself, as evidence of women's corruptibility and sexual transgression (direct and implied—Lady Dedlock is threatened by the letters Krook has and by the legibility of Hawdon's handwriting). Notice too that Esther's returning sense of duty and serenity is brought about by letters from people who function toward her as sister/rival/daughter/lover, and as father/husband—a complex but patriarchally sanctioned group.[5]

In recognizing the legitimacy and power of women's writing, Dickens also works to contain it within the acceptable bounds of domestic endeavor. Alison Milbanks argues that in this novel writing is a source of power (126); however, all the while, characters—especially women—are writing, they are being written/controlled by Dickens. Nevertheless, as he constantly tries to enclose women within Victorian boundaries, his narrative—as woman's writing—evinces a struggle against this form of enclosure. Esther is resisting such confines.

Ellen Moers notes this restlessness in this novel, citing the many times that women move about freely outside the home, which she reads as a rebellion against the confinement of woman's place (20–24). If one agrees with Judith Wilt that Esther's identity is unknown because her mother is unknown (307), then Esther's restless quest should be resolved through a connection with her mother. However, as Frank points out, she cannot identify with her mother because Honoria Dedlock is a fallen woman. That is why Honoria must wear a veil and why the poxed Esther can live without a mirror and with an ugly face. The heroine knows well that she must not be tied to a tainted past (71–74).

If one agrees with Frank's interpretation, Esther intuitively knows that her mother is a dissenting woman and not a good role model. However, when Esther does learn the truth about her mother, she does not reject her. Instead, the text effects an extensive separation between the two women because Dickens portrays Honoria as not only a fallen woman, but a woman of passion who, as Taylor Stoehr mentions, has defied social laws by having given herself to "a wild love affair" and indulging in "fits of rage and grief in the privacy of her boudoir" (105). Honoria is no fit mother for Dickens' heroine.[6] Sex complicates identity: illegitimate children, like Esther, do not know their identity (Allen 88). Yet, once Esther knows that Lady Dedlock is her mother, she first tries to protect her and then desperately pursues her.

J. Hillis Miller interprets the reconnection to the mother in a more positive way. He reads Lady Dedlock's flight, even if it ends in death, as a
flight to freedom—"freedom to be one's destined self" (87). As Esther races
after her mother and if she can identify with her, she might realize this
freedom, too. Miller argues that she does just this. The novel's conclusion
is "her liberation into an authentic life when she chooses to accept the self
she finds herself to be" (223). This is quite an optimistic outcome, which
is not supported by the language of the text. Esther fails to resolve the
conflict that has registered throughout her narrative. As a woman who
seeks to identify herself, she desperately desires to be imprinted by her
mother. At the same time, she constantly denies herself and shies away
from her mother. The novel ends on the printed page as a dash; the novel
ends but Esther's narrative does not. Her internal conflicts are not resolved.

Esther's narrative is riddled with turmoil over identity and self-assertion.
Esther is not just caught in a bind in always doing the selfless thing when
she clearly desires to do something else: her actions are also examples of
self-mistrust (Graver 10). Consider her relationship with Ada and Richard.
She watches as Ada clearly demonstrates her love for Richard; afterward
Esther writes: "For I was so little inclined to sleep myself that night that I
sat up working. It would not be worth mentioning for its own sake, but I
was wakeful and rather low-spirited. I don't know why. At least I don't
think I know why. At least, perhaps I do, but I don't think it matters"
(247; ch. 17). Esther's depression is not due to Richard's immaturity and
restlessness, nor to her concern for Ada, who is in love with the immature
and restless Richard. What Esther is trying to deny is that she loves Richard.[7] Frank suggests this, that Esther shuns passion and decides to marry
Jarndyce so that she will not experience passion, and will, at the same time,
live "vicariously through Ada and Richard" (77–78). Regardless of what
her desire is, she says that her desire does not matter. If so, why *indeed*
hint at it in writing? Erasing out of text any reference to her having desire
would have been the true act of self-denial. What she erases, instead, is the
specific desire itself as if she, as a woman, has no right to feel desire, but
feel desire she does.

Graver reasons that Esther includes the passage discussed to instruct
women that self-denial is a struggle and something one has to wrestle with
constantly, but that it is a worthy virtue and will result in reward (11)
(marriage to Allan). Is the reader to doubt the power of Esther's goodness
to save Richard? After all, is that not one of the missions of an angel-in-
the-house: not necessarily to marry the man of her dreams but, through
her moral influence, to save men from such destructive forces as Chancery
through her moral influence? And what better way to do this than within
the framework of marriage, where women are to exercise their greatest
power?

There is another conflict in this novel's promulgation of domestic ideology: Recalling the Dora/David/Agnes triangle in *David Copperfield* and comparing it to the Ada/Richard/Esther triad of *Bleak House*, one may notice a significant departure from the way David tells his story as a male writer and Esther tells hers. Clearly Jarndyce feels that the Ada/Richard marriage is a mistake, not because Ada is incapable of being a wife—although her inadequacies are very similar to Dora's—but because Richard has failed to commit himself to his gender obligations, that is, to secure a responsible occupation. As the narrator, David never blames himself for not providing a life-style commensurate with Dora's upbringing. Esther, however, finds fault with Richard. In *David Copperfield*, Dora has to die because she fails to fulfill her gender obligations in running the household, and she does not have a baby, lest she reproduce this aberration in her offspring. In *Bleak House*, Richard has to die, and Ada, who is the more resilient of the two, survives and produces a son (Moers 19). Further, Ada is not penalized for independently pursuing Richard after he leaves Bleak House; she did not get permission from Jarndyce, and Richard did not invite her. Yet when Richard opposes his guardian's wishes and does set up housekeeping without fulfilling his gender obligations as a provider and protector to his wife, the text expresses disapproval by killing him off. However, he would not have been in a domestic situation had Ada not run away to be with him. By not punishing Ada but by punishing Richard, the text subverts domestic ideology. Traditionally the man was encouraged to pursue a worldly occupation (as Richard was trying to do). But here Ada—the woman regarded as the temptress—forced a marriage that Richard did not initiate.

At another time Esther tries to tell that her attitude about Allan need not be mentioned, "for it hardly seems to belong to anything" (251; ch. 17). At still another time she tries to convince that it matters little that she should consider her mother as dead (597; ch. 43). Esther's writing is an attempt to erase herself from the narrative. She not only does not succeed, she effects just the opposite. The effort itself highlights her desires and needs when domesticity would deny that women possess such things.

Burying her doll is another attempt at self-erasure. Esther projects her shortcomings onto the doll and punishes it as she would herself, just as she endeavors to do through her writing. Indicating Esther's poor self-esteem, the doll stares at "nothing" as if Esther is nothing. Nevertheless, the doll is the only "person" in Esther's life (up to that point) who remains faithful to her. When she buries the doll, the extension of herself, it is a ceremonial betrayal of self (30; ch. 3).

Zwerdling suggests that she buries her selfishness, her self-indulgence in wanting a mother (104), an interpretation that gets to the heart of Esther's turmoil. The doll represents Esther's self, but Esther would see "self" as selfishness. The doll personifies a female identity (like her mother's) that can mirror Esther's femininity.[8]

After Guppy professes his passion for Esther, she returns to the business of paying bills and completing other household responsibilities when she cries, recalling the "dear old doll, long buried in the garden" (141; ch. 9). Why does she cry? For the same reason she cries when she realizes that she cannot marry Richard, cannot marry Allan, but must marry Jarndyce. She is, as Slater speculates, a woman who has no choice: "Esther is damaged as a character because she is ultimately denied the freedom to choose whom she will marry; she seems to be entirely manipulated, along with her lover, by the masterfully paternal figure of Mr Jarndyce" (167). That doll represents Esther's will, which she continually tries to repress and deny. She is supposed to die to herself and surrender to male authority, but the text betrays her inability finally to do so.

The last reference to this doll occurs when Esther is in church and sees Lady Dedlock for the first time:

And, very strangely, there was something quickened within me, associated with the lonely days at my godmother's; yes, away even to the days when I had stood on tiptoe to dress myself at my *little glass* after dressing my doll. And this, although I had never seen this lady's face before in all my life—I was quite sure of it—absolutely certain. (262; ch. 18; emphasis added)

Repeated, deliberate efforts to deny a self-identity appear throughout this passage. Esther recalls lonely days with her godmother, who preached domestic ideology: a woman had to practice "[s]ubmission, self-denial, diligent work . . . the preparations for a life begun with such a shadow on it" (33), with the shadow, of course, the disgrace of Esther's mother, (Miss Barbary's sister) to be borne by Esther. Thus Miss Barbary denies any other female role model to Esther than her own severe, nonsmiling, angelic self (31).

In her youth Esther is already a care giver. She dresses her doll, taking care of her only "dependent," maternally meeting the doll's "needs" before her own. Yet, if her doll is an object that Esther can project herself into, then to dress the doll is a way for Esther to tend to her own needs in an ideologically correct way.

Moreover, peering into the "little glass," especially when one has to stand on tiptoe to do so, is not an act of self-negation. In the mirror Esther sees that she is somebody, and later she sees herself again in Lady Dedlock. Then she tries to deny ever having seen Lady Dedlock before, which is to say, she denies ever having seen herself. Throughout the text, Esther is preoccupied with her physical appearance. According to Pam Morris, these are not acts of vanity; they signify Esther's "unappeasable anxiety about her own inner worth" (93).

The passage relates Esther's struggle to find herself while she is supposedly trying to lose herself. The doll, the mirror, and Lady Dedlock all reflect one image: Esther.

According to John Ward, Esther gains power to define herself matrilineally, through transference from her mother. Ward posits: "Dickens wishes us to conclude that the virtues of the mother have been meted out to the daughter, exhausting the parent, but empowering the child" (42). Jarndyce prophesies this transference when he muses, "I think it must be somewhere written that the virtues of the mothers shall occasionally be visited on the children, as well as the sins of the father" (247; ch. 17). This is the plot that the text seems to want to develop with Esther, that despite the sin of her father (an opiate addict and rogue), and despite what society would consider to be sin committed by Lady Dedlock (bearing an illegitimate child), by identification with her mother, Esther can finally negotiate her own identity, cultivating what she esteems to be virtues and discarding what she regards to be vices.

The mirrors in this novel complicate the theme of self-denial and negation of woman's right to her own identity. Mirror allusions abound in *Bleak House*; they are appropriate according to D. W. Winnicott's belief that a baby's first mirror must be a mother's face, so that Esther's failure to have a mother causes her to search for one, for without a mother she cannot develop a healthy self-image (1–25). The first appears when a coachman tells Esther that she might want to check herself in a looking glass before she appears at Chancery, as if to say, she could get one final grasp on her identity before the court takes it away and replaces it (44; ch. 3). After Chancery she becomes "Old Woman, and Little Old Woman, and Cobweb, and Mrs. Shipton, and Mother Hubbard, and Dame Durden" (112; ch. 8). These nicknames put Esther in constant peril of losing her identity, and so she frequently looks in the mirror to reclaim herself (Frances Armstrong 96).

Marianna Torgovnick interprets Esther's story as a "quest for her mother [which] is a quest for her own identity and . . . until Esther can find and then separate herself from her mother, she will never emerge into full, independent womanhood." When Esther finally sees her mother face to face, Torgovnick claims, then Esther can finally live as if she has some selfhood, but when next she is forced once again to adopt the identity of Dame Durden, the novel's ending becomes appropriate as a failed development of Esther's separation from her mother; she will never succeed as an entity separated from the breast; she will continue to search for the breast—or for a mother (52–54).

The text bears out Winnicott's theory and Torgovnick's application.[9] When Esther looks upon her mother as if she were peering into a looking glass at herself, it is as if the glass is broken (262; ch. 18). Recall, too, that when Lady Dedlock sits at her boudoir mirror, she sees not herself, but Mademoiselle Hortense (176; ch. 12). If Lady Dedlock's identity is not

intact—and it most assuredly is not (nobody knows who she really is)—
then how can Esther look upon her mother and gain any sense of identity?
Her identity will be as fragmented as is her mother's. By the time Esther
has been afflicted with pox and her face scarred, the glass is worse than
broken; it is gone: Charley removes it from the room so that Esther cannot
see how altered she is. The pox is necessary in the narrative because, prior
to Esther's illness, the appearance of Esther's face resembling her mother's
could have betrayed Lady Dedlock's secret. But there is more at work here:
the text would have Esther effaced. Notice the multiple references to veils,
worn by both Esther and Lady Dedlock. If that is not enough to nullify
these women's identities (and not just for the sake of plot), then making
Esther blind should.

From this point on, Esther does not need a mirror. Her friends and ac-
quaintances will identify who she is (Wilt 308). Ada, Richard, Jarndyce,
Miss Flite, the children in the villages—all identify her as the good, self-
denying woman. When John Jarndyce proposes to Esther in a letter,[10] she
turns to a looking glass and cries. Then she admonishes herself: " 'Oh,
Esther, Esther, can that be you?' I am afraid the face in the glass was going
to cry again at this reproach, but I held up my finger at it, and it stopped"
(617; ch. 44). Esther is clearly a woman divided into images of who she
should be and who she wants to be. Though the lesson of the narrative is
that discipline is expected of women, to deny themselves, the narrative itself
suggests that self-denial is no natural behavior for women. It is a trait
imposed or urged by domesticity that women must exercise. That self-
denial is a constant struggle for Esther also suggests a lack of acceptance
of such behavior, which is mandatory not only for her but for all women.

By the end of the novel, her husband asks her whether she ever looks in
the glass. Before the pox, she struggled to kill her self. After the pox, she
no longer has any self. At this point, though, her husband substitutes for
a mirror by calling her pretty. She is pretty to him and pretty to Dickens
because she is the perfect portrait of an ideal woman, and she, in turn,
thinks her own children are pretty, but she sees herself as ugly. Where does
this self-perception come from unless she does not accept the same value
system of her defacers?

Esther finishes her story with hoping that "they can very well do without
much beauty in me—even supposing—" (881; ch. 67). Dickens probably
wants the reader to find this rhetoric as the old Esther posturing as the
modest female, whose beauty is spiritual (Reed 304) or believe that her pox
scars have faded in proportion to the fading of her self (Sutherland 18)—
what Dickens would consider to be a feminine virtue—and, therefore, she
has become beautiful. Lowry Pei reads the dash to indicate that by the end
of her story, she still is unable to recognize herself (156). Is the ending of
the novel up to the reader? Is the woman not allowed to bring closure to
her own story (Giddings 195)? Esther is a woman who, although she out-

wardly conforms to the standards expected of her, still struggles within those limitations. The dash at the end is feminine discourse. Esther postures modesty but cannot stop there. Her narrative ends with a gap even as her narrative has been riddled with gaps, things that she is not supposed to say or feel. What Esther indicates with this dash is that she wants to feel beautiful. Either she is not really content with her domestic life and cannot state such a thing or else she feels good about herself because she has resolved so many inner conflicts, but she is not allowed to feel proud. Regardless, Esther's identity is still hanging on that dash, and the reader is not to witness its resolution. It bothers one, instilling a mystery as deep as the fog that brought us to Chancery.

This novel gives woman's voice (through Dickens) the space to articulate struggle and pain when women were supposed to aspire and moderate their behavior toward an angel-in-the-house ideal naturally and joyfully. Esther has constantly resisted her own dissent, and the text has portrayed her as forcing herself to conform. Through ink on the page, the female narrative inadvertently but severely undercuts the benevolence and the absolute value of the domestic ideology that the Dickensian text has attempted to construct and advocate.

NOTES

1. W. J. Harvey considers that the two narratives occur in almost exactly equal portions, the Esther chapters totaling thirty-three and the omniscient, thirty-four (90). However, Robyn Warhol identifies, besides Esther and a single third person, a polyvocal narrative, such as the voice of the "fashionable intelligence" in Chapter 2 and another voice that reports public occurrences at Tom-all-Alone's (149–50).

For additional discussions identifying the characteristics of each point of view, see Albert D. Hutter's "The High Tower of His Head: Psychoanalysis and the Reader of *Bleak House*" (83), Michael Slater's *Dickens and Women* (255–57), Leonard W. Dean's "Style and Unity in *Bleak House*" (60–61), Diane L. Jolly's "The Nature of Esther" (35), Michael S. Kearns' " 'But I Cried Very Much': Esther Summerson as Narrator" (123), Jacob Korg's Introduction, *Twentieth Century Interpretations of* Bleak House (15–16), Marianna Torgovnick's *Closure in the Novel* (43), Armour Craig's "The Unpoetic Compromise" (58–63), Grahame Smith's "Structure and Idea in *Bleak House*," James Davies' *The Textual Life of Dickens's Characters* (53–94), Bert Hornback's "The Other Portion of *Bleak House*," Alison Milbank's *Daughters of the House: Modes of the Gothic in Victorian Fiction* (83), Pam Morris' *Dickens's Class Consciousness: A Marginal View* (90–91), Thomas Vargish's *The Providential Aesthetic in Victorian Fiction* (131–32), Carol Senf's "*Bleak House*: Dickens, Esther, and the Androgynous Mind," Thorell Tsomondo's " 'A Habitable Doll's House': Beginning in *Bleak House*," Suzanne Graver's "Writing in a 'Womanly' Way and the Double Vision of *Bleak House*," and Karen Chase's *Eros and Psyche: The Representation of Personality in Charlotte Brontë, Charles Dickens, and George Eliot* (112–35).

2. Slater records Dickens' telling an American woman how difficult it was for him to write Esther's point of view: that it "cost him no little labor and anxiety" (qtd. in 255).

3. See Robyn Warhol's discussion in *Gendered Interventions: Narrative Discourse in the Victorian Novel* (150). Also see Jacob Korg's introduction to *Twentieth Century Interpretations of* Bleak House.

4. J. Hillis Miller alludes to this dynamic of the narrative in his introduction to *Bleak House:* "*Bleak House* is a document about the interpretation of documents" (11).

5. I am indebted to Dr. Anne Wallace of the University of Southern Mississippi for this observation.

6. See the discussion in Chapter 9 of Dickens' treatment of women who display passion in his novels.

7. Barickman et al., however, suggest that Esther loves Ada and is jealous of Richard. They interpret Ada as a surrogate lover for Esther, someone she can kiss and caress and address in endearing terms when she is not able to do so with Allan. Their interpretation that the Esther/Ada relationship is a denial of Esther's sexuality (80–81).

Geoffrey Carter develops a convincing argument that regards Esther as a lesbian. He cites the scene when Esther creeps up to Ada and Richard's door on their wedding night, describing it as "voyeurism masquerading as selfless love" (143). He also analyzes the scenes of Esther's sickness, concluding that the narrative builds "sexual hysteria, set up by weeks of subtly sadistic postponement of gratification" (144). In reading the scene of Esther's excitement and subsequent rendezvous with Ada at Boythorn's estate (ch. 36), one may understand how Carter has drawn his conclusions:

There were more than two full hours yet to elapse before she could come, and in that interval, which seemed a long one, I must confess I was nervously anxious about my altered looks. I loved my darling so well that I was more concerned for their effect on her than on any one. . . . I did not mean to do it, but I ran upstairs into my room and hid myself behind the door. There I stood trembling, even when I heard my darling calling. . . . Oh, how happy I was, down upon the floor, with my sweet beautiful girl down upon the floor too, holding my scarred face to her lovely cheek, bathing it with tears and kisses, rocking me to and fro like a child, calling me by every tender name that she could think of, and pressing me to her faithful heart. (523–34)

Albert Guerard similarly interprets such passages as erotic. In fact, he considers Ada and Esther as forming the most intense erotic relationship in the novel.

8. Pam Morris supports this notion to a degree. She interprets the doll as Esther's pretend mother, a "smiling angel," in contrast to her "frowning angel godmother" (92). Crawford Kilian also interprets the doll as a mother; the burial mimics the mother's abandonment of Esther (323).

9. Torgovnick argues that by the time Esther joins Bucket in pursuit of Lady Dedlock, the text gives evidence of Esther's development into selfhood. For example, when Bucket praises Esther, she does not fall into her usual self-deprecation. Nor does she attempt to be cheerful (51). In other words, Torgovnick does not consider Esther's usual acts of self-denial characteristic of a Victorian woman type. Instead, she interprets Esther's self-denial as symptomatic of a woman who has

failed to experience the first and second mirror stages of identity development (43–56).

10. Note that he does propose in a letter, which is Esther's medium—*her* expression of self. By so doing, he has infiltrated her private domain and her self has been violated.

PART IV

"The Bearings of This Observation Lay in the Application of It" (Captain Bunsby); or, Reference Aids

Bibliographical Essay: The Archive of Criticism on Dickens' Women

Ever since their debut on the literary stage nearly two centuries ago, Dickens' characters have been seducing millions of readers. This splendid cast has been so diverse, dictionaries and encyclopedias have appeared to catalog its members. Bibliographies have chronicled an equally diverse mass of criticism about those characters, for historically, the critics have rarely agreed on Dickens as a character maker. When in 1856 George Eliot praised Dickens for his power and gift of depicting unforgettable external traits of people, she also bemoaned his failure in giving them psychological depth (qtd. in Churchill 171). And a century later, Dorothy Van Ghent (1950) and E. D. H. Johnson (1969) would say more or less the same.[1] However, in the same year Johnson tendered his perspective, another well-known Dickens critic, V. S. Pritchett, argued that all of Dickens' characters magnify their inner life (qtd. in Churchill 177). Dickens' emphasis on physical description, to Juliet McMaster (1987), does not preclude the internal but signifies the characters' souls (xiii–7). Earlier, J. Hillis Miller (1959) defined the psychological reality of the Victorian, reflected in Dickens' novels, as a search for something outside self that would validate self.[2] If one accepts Miller's theory, one will understand the conflicting analyses of the critics. If Victorians reached outside themselves for that which transcended them in order to realize authentic identity, Dickens, himself a Victorian, would not have been compelled to develop the internal nature of his characters. Then the psychological drama apparent throughout his work evidences anything but superficial character formation.

Many critics have accused Dickens of being sentimental and his char-

acters of being overly manipulated by a novelist's propensity for melo-
drama. Even though the work of Jane Tompkins has done much to validate
the sentimental and sensational as art forms and as nineteenth-century literary conventions,[3] as early as 1844, Richard Henry Hornes commended
Dickens for portraying characters that are *not* merely sentimental (qtd. in
Churchill 170). Yet, in 1899 James Oliphant criticized him for not being
subtle enough, asserting that the characters were only "shadows" (34–35).
Douglas Bush (1958) insisted that Dickens "never approached sentimentality" (20). Not "sentimental" but "flat" was the characterization of both
Lauriat Lane (1961) and E. M. Forster (1927).[4] Instead George Santayana
(1921) held that Dickens created a "fresh world" because of characters in
whom readers can recognize themselves. Probably the most frequent criticism of his characters was that they are caricatures (although many concede
that Dickens was a master at creating caricatures). W. Walter Crotch
(1972), however, contended that they are not (75).

Just as amazing is the polarity among critics about the effectiveness of
Dickens' characterizations. One learns to know oneself better through his
people, George Gissing (1898) wrote, but Dickens often illustrated manners
rather than developing individual characters ("Humour" 10–11). Both
George Henry Lewes (1872) and Anthony Trollope (1882) called his characters mere puppets.[5] Although Lewes seemed to want to correct the critics
who had shown so little appreciation for Dickens (57), he fell short by
commenting that the characters "have nothing fluctuating and incalculable
in them" (65). Some of the very characters that he listed as being too
mechanical and lacking growth, such as Esther Summerson and Edith Dombey, have been the focus of many an article analyzing that very growth;
critics since Lewes have recognized the development and force of such characters. Lewes himself reasoned that Paul *(D&S)* and Little Nell *(OCS)* must
have seemed real enough to many people, for at both of their deaths, Britain
plunged into national mourning (68). Trollope thought Dickens' characters
were not real in the way that Thackeray's were, but he conceded that the
former moved readers in a way that the latter did not (75). Whereas T. S.
Eliot (1932) proclaimed the characters as real as flesh and blood, John
Kucich (1981) thought them mechanical and not organic (219). Thomas
Vargish (1985) saw them as realistic and individualistic (89–91).

The point of this survey has been to emphasize the historical variation
in the assessment of Dickens' characters. Much of the disagreement lies in
differing expectations of what characters should do in a novel. Does a
reader want them to be real enough to be engaged in their conflicts? How
real do people have to be in one's own life before one can care what happens to them? In reality, how many people allow others to venture into the
inner sanctum of their soul? But that does not mean that others are not
involved in their lives, nor that others do not know them well through their
external actions and attributes.

Are Dickens' characters stereotypical? There is only one Mr. Pickwick, but many real people are Pickwickian. The same can be said of Mr. Micawber. And what would Christmas be without Tiny Tim? Everyone has known Mrs. MacStinger, Uriah Heep, Mr. Turveydrop, Mrs. Pardiggle, and so many other characters who do not stay inside their novels. These are not stereotypes; they are types of real people who become more knowable because of their revelation of ourselves to ourselves by Dickens.

Does one expect them to be melodramatic, as is typical of many nineteenth-century works devoted to the sentimental and the sensational? If so, and if they are, what effect do they have on modern readers? What person is not moved to laugh in reading the courtship scene between Mr. Bumble and Mrs. Corney? What a stoic a reader must be not to feel infuriated by the maltreatment of Smike under the cruel hands of Squeers. Everyone knows what it is like to love someone who has an addiction that hurts most of the people he loves, as is the case with Little Nell and her love for her grandfather. Dickens' characters act out our worst anxieties and fears as well as our most wonderful aspirations and hopes.

From such a complicated array of both characters and criticism about them, one can only conclude that Dickens' characterization is complex and diverse, and appropriately so, insofar as people are complex and diverse, and so are our levels of perceptions of other people.

One must keep this broad perspective in mind when one studies Dickens' women. By and large, the greatest criticism of Dickens has been leveled against his portrayal of women, and most of it, until recent years, has been negative. Historically, the critical canon has packaged Dickens into a locus classicus of pure patriarchal tyranny. "Patriarchy" refers to an ideology privileging male over female, empowering male to signify female as to who she is and what role she must play within the household and social realm.

With rising sensitivity to or at least awareness of the "new woman" ideology, turn-of-the century critics rated Dickens' women as either unbelievable or unrealized or perceived them as portrayed pejoratively. William Dean Howells (1901) judged Dickens' heroines as moral fabrications, constructed for "our own good," rather than as "an artistic triumph" (126). In his preface to *Getting Married* (1908), George Bernard Shaw quoted and echoed George Gissing's sentiments regarding Dickens' women: "The most convincingly real ones are either vilely unamiable or comically contemptible; whilst [Dickens'] attempts to manufacture admirable heroines by idealizations of home-bred womanhood are not only absurd but not even pleasantly absurd: one has no patience with them" (328).

Many critics, as did Howells earlier, faulted Dickens for sacrificing characterization and realistic portrayals of women to advance a moral. A Dickens biographer, Stephen Leacock (1936), concluded that the Dickensian woman was either a mindless entity or a fabricated abstraction of what men wanted her to be (220–22). C. J. Woolen, in a 1940 article, criticized

Dickens for not painting "real women" (178), and in that same year, Audrey Lucas repeated this evaluation, adding that Dickens' women had to be painted white or black to make clear their moral value (706–28). In reviewing the changing ideal of the Victorian heroine in novels, Patricia Thomson (1956) assailed Dickens for heroines that "may be incandescent with virtue, but [they] do not strike a responsive spark" (16–17, 93).

Many critics have blamed Dickens for simply lacking sensitivity toward women. Angus Wilson (1970), for one, underscored the "absence of any real sympathy with, or understanding for, 'women' in the novels" (*World* 59). Women find power in Dickens' world, according to Sylvia Manning (1975), but only in terms of how they take care of their men (72–75). Jenni Calder (1976), a well-known critic of Victorian women and marriage, estimated that "Dickens' limited view of women's fulfilment [*sic*] seriously damaged his novels" (100). Similarly, Carolyn Heilbrun (1978) staunchly pronounced: "There is no arguing the fact that, in the novels we have he simply could not conceive of women as complex human beings" (52). Edward M. Eigner (1989) found heroines who were only empowered to save men (130–42).

Still others regard Dickens' women as male-dominated figures and no more than illusions. Alexander Welsh's chapter on the hearth (1971) deduced that the Victorian woman was like a religious icon, worshipped as a timeless divinity in the midst of prevailing mortality. Following a similar theme, Frances Armstrong (1990) identified Dickens' women as male-created fantasies of homemakers that reproduced childhood homes. Camille Colatosti (1980) interpreted Susan Weller's deathbed speech as Dickens' "attempts to reconfirm both male power and female submissiveness" (2). In *Great Expectations* Carl Hartog (1982) read Dickens as keeping women "in check," or in submission to men (248). Kathryn Sutherland (1983) complained that Dickens' women are either effaced or defaced, and further, "their unsublimated sexuality is the butt of the cruel and horrified fun, and only if they prove to be excellent cooks or housekeepers and passionless mothers (particularly to their husbands) . . . can they hope for Dickens's approval" (17–18). Similarly, Merryn Williams (1984) determined the main theme of *Bleak House* to be that a woman belongs in the home (85). As late as 1990, Doreen Roberts decided that Dickens' novels are populated by "bad-tempered, bossy, middle-aged wives who keep their husbands in subjection by a regime of merciless nagging, complaint and hysterics" (299).

Aside from critics who have either discarded Dickens' women as unworthy of exploration or regarded them only as lineal creations, others have urged an appreciation for diversity and depth, such as Ross Dabney (1967), who provided a reassessment of his women and marriage; Albert Guerard (1976), a psychoanalytical study of the women in *Little Dorrit, Bleak House*, and *The Old Curiosity Shop*; Dianne Sadoff (1982), a demythologization of the paterfamily; Michael Slater (1983) and Doris Alexander (1991), a biographical backdrop for Dickens' female creations; Arthur Adrian (1984), an exploration of mothers; Peter Brooks (1984), a structuralist reading of *Great Expectations* that concentrates on the incestuous aspects of the Estella/Pip relationship; Barbara Weiss (1984), conflicts of the marriage ideal; D. A. Miller (1988), a discussion of the forms of social control of women in *Bleak House*; and Laurie Langbauer (1990), a study of romance as a site of female rebellion.

Concerning the criticism of the 1970s, Andrew McDonald warned that it

has increasingly tended to look on Dickens as an epitome of Victorian hypocrisy, and to find under his mask of moral posing and sentimentality a monster of cant, and worse . . . to dismiss pristine characters like Florence as merely the vehicles of this cant is to overlook the ways in which Dickens's psychological preoccupations emerge in unexpected regions of the novels. (2)

McDonald viewed the women in *Dombey and Son* through a wide-angle lens. When Mrs. Brown forces Flo to disrobe and don rags, McDonald did not isolate this incident but connected it with Alice Marwood's being forced to wear rags, too, and later made to prostitute by her mother (the same woman who tyrannizes Flo). McDonald then connected Flo and Alice with Edith and with the work the novel has engaged in defining prostitution through her. Forced also by her mother, Edith sells herself to Dombey and delivers herself as mistress to Carker as Alice did earlier (3–13). In light of Alice's and Edith's tragic consequences, the scene with Flo evidences women's lack of power to determine their own fate, a point that broadens what Dickens is doing with women in this novel.

Margaret Flanders Darby (1987) also offered a wider perception of Dickens' women. She claimed that these characters "have been read unimaginatively from [Dickens'] day to ours. They have been dismissed or evaded in critical readings, judged a mistake" (24). She studied characters and incidents as integral, not separable from the rest of the text. For example, Darby correlated Lizzie's rescue of Eugene Wrayburn *(OMF)* with Hexam's activity on the Thames. Unlike her father, Lizzie pulls a man out of the river, not to rob, but to save him. This contrast demonstrates Lizzie's moral ascendancy over her father (31). In such interpretations Darby resolved text to domestic ideology. In the cited example, she posited that Lizzie, as an angel-in-the-house, should be morally superior to any man (including father, husband, suitor, and brother); such was to be expected of women within the domestic order. Where as some readers might analyze Lizzie's rescue as gender reversal (when a woman physically drags a man from the river and when a woman protects a man from violent acts of the world) and speculate how that scene is related to domestic ideology, Darby would remind the reader that Eugene keeps Lizzie "in her place" through sexual threats (31), thus confirming the text's reinforcement of domestic ideology.

Nancy Armstrong (1987) is one critic who traced the feminine ideal through Victorian novels and exposed complications to that ideal. Even so, Armstrong inferred that Dickens exercised considerable control over the ideological operations in his novels, theorizing that the Victorian novel intends "to train women to be desirable and thus rise in social ranks" (19). According to that priority, novels augment the power of domestic ideology by pedagogically compelling characters to conform or suffer the consequences. Examining Louisa in *Hard Times*, Armstrong argued that, by the novel's end, Louisa is "returned to her father in a state of infantile dependency" because her passion has to be subdued (55). Armstrong reached this conclusion through the juxtaposition of Sissy Jupe, an angel-in-the-house who wants above all else to find her lost father (55). By concurrently exploring what is going on with other characters in the same novel and by drawing parallels and indicating relationships, Armstrong practiced a procedure followed in this study. However, where Armstrong interpreted the activity in Victorian novels as phallomorphic, this study identified text that conflicts with patriarchal power interests.

Of all the work that has been done to revise critical assessments of Dickens, *Corrupt Relations: Dickens, Thackeray, Trollope, Collins, and the Victorian Sexual System* (1982) is most consonant with this study in its analysis. Richard Barickman, Susan MacDonald, and Myra Stark (through a collaborative effort) documented and analyzed female characters who seem to break through the narrative,[6] steal the writer's pen, and blatantly defy gender enclosure; or text that seems in conflict with itself over domestic ideology. These critics considered Dickens' work palimpsestic, that is, characterized by a story written over the author's subtext: its "surface designs conceal or obscure deeper, less accessible (and less socially acceptable) levels of meaning" (14–18). Barickman's team did not suggest a deliberate problematizing of patriarchal rule; however, they did identify many ways the narrative undercuts the virtue of male dominance. Because of the scope of their project, Barickman et al. offered only a sampling of such conflicts throughout Dickens' novels. Similarly searching for departures from ideology and having benefited from their ground-breaking work, this study has been able to examine Dickens' novels more thoroughly.

Additionally, David Cowles' agenda is useful insofar as he noted Dickens' text to contain multiple significant contradictions about gender issues. In his article (1991), Cowles wrote: "Throughout Dickens's works, treatment of women probably engenders more unintentional self-contradiction than any other topic. Like all great artists, Dickens typifies as much as he transcends the conceptual languages of his age" (80). Cowles pointed out incidents in which Dickens clearly attempts to manipulate readers to feel about a character one way, only at another turn to cause them to feel quite differently. In an analysis of *Hard Times*, Cowles commented that Dickens frequently condemns Tom "for his insensitive, gender-based demands on Louisa's devoted services," and expects readers to sympathize with the exploited sister. At other times Dickens condemns Louisa as the exploiter, for example, when she leads Tom to a circus. Readers are expected to censure Louisa for her domination of Tom and for her encouragement to do wrong (79–82). In Cowles' example, the contradiction cited is not so clear. Yes, Tom is selfish and demanding of his sister, but the text, as a whole, paints a chilling picture of Louisa. Tom's failure to be good, as well as Mr. Bounderby's failure to reform, are both due to Louisa's failure to perform her womanly duty in guiding men to higher moral accountability. Tom's selfishness and waywardness result from the earlier episode with Louisa, who led the boy astray despite woman's charge to instill moral and spiritual values in him. Therefore, readers are not to sympathize with Louisa. One does find contradictions in *Hard Times*, too, but it is because they exist inside the text that they are contradictions and must be discussed as such. Throughout, this study has considered women as an integral part of the whole of the novel and resisted isolating them from their fictive milieu. Additionally, like that of James Marlow (1994), this analysis considers Dickens texts not by excerpting them, but by contextualizing them within the author's entire corpus (21), indicating their associations with other novels in the Dickens canon to calibrate their ideological mechanisms.

Recent additions to the ranks of critics who have come to appreciate the complexities of Dickens' women are numerous. Briefly, as they pertain to this study, the theories of several critics have been considered: Pam Morris (1991), who asserts that women are vulnerable to males and that Dickens' work consists of a "double fiction" that contains female subversion; Patricia Ingham (1992), who suggests that all depictions of women are through one male's perspective, voyeuristically presented to male characters that contain and prescribe female definition; Nicholas Morgan (1993), who does not seem to find contradictions but believes in the importance of unlayering Dickens' work to uncover its dynamic meaning; Elsie Michie (1993), who writes that women in Dickens' novels are property who struggle to possess themselves; Natalie McKnight (1993), who characterizes Dickens' text as conflicted by representing silence in women as both attractive to others and dangerous to themselves; Kimberly Reynolds and Nicola Humble (1993), who suggest that not all Victorian novels, including Dickens', portrayed women as angel/fallen models; David Holbrook (1993), who points out that Dickens associated murder and death with women and was unable to reconcile the ideal with the libidinal; Constance Harsh (1994), who sees the novels as critical of paternalism, marriage laws, and patriarchal industrialization; Gail Turley Houston (1994), who points out that Dickens' women were perpetual nurturers who never seemed to need nurturing themselves; Harry Stone (*Night* 1994), who suggests that after his separation Dickens suddenly infused his characters with passion that would prove dangerous to them; and David Suchoff (1994), who reads Dickens as painting a sympathetic portrait of women oppressed by patriarchy.

Dickens critics have created a splendid and manifold archive of study. That there appears to be room for more is testimony to Dickens' artistry and cultural legacy, of special interest to investigations of gender ideologies.

NOTES

1. It would not be fair to infer that either Van Ghent or Johnson actually bemoaned Dickens' lack of psychological depth. Van Ghent did conclude that Dickens' characters typically lacked complex inner lives but suggested that often the inner life was "transposed to other forms than that of character." For example, she referred to the "gropings and pausings of the black beetles on Miss Havisham's hearth." The insect activity obviously is a metaphor for Miss Havisham's despair (217). Johnson found Dickens' characters to succeed because he artfully created "consistent and emphatically defined patterns of individualized responses to external circumstances." Ingeniously Dickens was able to make them real through their actions (115–16). An argument could be made that the reader is able to learn a great deal about the internal makeup of characters through their actions, reactions, and interactions.

2. For a fuller explanation of his theory, see especially the conclusion to *Charles Dickens: The World of His Novels* (328–34).

3. See her *Sensational Designs: The Cultural Work of American Fiction, 1790–1860*, and in particular her introduction. She investigated why modern criticism often devalues those literary works containing the seeming defects of "an absence of finely delineated characters, a lack of verisimilitude in the story line, an excessive reliance on plot, and a certain sensationalism in the events portrayed" (xii). She concluded that stereotypical characters serve as "instruments of cultural self-definition," communicating a tremendous amount of important information about culture (xvi–xvii).

Also see Jonathan Loesberg's article, "The Ideology of Narrative Form in Sensation Fiction." Loesberg further validated the nonseriousness of plot and dialogue as well as exaggeration of incident over development of character as an artform in this genre.

4. However, Lane also explained that he was not being critical. His theory, expressed in the introduction to *The Dickens Critics*, argued that all characters in literature are flat and that it is not necessarily the task of literature to produce verisimilitude. Instead, art should exceed ordinary experience. To Lane, Dickens created characters that would increase a reader's awareness of life (15).

Forster's comment is more critical; nonetheless, he did add that Dickens' characters seem to give the reader a "wonderful feeling of human depth" (75).

5. Both articles are in Ford and Lane's *The Dickens Reader*. See Lewes (65) and Trollope (75).

6. Ellen Moers (1973) also found dissenting women in *Bleak House*. She assumed that Dickens deliberately depicted strong, independent women but with an ambivalence as to how he really felt about women's issues of the day (13).

Along similar lines, Laurie Langbauer (1991) analyzed the dynamics of romance in several of Dickens' novels, as it becomes "the imaginary locus of dissatisfaction, rebelliousness" (127–87). She investigated specific connections between women and romance and argued those connections in terms of sexual power.

Bibliography

Acton, William. *The Functions and Disorders of the Reproductive Organs in Child-hood, Youth, in Adult Age, and in Advanced Age, Considered in Their Phys-iological, Social and Moral Relations.* 4th ed. London, 1865.

———. *Prostitution.* 1870. Ed. and introd. Peter Fryer. New York: Praeger, 1969.

Adrian, Arthur. *Dickens and the Parent–Child Relationship.* Athens: Ohio Univer-sity Press, 1984.

Aers, David, Jonathon Cook, and David Punter. *Romanticism and Ideology: Studies in English Writing 1765–1830.* London: Routledge, 1981.

Agress, Lynne. *The Feminine Irony/Women on Women in Early Nineteenth-Century English Literature.* Cranbury, England: Associated University Presses, 1978.

Alexander, Doris. *Creating Characters with Charles Dickens.* University Park: Pennsylvania State University Press, 1991.

Allen, Dennis W. *Sexuality in Victorian Fiction.* Norman: University of Oklahoma Press, 1993.

Althusser, Louis. "From 'Ideology and Ideological State Apparatuses.' " *Critical Theory Since 1965.* Ed. Hazard Adams and Leroy Searle. Tallahassee: Uni-versity Press of Florida, 1986. 239–50.

———. *"Lenin and Philosophy" and Other Essays.* Trans. Ben Brewster. New York: Monthly Review Press, 1971.

Altick, Richard. *The Presence of the Present: Topics of the Day in the Victorian Novel.* Columbus: Ohio State University Press, 1991.

Armstrong, Frances. *Dickens and the Concept of Home.* Ann Arbor, MI: UMI Research Press, 1990.

Armstrong, Nancy. *Desire and Domestic Fiction: A Political History of the Novel.* New York: Oxford University Press, 1987.

Auerbach, Nina. *Woman and the Demon.* Cambridge, MA: Harvard University Press, 1982.

Baker, George Pierce. *Charles Dickens and Maria Beadnell: Private Correspondence.* Boston: Bibliophile Society, 1908.

Barickman, Richard, Susan MacDonald, and Myra Stark. *Corrupt Relations: Dickens, Thackeray, Trollope, Collins, and the Victorian Sexual System.* New York: Columbia University Press, 1982.

Barthes, Roland. "The Photographic Message." *Image, Music, Text.* Trans. Stephen Heath. New York: Hill and Wang, 1977.

———. *The Pleasure of the Text.* Trans. Richard Miller. New York: Hill and Wang, 1975.

Belcher, Diane Dewhurst. "Dickens's Mrs. Sparsit and the Politics of Service." *Dickens Quarterly* 2.3 (September 1985): 92–97.

Bennett, William Crosby. "The Mystery of the Marchioness." *Dickensian* 36 (1940): 205–8.

Blake, Andrew. *Reading Victorian Fiction: The Cultural Context and Ideological Content of the Nineteenth-Century Novel.* New York: St. Martin's Press, 1989.

Boyle, Thomas. *Black Swine in Sewers of Hampstead: Beneath the Surface of Victorian Sensationalism.* New York: Viking, 1989.

Brooks, Peter. *Reading for the Plot: Design and Intention in Narrative.* New York: Knopf, 1984.

Bullough, Vern L. *Sexual Variance in Society and History.* New York: John Wiley, 1976.

Bush, Douglas. "A Note on Dickens' Humor." Ed. William Ross Clark. *Discussions of Charles Dickens.* Boston: Heath, 1961. 17–23.

Calder, Jenni. *Women and Marriage in Victorian Literature.* London: Thames, 1976.

Carmichael, Virginia. "In Search of Beein': *Nom/Non du Pere* in *David Copperfield.*" *ELH* 54 (Fall 1987): 653–67.

Carter, Geoffrey. "Sexuality and the Victorian Artist: Dickens and Swinburne." Don Richard Cox, ed. *Sexuality and Victorian Literature.* Knoxville: University of Tennessee Press, 1984. 141–60.

Charles, Edwin. *Some Dickens Women.* New York: Stokes, 1945.

Chase, Karen. *Eros and Psyche: The Representation of Personality in Charlotte Brontë, Charles Dickens, and George Eliot.* New York: Methuen, 1984.

Chesterton, G. K. *Appreciation and Criticism of the Works of Charles Dickens.* New York: Haskell, 1966.

Churchill, Reginald C. *A Bibliography of Dickensian Criticism, 1836–1975.* New York: Garland, 1975.

Clark, William Ross, ed. *Discussions of Charles Dickens.* Boston: Heath, 1961.

Cockshut, A. O. J. *The Imagination of Charles Dickens.* New York: New York University Press, 1962.

Colatosti, Camille. "Male vs. Female Self-Denial: The Subversion Potential of the Feminine Ideal in Dickens." *Dickens Studies Annual* 19 (1990): 1–24.

Collins, Philip. *Dickens: The Critical Heritage.* London: Routledge, 1971.

Cott, Nancy F. *The Bonds of Womanhood.* New Haven, CT: Yale University Press, 1977.

———. "Passionlessness: An Interpretation of Victorian Sexual Ideology, 1790–1850." *Signs* 4 (1978): 219–36.

Cowie, L. W. "Bridewell." *History Today* 23.5 (May 1973): 350–58.

Cowles, David. "Having It Both Ways: Gender and Paradox in *Hard Times." Dickens Quarterly* 8 (June 1991): 79–84.

Cox, Don Richard, ed. *Sexuality and Victorian Literature.* Knoxville: University of Tennessee Press, 1984.

Craig, G. Armour. "The Unpoetic Compromise." Ed. Jacob Korg. *Twentieth Century Interpretations of* Bleak House. Englewood Cliffs, NJ: Prentice-Hall, 1968. 58–63.

Crotch, W. Walter. *The Secrets of Dickens.* New York: Haskell House, 1972.

Dabney, Ross H. *Love and Property in the Novels of Dickens.* Berkeley: University of California Press, 1967.

Darby, Margaret Flanders. "Four Women in *Our Mutual Friend." The Dickensian* 83 (Spring 1987): 24–39.

Davidoff, Leonore, and Catherine Hall. *Family Fortunes: Men and Women of the English Middle Class, 1780–1850.* Chicago: University of Chicago Press, 1987.

Davies, James A. *The Textual Life of Dickens's Characters.* Houndsmell, England: Macmillan, 1989.

Dean, Leonard W. "Style and Unity in *Bleak House.*" Ed. Jacob Korg. *Twentieth Century Interpretations of* Bleak House. Englewood Cliffs, NJ: Prentice-Hall, 1968. 45–57.

Dickens, Charles. *Barnaby Rudge.* 1841. Ed. and introd. Gordon Spence. New York: Penguin, 1973.

———. *Bleak House.* 1852. Afterword. Geoffrey Tillotson. New York: Signet, 1964.

———. *David Copperfield.* 1850. Ed. Jerome Buckley. New York: Norton, 1990.

———. *Dombey and Son.* 1848. Boston: DeWolfe, Fiske, n.d.

———. *Great Expectations.* 1860. Introd. Edward Wagenknecht. New York: Washington Square Press, 1956.

———. *Hard Times.* 1854. Eds. George Ford and Sylvère Monod. New York: Norton, 1990.

———. *Little Dorrit.* 1855. Ed. John Holloway. New York: Penguin, 1967.

———. *Martin Chuzzlewit.* 1843. Ed. and introd. Margaret Cardwell. Oxford: Oxford University Press, 1982.

———. *The Mystery of Edwin Drood.* 1870. Concluded by Leon Garfield. New York: Pantheon, 1980.

———. *Nicholas Nickleby.* 1838. Afterword. Steven Marcus. New York: Signet, 1980.

———. *The Old Curiosity Shop.* 1840. Ed. Angus Easson. New York: Penguin, 1972.

———. *Oliver Twist.* 1837. Ed. Fred Kaplan. New York: Norton, 1993.

———. *Our Mutual Friend.* 1864. Afterword. J. Hillis Miller. New York: Signet, 1964.

———. *The Pickwick Papers.* 1836. Ed. and introd. Edgar Johnson. New York: Dell, 1964.

———. *A Tale of Two Cities.* 1859. New York: Bantam, 1981.

Dixon, Hepworth. *The London Prisons*. New York: Garland, 1985.

Donovan, Robert A. "Structure and Idea in *Bleak House*." Ed. Jacob Korg. *Twentieth Century Interpretations of* Bleak House. Englewood Cliffs, NJ: Prentice-Hall, 1968. 34–44.

Douglas, Ann. *The Feminization of American Culture*. New York: Anchor, 1977.

Du Cann, C. G. L. *The Love Lives of Charles Dickens*. Westport, CT: Greenwood, 1961.

Eagleton, Terry. *Criticism and Ideology*. New York: New Left, 1976.

———. *Ideology*. New York: Verso, 1991.

Easson, Angus. "Dickens's Marchioness Again." *Modern Language Review* 65 (1970): 517–18.

Eigner, Edwin M. *The Dickens Pantomime*. Berkeley: University of California Press, 1989.

Eliot, T. S. *Wilkie Collins and Dickens*. Eds. George H. Ford, and Lauriat Lane, Jr. *The Dickens Critics*. Ithaca, NY: Cornell University Press, 1961. 151–52.

Ellis, Mrs. Sarah. *The Wives of England: Their Influence and Responsibility*. New York: Langley, 1843.

———. *The Women of England: Their Social Duties, and Domestic Habits*. New York: Langley, 1843.

Fernando, Lloyd. *"New Women" in the Late Victorian Novel*. University Park: Pennsylvania State University Press, 1977.

Finnegan, Frances. *Poverty and Prostitution: A Study of Victorian Prostitutes in York*. Cambridge: Cambridge University Press, 1979.

Ford, George H., and Lauriat Lane, Jr., eds. *The Dickens Critics*. Ithaca, NY: Cornell University Press, 1961.

Forster, E. M. *Aspects of the Novel*. New York: Harcourt, Brace, 1927.

Forster, John. *The Life of Charles Dickens*. New York: Baker and Taylor, 1911.

Frank, Lawrence. "Through a Glass Darkly: Esther Summerson and *Bleak House*." Ed. Eliot L. Gilbert. *Critical Essays on Charles Dickens's* Bleak House. Boston: G. K. Hall, 1989. 64–83.

Giddings, Robert, ed., *The Changing World of Charles Dickens*. London: Vision, 1983.

Gilbert, Elliot L., ed. *Critical Essays on Charles Dickens's* Bleak House. Boston: G. K. Hall, 1989.

Girouard, Mark. *Life in the English Country House: A Social and Architectural History*. New Haven, CT: Yale University Press, 1978.

Gissing, George. *Charles Dickens: A Critical Study* (1903). New York: Haskell, 1974.

———. "Humour and Pathos." Ed. William Ross Clark. *Discussions of Charles Dickens*. Boston: Heath, 1961. 8–16.

Goldfarb, Russell M. *Sexual Repression in Victorian Literature*. Lewisburg, PA: Bucknell University Press, 1982.

Gorham, Deborah. *The Victorian Girl and the Feminine Ideal*. Bloomington: Indiana University Press, 1982.

Graver, Suzanne. "Writing in a 'Womanly' Way and the Double Vision of *Bleak House*." *Dickens Quarterly* 1 (March 1987): 1–14.

Greg, W. R. "Why Are Women Redundant?" *Literary and Social Judgments*. New York: Henry Holt, 1876.

Grubb, Gerald G. "Dickens' Marchioness Identified." *Modern Language Notes* 68 (1953): 162–65.

Guerard, Albert. *The Triumph of the Novel: Dickens, Dostoevsky, Faulkner*. Chicago: University of Chicago Press, 1976.

Halttunen, Karen. *Confidence Men and Painted Women: A Study of Middle-Class Culture in America, 1830–1870*. New Haven, CT: Yale University Press, 1982.

Hardy, Barbara. *The Moral Art of Dickens*. London: Athlone, 1970.

Harsh, Constance. *Subversive Heroines: Feminist Resolutions of Social Crisis in the Condition-of-England Novel*. Ann Arbor: University of Michigan Press, 1994.

Hartog, Curt. "The Rape of Miss Havisham." *Studies in the Novel* 14 (Fall 1982): 248–65.

Harvey, W. J. *Character and the Novel*. Ithaca, NY: Cornell University Press, 1965.

Heilbrun, Carolyn G., and Margaret R. Higonnet, eds. *The Representation of Women in Fiction*. Baltimore: Johns Hopkins University Press, 1983.

Holbrook, David. *Charles Dickens and the Image of Woman*. New York: New York University Press, 1993.

Hornback, Bert G. "The Other Portion of *Bleak House*." Ed. Robert Giddings. *The Changing World of Charles Dickens*. London: Vision, 1983. 180–95.

Houghton, Walter. *The Victorian Frame of Mind, 1830–1870*. New Haven, CT: Yale University Press, 1957.

Houston, Gail Turley. *Consuming Fictions: Gender, Class, and Hunger in Dickens's Novels*. Carbondale: Southern Illinois University Press, 1994.

Howells, William Dean. *Heroines of Fiction*. London: Harper, 1901.

Hutter, Albert D. "The High Tower of His Head: Psychoanalysis and the Reader of *Bleak House*." Ed. Elliot L. Gilbert. *Critical Essays on Charles Dickens's Bleak House*. Boston: G. K. Hall, 1989. 83–99.

Ingham, Patricia. *Dickens, Women and Language*. Toronto: University of Toronto Press, 1992.

Johnson, E. D. H. *Charles Dickens: An Introduction to His Novels*. New York: Random House, 1969.

Johnson, Wendell Stacy. *Living in Sin: The Victorian Sexual Revolution*. Chicago: Nelson-Hall, 1979.

Jolly, Diane L. "The Nature of Esther." *The Dickensian* 86 (Spring 1990): 29–39.

Jordan, John O. "The Purloined Handkerchief." *Dickens Studies Annual* 18. Ed. M. Timko, F. Kaplan and E. Guiliano. New York: AMS Press, 1989: 1–17.

Kearns, Michael S. "But I Cried Very Much: Esther Summerson as Narrator." *Dickens Quarterly* I.4 (December 1984): 121–29.

Kelly, Joan. *Women, History and Theory: Essays of Joan Kelly*. Chicago: University of Chicago Press, 1984.

Kennard, Jean E. *Victims of Convention*. Hamden, CT: Archon, 1978.

Kettle, Arnold. "Dickens: *Oliver Twist*." Eds. George H. Ford and Lauriat Lane, Jr. *The Dickens Critics*. Ithaca, NY: Cornell University Press, 1961. 252–70.

Kilian, Crawford. "In Defense of Esther Summerson." *Dalhousie Review* 54 (1974): 318–28.

Kirchhoff, Frederick. *John Ruskin*. Boston: Twayne, 1984.

Korg, Jacob, ed. *Twentieth Century Interpretations of* Bleak House. Englewood Cliffs, NJ: Prentice-Hall, 1968: 1–20.

Kucich, John. *Excess and Restraint in the Novels of Charles Dickens*. Athens: University of Georgia Press, 1981.

Lane, Lauriat, Jr. "Introduction: Dickens and Criticism." Eds. George H. Ford and Lauriat Lane, Jr. *The Dickens Critics*. Ithaca, NY: Cornell University Press, 1961. 1–18.

Lane, Margaret. Preface. *Ruth*. 1853. By Mrs. Gaskell. London: Dent, 1967.

Langbauer, Laurie. *Women and Romance: The Consolations of Gender in the English Novel*. Ithaca, NY: Cornell University Press, 1990.

Langland, Elizabeth. "Nobody's Angels: Domestic Ideology and Middle-Class Women in the Victorian Novel." *PMLA* 107 (2) (March 1992): 290–304.

———. *Society in the Novel*. Chapel Hill: University of North Carolina Press, 1984.

Leacock, Stephen. *Charles Dickens: His Life and Work*. Garden City, NY: Doubleday, 1936.

Leavis, F. R., and Q. D. Leavis. *Dickens the Novelist*. New Brunswick, NJ: Rutgers University Press, 1979.

Levine, George. *The Realistic Imagination: English Fiction from Frankenstein to Lady Chatterly*. Chicago: University of Chicago Press, 1981.

Loesberg, Jonathan. "The Ideology of Narrative Form in Sensation Fiction." *Representations* 13 (Winter 1986): 115–38.

Lucas, Audrey. "Some Dickens Women." *Yale Review* 29 (June 1940): 706–28.

Lucas, John. *The Melancholy Man: A Study of Dickens's Novels*. Totowa, NJ: Barnes & Noble, 1970.

Manheim, Leonard F. "Floras and Doras: The Women in Dickens' Novels." *Texas Studies in Literature and Language* 7 (Spring 1965): 181–200.

Manning, Sylvia. "Dickens, January, and May." *The Dickensian* 71 (May 1975): 67–75.

Marcus, Stephen. *The Other Victorians: A Study of Sexuality and Pornography in Mid-Nineteenth-Century England*. New York: Basic, 1964.

Marlow, James E. *Charles Dickens: The Uses of Time*. Selinsgrove, PA: Susquehanna University Press, 1994.

Mayhew, Henry. *Selections from* London Labour and the London Poor. Introd. John L. Bradley. London: Oxford University Press, 1965.

McDonald, Andrew. "The Preservation of Innocence in *Dombey and Son*: Florence's Identity and the Role of Walter Gray." *Texas Studies in Literature and Language* 18 (Spring 1976): 1–17.

McKnight, Natalie. *Idiots, Madmen, and Other Prisoners in Dickens*. New York: St. Martin's Press, 1993.

McMaster, Juliet. *Dickens the Designer*. Totowa, NJ: Barnes & Noble, 1987.

Meynell, Alice. "Victorian Caricature." *Essays*. London: Burns Oates and Washbourne, 1925. 161–64.

Michie, Elsie B. *Outside the Pale: Cultural Exclusion, Gender Difference, and the Victorian Woman Writer*. Ithaca, NY: Cornell University Press, 1993.

Milbank, Alison. *Daughters of the House: Modes of the Gothic in Victorian Fiction.* New York: St. Martin's Press, 1997.

Miller, D. A. *The Novel and the Police.* Los Angeles: University of California Press, 1988.

Miller, J. Hillis. *Charles Dickens: The World of His Novels.* Cambridge, MA: Harvard University Press, 1959.

Mise, Raymond W. *The Gothic Heroine and the Nature of the Gothic Novel.* New York: Arno, 1980.

Modleski, Tania. *Loving with a Vengeance: Mass Produced Fantasies for Women.* Hamden, CT: Archon, 1982.

Moers, Ellen. "*Bleak House*: The Agitating Women." *The Dickensian* 69 (January 1973): 13–24.

Morgan, Nicholas H. *Secret Journeys: Theory and Practice in Reading Dickens.* Rutherford, NJ: Fairleigh Dickinson University Press, 1992.

Morris, Pam. *Dickens's Class Consciousness: A Marginal View.* New York: St. Martin's Press, 1991.

Murray, Janet H. Introd. *Miss Miles.* 1890. By Mary Taylor. New York: Oxford University Press, 1990.

Needham, Gwendolyn. "The Undisciplined Heart of David Copperfield." *Nineteenth-Century Fiction* 9 (1954): 81–107.

Nield, Keith, ed. *Prostitution in the Victorian Age.* Westmead, England: Gregg International, 1973.

Oliphant, James, M. A. *Victorian Novelists.* New York: AMS Press, 1989.

Osborne, Charles, ed. *Letters of Charles Dickens to the Baroness Bardett-Coutts.* New York: Dutton, 1932.

Page, Norman. *A Dickens Companion.* New York: Schocken, 1984.

Pearsall, Ronald. *The Worm in the Bud: The World of Victorian Sexuality.* Toronto: Macmillan, 1969.

Pei, Lowery. "Mirrors, the Dead Child, Snagsby's Secret, and Esther." *ELN* 16 (December 1978): 144–56.

Phelps, Elizabeth Stuart. *The Story of Avis.* Boston: Houghton, 1879. Ed. and introd. Elizabeth Hardwick. New York: Arno, 1977.

Raina, Badri. *Dickens and the Dialectic of Growth.* Madison: University of Wisconsin Press, 1986.

Reed, John. *Victorian Conventions.* Athens: Ohio University Press, 1975.

Reynolds, Kimberley, and Nicola Humble. *Victorian Heroines: Representations of Femininity in Nineteenth-Century Literature.* New York: New York University Press, 1993.

Rice, Thomas J. "*Barnaby Rudge*, a Vade Mecum for the Theme of Domestic Government in Dickens." *Dickens Studies Annual* 7 (1989): 81–107.

Ricoeur, Paul. *Lectures on Ideology and Utopia.* New York: Barnes & Noble, 1974. Roberts, Doreen. "*The Pickwick Papers* and the Sex War." *Dickens Quarterly* 7.3 (September 1990): 299–311.

Ruskin, John. *The Ethics of Dust: Ten Lectures to Little Housewives on the Elements of Crystallization.* Chicago: Donohue, 1890.

———. "Of Queens' Garden." *Sesame and Lilies.* 1864. New York: Dutton, 1907.

Sadoff, Dianne F. *Monsters of Affection: Dickens, Eliot and Brontë on Fatherhood.* Baltimore: Johns Hopkins University Press, 1982.

Santayana, George. "Dickens." *The Dial* 71 (1921): 537–49.

Schroeder, Natalie E., and Ronald A. Schroeder. "Betsey Trotwood and Jane Murdstone: Dickensian Doubles." *Studies in the Novel* 21 (Fall 1989): 268–78.

Senf, Carol A. "*Bleak House*: Dickens, Esther, and the Androgynous Mind." *Victorian Newsletter* 64 (Fall 1983): 21–27.

Shaw, George Bernard. Preface. *Getting Married.* 1908. *Complete Plays with Prefaces*, Vol. 4. New York: Dodd, 1963.

Shaw, Marion. *Alfred Lord Tennyson.* Atlantic Highlands, NJ: Humanities Press International, 1988.

Showalter, Elaine. "Guilt, Authority, and the Shadows of *Little Dorrit*." *Nineteenth-Century Fiction* 34 (June 1979): 20–40.

———. "Victorian Women and Insanity." *Madhouses, Mad-Doctors, Madmen: The Social History of Psychiatry in the Victorian Era.* Ed. Andrew Scull. Philadelphia: University of Pennsylvania Press, 1981. 313–39.

Sigsworth, E. M., and T. J. Wyke. "A Study of Victorian Prostitution and Venereal Disease." Ed. Martha Vicinus. *Suffer and Be Still: Women in the Victorian Age.* Bloomington: Indiana University Press, 1980.

Slater, Michael. *Dickens and Women.* London: Dent, 1983.

Smith, Grahame. "Structure and Idea in *Bleak House*." *ELH* 29 (1962): 175–201.

Smith, Henry Nash. "The Scribbling Women and the Cosmic Success Story." *Critical Inquiry* 1 (1974): 47–70.

Smith, Mary Daehler. "All Her Perfections Tarnished: The Thematic Function of Esther Summerson." *Victorian Newsletter* 38 (Fall 1970): 10–14.

Smith-Rosenberg, Carroll, and Charles Rosenberg. "The Female Animal: Medical and Biological Views of Woman and Her Role in Nineteenth-Century America." *Journal of American History* 60 (September 1973): 332–56.

Stoehr, Taylor. "The Novel's Dream." Ed. Jacob Korg. *Twentieth Century Interpretations of* Bleak House. Englewood Cliffs, NJ: Prentice-Hall, 1968. 105–6.

Stone, Harry. "The Love Pattern in Dickens' Novels." *Dickens the Craftsman: Strategies of Presentation.* Ed. Robert B. Partlow, Jr. Carbondale: Southern Illinois University Press, 1970.

———. *The Night Side of Dickens: Cannibalism, Passion, and Necessity.* Columbus: Ohio State University Press, 1994.

Suchoff, David. *Critical Theory and the Novel: Mass Society and Cultural Criticism in Dickens, Melville, and Kafka.* Madison: University of Wisconsin Press, 1994.

Sutherland, Kathryn. "Dickens and Women." *Critical Quarterly* 25 (Fall 1983): 17–19.

Taylor, Gordon Rattray. *The Angel Makers: A Study in the Psychological Origins of Historical Change, 1750–1850.* New York: Dutton, 1974.

Taylor, Mary. *Miss Miles.* 1890. New York: Oxford University Press, 1990.

Therborn, Göran. *The Ideology of Power and the Power of Ideology.* London: Verso, 1980.

Thompson, John B. *Studies in the Theory of Ideology.* Berkeley: University of California Press, 1984.

Thomson, Patricia. *The Victorian Heroine: A Changing Ideal, 1837–1873*. London: Oxford University Press, 1956.

Tompkins, Jane. *Sensational Designs: The Cultural Work of American Fiction, 1790–1860*. New York: Oxford University Press, 1985.

Torgovnick, Marianna. *Closure in the Novel*. Princeton, NJ: Princeton University Press, 1981.

Tsomondo, Thorell. " 'A Habitable Doll's House': Beginning in *Bleak House*. *Victorian Newsletter* 62 (Fall 1962): 3–7.

Uglow, Jennifer. Introduction. *Lady Audley's Secret*. 1862. By Mary E. Braddon. New York: Penguin, 1985.

Van Ghent, Dorothy. "The Dickens World: A View from Todgers." Eds. George H. Ford and Lauriat Lane, Jr. *The Dickens Critics*. Ithaca, NY: Cornell University Press, 1961. 213–32.

Vargish, Thomas. *The Providential Aesthetic in Victorian Fiction*. Charlottesville: University Press of Virginia, 1985.

Vicinus, Martha, ed. *Suffer and Be Still: Women in the Victorian Age*. Bloomington: Indiana University Press, 1973.

Walkowitz, Judith R. *Prostitution and Victorian Society: Woman, Class, and the State*. Cambridge: Cambridge University Press, 1980.

Ward, John. " 'The Virtues of the Mothers': Powerful Women in *Bleak House*." *Dickens Studies Newsletter* 14 (June 1983): 37–42.

Warhol, Robyn R. *Gendered Interventions: Narrative Discourse in the Victorian Novel*. New Brunswick, NJ: Rutgers University Press, 1989.

Warner, Susan. *The Wide Wide World*. New York: Grosset, 1850.

Watt, George. *The Fallen Woman in the Nineteenth Century English Novel*. London: Croom Helm, 1984.

Weiss, Barbara. "The Dilemma of Happily Ever After: Marriage and the Victorian Novel." Eds. Anne C. Hargrove and Maurine Magliocco. *Portraits of Marriage in Literature*. Macomb: Western Illinois University Press, 1984. 67–86.

Welsh, Alexander. *The City of Dickens*. Oxford: Clarendon Press, 1971.

Welter, Barbara. "The Cult of True Womanhood: 1820–1860." *American Quarterly* 19 (Spring 1966): 151–74.

———. *Dimity Convictions: The American Woman in the Nineteenth Century*. Athens: Ohio University Press, 1976.

Williams, Merryn. *Women in the English Novel, 1800–1900*. New York: St. Martin's Press, 1984.

Wilson, Angus. "The Heroes and Heroines of Dickens." *Dickens: A Collection of Critical Essays*. Ed. Martin Price. Englewood Cliffs, NJ: Prentice-Hall, 1967. 16–23.

———. *The World of Charles Dickens*. New York: Viking, 1970.

Wilt, Judith. "Confusion and Consciousness in Dickens's Esther." *Nineteenth-Century Fiction* 32 (December 1977): 285–309.

Winnicott, D. W. "Transitional Objects and Transitional Phenomena." *Playing and Reality*. London: Tavistock, 1971. 1–25.

Winter, Sarah. "Domestic Fictions: Feminine Deference and Maternal Shadow Labor in Dickens' *Little Dorrit*." *Dickens Studies Annual* 18 (1989): 243–54.

Wohl, Anthony S., ed. *The Victorian Family: Structure and Stresses*. London: Croom Helm, 1978. 1–33.

Woolen, C. J. "Some Thoughts on Dickens's Women." *The Dickensian* 36 (1940): 178–80.

Zabel, Morton Dauwen. "*Bleak House*: The Undivided Imagination." Eds. George H. Ford and Lauriat Lane, Jr. *The Dickens Critics*. Ithaca, NY: Cornell University Press, 1961. 325–48.

———. "Dickens: The Reputation Revised." Ed. William Ross Clark. *Discussions of Charles Dickens*. Boston: Heath, 1961. 1–7.

Zwerdling, Alex. "Esther Summerson Rehabilitated." *Charles Dickens: New Perspectives*. Ed. Wendell Stacy Johnson. Englewood Cliffs, NJ: Prentice-Hall 1982. 94–113.

Index of Dickens' Characters

General Index

About the Author

BRENDA AYRES is Associate Professor of English at Middle Georgia College.

ISBN 0-313-30763-6

90000>

EAN

9 780313 307638

HARDCOVER BAR CODE